RAISING
SUGARCANE

A memoir by BARRY RAFFRAY

Gotham Books

30 N Gould St.
Ste. 20820, Sheridan, WY 82801
https://gothambooksinc.com/

Phone: 1 (307) 464-7800

© 2024 *Barry Raffray*. All rights reserved.

No part of this book may be reproduced, stored in a retrieval system, or transmitted by any means without the written permission of the author.

Published by Gotham Books (November 14, 2024)

ISBN: 979-8-3305-5223-8 (P)
ISBN: 979-8-3305-5224-5 (E)

Because of the dynamic nature of the Internet, any web addresses or links contained in this book may have changed since publication and may no longer be valid.

The views expressed in this work are solely those of the author and do not necessarily reflect the views of the publisher, and the publisher hereby disclaims any responsibility for them.

CONTENTS

ACKNOWLEDGEMENT ix
Dedication to Daddy and Momma xi
Introduction xv
CHAPTER 1 1
BEFORE I WAS LITTLE: AGES ZERO THROUGH FIVE - MY DADDY 1
WHEN I WAS LITTLE: THE BIRTH AND CIRCUMCISION 15
THE BAPTISM 16
VERY YOUNG YEARS: FROM ZERO TO AGE FOUR OR FIVE 19
MOSES (NOT FROM THE BIBLE) 19
CHAPTER 2 22
A LITTLE LATER IN MY LIFE: AGES SIX, SEVEN, EIGHT, AND NINE 22
VERY COLD TIMES 25
TRIPS TO NEW ORLEANS 27
MY FIRST WHOLE CAN OF BEER 32
DIGRESS A LITTLE 33
BACK TO THE EARLY FIFTIES 34
PICNICS 36
POTTY PANTS (BAD TIME) 38
THE HOT WATER BOTTLE 41

LEARNING TO RIDE A BICYCLE 43
SMOKING CIGARETTES AND WATCHING THE GRASS GROW (DON'T TELL ME I'VE NOTHING TO DO) 45

CHAPTER 3 49

DOCTOR/DENTIST VISITS: AGES EIGHT AND NINE 49
DEAD MAN'S MONEY 52
THE BLACKSMITH SHOP 53
THE NOT SO GREAT ROCK THROWING CONTEST 55
CAUGHT UP A TREE 57
WALKING THE FENCE 59
THE CURE-ALLS (CASTER AND MINERAL OIL AND MILK OF MAGNESIA, ETC) 62
HEAT STROKE 64

CHAPTER 4 66

WART TREATMENT: AGES NINE AND TEN 66
DOMESTIC HELP (MRS. IDA WASHINGTON AND MRS. SISTER LINK) 67
RIDING MY BICYCLE 70
MY FIRST DRIVE-IN MOVIE 73
FIRST (AND ONLY) TRAIN RIDE 76
THE CATHOLIC SCHOOL EXPERIENCE AGES TEN, ELEVEN, TWELVE, AND THIRTEEN 79

CHAPTER 5 83

MY COMMUNION AND OTHER THINGS 83
THE BAJON BOYS (FROM MRS. BARLOW'S CLASS WINDOW) 90

MY FIRST HIGH SCHOOL BASKETBALL GAME - ALMOST 94
THE 4440 WINCHESTER 99
HI-LIFE (SOME HOT STUFF) 102
STILL RIDING MY BICYCLE 104

CHAPTER 6 108
MORE DOCTOR STUFF: AGES TWELVE AND THIRTEEN 108
THE GLOVE 110
NOU NOU IN THE CORN CRIB-SMOKING 113
SLED-RIDING DOWN THE LEVEE 114
MY FIRST NEW (USED) BIG BICYCLE 117
THE CORNCRIB FIRE 120
JESSY'S CANAL (ON THE PLANTATION) 122

CHAPTER 7 127
THE BOUCHERIE/PIG PROCESSING 129
BEEF BUTCHERING 132
CHICKEN PROCESSING 133
PROCESSING VEGETABLES 136
GROWING POTATOES 138
GROWING CORN/TENDING TO COWS 139
THE PROCESS OF MAKING BUTTER 141
TAKING ADVANTAGE OF FOOD STUFF 143
MY BIG BROTHER'S OLD RADIO PROGRAMS 144

CHAPTER 8 147

MY FIRST AIRPLANE RIDE: AGES THIRTEEN AND FOURTEEN 147
1955 A VERY IMPORTANT YEAR 148
MY EARLY TEENAGE YEARS: AGES FOURTEEN THROUGH SIXTEEN - EIGHTH, NINTH AND TENTH GRADES 150
HEAD LIGHTING FOR RABBIT 152
HEAD LIGHTING WITH THE MABILES 156
MY LAST RABBIT HUNTING TRIP WITH MY DADDY 157
SUGAR CANE PLANTING 159
SUGAR CANE HARVESTING 160
MEETING MY TO BE BROTHER-IN-LAW 163
MEETING THE MICHELLES OF PLAQUEMINE 165

CHAPTER 9 170
MAKING POPGUNS AND OTHER TOYS (WEAPONS): AGES EIGHT THROUGH SIXTEEN 170
SLING SHOTS OR NEGRO (POLITE) SHOOTERS 175
MAKING A CORN COB PIPE 177
RUBBER BAND (STRIP) SHOOTERS 178
BOW AND ARROWS AND WILLOW REEDS 178
MUD-SLINGING WILLOW REEDS 180

CHAPTER 10 182
OUR HOUSE IN WHITE CASTLE AGES FOURTEEN AND FIFTEEN 182
THE TASTE OF FRESH BREAD 182
FRIENDSHIPS IN WHITE CASTLE 184
NICKY (CROWBAR) GUERCIO 186

HALLOWEEN IN THE CITY 194
MY BROTHER GOT MARRIED 199
CROP DUSTING ON THE PLANTATION 200
MY UNCLE'S 1954 DESOTO 208
BURNING UNC'S CAR UP 211

CHAPTER 11 215
HANGING WITH ALVIN (SLIM) BARBIER: AGES
FIFTEEN AND SIXTEEN 215
MEETING DAVIS CALLEGAN AGAIN 217
THE GUITAR 219
MR. ALEX'S 1954 CHEVY 220
LEON MILLER BASEBALL STORY AS DADDY TOLD IT
.... 223
MY SISTER'S WEDDING 225
NINTH AND TENTH GRADE SHENANIGANS 229
OTHER WILD TIMES IN AG CLASS................................... 232

CHAPTER 12 237
SNEAKING INTO CLASSROOMS DURING RECESS:
AGES SIXTEEN AND UP 237
A PROBLEM WITH TEST PAPERS 240
MORE TENTH GRADE WOES 243
SHRIMPING IN THE BIG MUDDY 245

CHAPTER 13 252
MOVE TO THE BIG HOUSE NEXT TO OURS ON THE
PLANTATION: AGES SEVENTEEN AND UP 252
VALUABLE RECORDS LOST FOREVER........................... 253

LATE TEENAGE YEARS: AGES SEVENTEEN AND
EIGHTEEN - ELEVENTH AND TWELFTH GRADES 255
TED HYMEL AND I 257
UNCLE NOLAN'S PASSION 259
THE FEE FEE EXPERIENCE (BOY WHAT A RIDE) 262
THE BOBBY SQUIRREL STORY 263
RIDING WITH STEVE (I DOUBT YOU) LANDRY 266
PLAYING CARDS FOR MONEY 268
MR. PERCLE- JUNIOR/SENIOR YEARS 269
CHAPTER 14 275
ME AROUND THE HOUSE: AGES EIGHTEEN AND UP 275
TRYING TO GET MY UNCLE TO TALK 276
MY SENIOR YEAR. 279
ATTENDING PROMS 280
JOINING THE ARMY 285
GRADUATION MAY 1962 286
AFTER GRADUATION - ARMY BOUND 291

ACKNOWLEDGEMENT

This is a reprinting of my first book. I want to take the opportunity to apologize for several errors made in the first printing. First and foremost, for the misspelling of some of my childhood friends. I believe that I've corrected them in this book.

The story about the GLOVE. In the first printing, I said that Leon Miller gave the first baseman mitt to Sonny Barbier which is not correct. He gave the mitt to Dicky Barbier.

Another correction I made is in the section where I wrote about our school janitor whom I referred to as Easy Ed Brown. His name was Bill Brown. So it is Easy Bill Brown. I found out from Mrs. Bill Brown the Easy Bill lived and worked on Cedar Grove Plantation as a mechanic for several years. This would have been when I was very young or even before my time. He worked for Mr. George Cunningham who was our Shop Manager before Mr. Ashley (Lou Lou) Henry. I do remember Mr. George and his wife, Miss Lizzy. They built a very nice brick house at the corner of Adams Drive in White Castle. It is still there.

Back to Mr. Bill Brown. He was wounded during World War II and did not have the full use of this left arm. At school he always work at a study pace and did not get in a rush and always remained calm whatever the situation. As I mention above he picked up the moniker- Easy Bill Brown. He always got the job done.

I also want to mention Floyd "Shackie" Pansano who married Norma Ann Brown. They were both raised on Cedar Grove Plantation.

A couple years after I published my book, "Raising Sugar Cane", I talked with Shackie and he told me that I had mentioned everybody on Cedar Grove except him. I said, NO WAY". After hanging up the telephone, I ran and got a copy of my book, and much to my surprise he was right. So I am mentioning him now. Shackie and Norma Ann live in Corpus Christi, Texas

  Barry Raffray

Dedication to Daddy and Momma

My Daddy was a sugar cane farmer. My Grandpa was a sugar cane farmer. My Great Grandpa was a surveyor. This is as far as I can go back with the occupations of my ancestors.

When my Daddy and Momma was married, at least three generations lived in one four or five room house. This happened to my Daddy and Momma. There may have even been a cousin or two that lived with them also.

My Daddy, his brother and sister, lived with their Daddy and Step Mother and my daddy's Grandpa and Grandma. By the time that daddy married momma, his sister had moved out but his brother and maybe cousin Clarence Breaux was still living with them.

Daddy used to tell me that they could count the chickens and ginney hens under the house from inside the house looking through the holes in the floor. They could also see daylight and the stars through the cracks in the walls. And there was not any glass window panes. In fact, there was not window panes at all. If they had anything in the window, it was mosquito netting used to help try and keep mosquitoes and flies out of the house.

I will tell about how it was when I was little in the 1940s, 1950s and early 1960s. There is nothing to compare with the hard times that my Daddy and Momma had when they were little and later when raising a family. But they work hard, lost three kids at birth and raised three kids up to be good, honest, citizens and saw more changes in their lifetime than I will ever see in mine.

I dedicate this book to my Momma and Daddy.

Without them, there would be no me.

Josie Correl Raffray
Born Sept. 29, 1914 Died April 08, 1980

Newton Joseph Raffray Sr.
Born Aug. 07, 1912 Died Dec. 14, 1984

Both are buried in the White Castle Catholic cemetery.

Introduction

This book is about the life of a little boy born during WW II raised on a sugarcane plantation in Southern Louisiana. These were hard times for poor folks who had to work very hard to earn meager living wages to support their families. Although money was scarce, living and working on the land allowed you to grow and raise much of the food that the city people could not do. Generally, one had food or the means to get food if they were inclined to do so by working extra time on land provide after their normal work day was completed. Some landowners would not allow workers to use their land for gardens.

Times were hard and folks were poor but most of us did not know we were poor because all of our friends and neighbors had the same things we had- nothing. You made the most with what you did have. It was a simple time when you could grow you own food and make your own toys to entertain yourself and friends. As a youngster, I had plenty fun times growing up on the plantation. This book is about some of those times as best as I can recall them.

Most of this book is written in the manner that we talked before education came into play. If this story were told with proper English and punctuations, the reader would miss out on the flavor of the times of these happenings.

CHAPTER 1

BEFORE I WAS LITTLE: AGES ZERO THROUGH FIVE - MY DADDY

My daddy was born August 7, 1912 near White Castle, Louisiana in an area referred to as "New Camp." He lived in a small shotgun one-story house in the middle of a sugar cane field with a large drainage canal running along one side of it.

Desire Franklin Raffray, Artamise Breaux Raffray, Clarence Breaux, Maude Daigle, Newton J. Raffray, Anna Sanchez Raffray, and Adam Raffray

Daddy's daddy (Adam Raffray - born May 25, 1885, died June 29, 1966)

Daddy's daddy, Adam, worked the fields nearby. They lived between highway La. 993 and highway La. 3001 on a dirt road. The old dirt road is now part of highway La. 404. The house was about one quarter mile from Rodusta's store which was located on Hw. 3001.

Anna Sanchez (my paternal Grandmother)

Daddy's momma, Anna Sanchez, was born Sept.22, 1886, and died May 13, 1923 when daddy was twelve years old. Some years later they moved to Lone Starr into a larger house. Lone Starr is located on highway 993 about two miles farther from White Castle than the other house on the dirt road.

They moved/evacuated from Lone Starr during the 1927 high water which flooded the area and got into their house as it did everybody's in that area.

Anna Sanchez (my paternal grandmother)

In the future years, dad lived and worked on/at Richland for the Supple family as a tenant farmer and later moved to Cedar Grove Plantation where he worked for the Soniat and then the Burton families for just over forty years as an overseer and later as plantation manager. He died on December 12 in 1984 while living on Cedar Grove and still working for the heirs of the William T. Burton estate. He was 72 years old at the time of his death.

My daddy was pulled out of the 2nd grade when he was 7 years old to work in the sugar cane field by his dad who was a tenant farmer. He would deliver the breakfast and the lunches to the field workers. This entailed getting up very early in the mornings and going by every worker's house and picking up their breakfast buckets. He would deliver to the workers wherever in the field they were working then gather the pails and bring back to the worker's houses so their wives or moms would clean them to place the lunch for that day into them. Before 11 a.m., dad would again go by the workers houses and gather the lunch pails and deliver to the different areas in the field where each worker was at that time. I do not know if he had a mule to transport the food pails or had to do it all by walking but do it he did. During these old days, the workers would eat in the field where they were when the clock struck 12 noon. Come 1 p.m. all the workers went back doing their jobs be it with shovels, hoes, ditch blades, cane knives, plowing behind a mule or whatever it was they were working at. I think daddy again would collect all the lunch pails and deliver them back to their respective homes for use the next day.

This activity surly kept a little boy of 7 or 8 years old very busy for most of the daylight hours. I am sure that he had other chores around the house/yard to do also. Things like shucking, shelling and grinding corn for the chickens and guinea hens that was raised for eggs and meat to eat. Also sloping the hogs and feeding the cows and milking them, etc. etc.

There was always plenty work to do when growing up in the country or on a farm. I experience that myself as did my brother and sister and everyone else that was raised on a farm. It did not make any difference weather you owned it or not- you worked your butts off to survive.

Daddy worked for his dad until he was in his twenties. He quit working in the field one time and moved to New Orleans for about a month or so. He got a job in a factory and was doing really good. Since he knew how to work and was a hard worker, he got several promotions in the short time he worked there. I often wondered what kind of life I would have had if grandpa would not have gone to New Orleans and begged daddy to come back to the farm because he just could not make the crop without him. Of course daddy quit the job and came back to the White Castle area. His boss in New Orleans was sorry to see him go.

Daddy and momma were married and grandpa would pay daddy 25 cents a week. This is what daddy used to tell us. I do not know if this was salary or just expense money. Daddy should have been a partner with his dad. But I don't think that he was. Maybe the 25 cents was just spending money so dad and mom could go paint the town red when not having to work on a weekend. Even during my time spent with my grandpa, he was kind of tight with money. Maybe that was because he never had very much of it during his lifetime.

Daddy lived on Cedar Grove in 1927 and worked with his dad farming part of the land from 1928 to 1942. At this time, I believe he went to Supple plantation (also called Catherine Plantation), to farm for two years as a tenant farmer before moving back to Cedar Grove in February 1944 to start working as and overseer for the owners at that time. Daddy told me that he left Supple after having a falling out with their Field Supervisor who tried to tell him when and how to work the land. Mr. Callegan was trying to force his will upon my daddy and he would not have any of it.

The Burton-Sutton Oil Company purchased Cedar Grove plantation at an auction in New Orleans in 1939 from the L.M. Soniat family who had owned it since before 1920. Sometime in the 1950s, the property was transferred to William T. Burton Industries Inc. Daddy was one of the overseers and stayed on to work for the new owners. Daddy became plantation manager for Cedar Grove Plantation in 1961.

Josie Correl (my mom), Nolan Correl (my uncle), and Josephine Quatrevingt Correl (my grandma)

Momma was born in Grosse Tete (pronounced Grow State), Louisiana, on September 29, 1914. Her daddy, Anthony Correl, (born 1889, died 1944), was a sugar cane tenant farmer there. My momma's mom, Josephine Quatrevingt was born 1893, and died in 1917), when my momma was three or four years old. Momma's brother, Nolan, was about two years old at the time. Momma always said that she thought her momma knew that she was dying because several weeks before she died, she dressed herself and the kids and went to town and had a photograph made of her. This is something that cost much money at the time and she did not care to have done before this time in her life.

Ernest Correl (my maternal great grandfather)

Momma's grandparents on her daddy's side were Ernest Correl and Pauline Quatrevingt. We do not have the years of birth or death only the year married which was December 31, 1884.

Juliet Himel (my maternal great grandmother)

Momma's grandparents on her mother's side were Oscar Quatrevingt (born 1852, died 1930) and Juliet Himel, (no other info). Momma used to tell me that her grandmother Himel's family used to own Ceily Plantation near Thibodeaux, Louisiana. It consisted of over 3000 acres of land. It was a large sugarcane plantation with its own sugar mill. They lost the plantation because of a few dollars owed to creditors. In those days, the High Sheriff would take your property to pay creditors. It did not make any difference how much you owed. You could owe $500 and your property worth $5000. They would take the whole thing to pay the debt. A new law came into effect in the 1950s that changed this forever. The property went to a Sheriff's sale to the highest bidder. Any money left over went to the family whose property they took and sold. This change in the law was many years too late to help the Himel family. When I was a teenager, the Harvey Peltier family of Thibodeaux owned this plantation. I do not know if these are the folks who got it for near nothing or acquired it later.

My momma told me that she learned to speak in Spanish before she learned English and some Cajun French. During her adult years she could not speak or understand Spanish anymore. I guess they quit speaking Spanish when she was very young. Momma also told us the story of her daddy's people and how an ancestor left Spain for the United States when he was a teenager because he did not want to serve seven years in the Spanish Navy. Upon arrival in America, he changed his name from Corallas to Correl. Maybe to cover his tracks or perhaps it was just the spelling of the person checking him in that misspelled his name.

Momma's momma has a similar story in her family's history. Her ancestor upon arrival into the United States, name was changed from Schwab to Quatrevingt. He was supposedly from France. We were told he was from a French/German border town. Upon arrival into America, the person checking them in could not understand what he was saying and since he was the eightieth person to step off the boat he became Eighty. Quatrevingt in French is the number eighty.

We do not know where in America that my Momma's folks entered. I surmise that it was New Orleans only because of the close proximity to the area that they settled in.

My Momma's Daddy and his sister (Correl) married a brother and sister (Quatrevingt). The off-springs from these two marriages are double first cousins which makes them my double second cousins and their off spring (my age) my double third cousins.

On my grandmother's deathbed, she asked her best friend, Maude Fleming to look after and marry my momma's daddy. This is the way that I remember my momma telling me this story.

Maude did marry my grandpa Tony some time after my grandma died. They had two girls and a boy. They were named Mildred, Muriel, and Anthony Jr.

Some years later, my grandpa Tony got injured some way and was laid up for years in the bed. He never did recover and died at 55 years of age.

During the early years of my grandpa's second marriage, to Mama Maude, my momma and Uncle Nolan went to live with Nan Noon and Paran Charlie Ponsano at Richland. Nan Noon and Paran Charlie never had any children. Nan Noon was grandpa Tony's sister-in-law. She was my grandma's sister. I guess Mama Maude had her hands full with her three kids and allowed/wanted momma and Unc to live somewhere else. Maybe the house was too small. I just don't know.

Josie Correl

    Momma often told me of the times when she and Uncle Nolan were in grade school and how he did not like school and sometimes made her miss the bus ride to school. I am not sure if the "bus" was pulled by mule/horse or not. Unc would make her hide in the woods or in a culvert with him until after the bus went by. Nan Noon must have just let this go on or did not know anything about it. I do not remember what grade mom was in when she quit going to school. She could read and write very well and was a first class seamstress.

    Momma and Uncle Nolan lived with Nan Noon until they were in their late teens. Momma married daddy and Unc went into the Army. He served over four years during WWII. He was in the second Wave during the Allied invasion at Normandy Beach, France. He once told me that the first Wave had over 90%

causalities. He received a number of metals for his wartime service. I remember seeing them stored in an old cigar box when I was a kid. I do not know what happened to his metals or what they were for.

I am really saddened when I think about this now. We could never get him to talk about what he seen and had been through. He came home to become a first rate auto mechanic for the Doiron brothers Plymouth dealership for almost 45 years.

After momma and daddy married, they moved in with my daddy's dad and grandpa and their wives. For a time they had three generations of Raffrays living in one small frame house. This had to be very hard for my momma. Eventually, I do not know when, they got their own place to live. Wherever and whenever it was, Uncle Nolan lived with them before the war and also after the war. He was my roommate for the first 24 and a half years of my life - until I got married and moved out.

WHEN I WAS LITTLE: THE BIRTH AND CIRCUMCISION

I was born a little boy on the 18th day of May in 1943. This was during the time of the Big War- WW II of course. I did not know anything about that at the time. I came to learn about it in the years to come.

I am told that I was a big little boy at birth. Well over eight pounds and something. My momma, being a small woman, about five foot two inches, must have hollowed a lot to get me out of there. They say she did not know where she was till three or two days later. I do not know if this is true or not, but if I would have gone through what she did, I would have wanted a lot of drugs and would not know where I am at either.

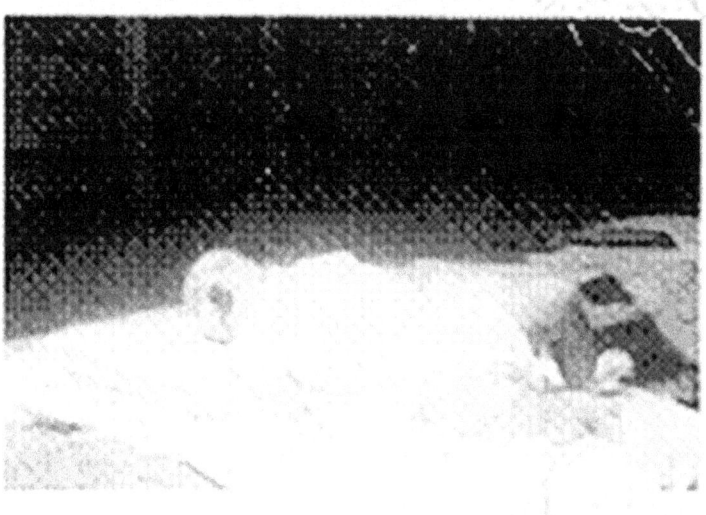

Fat baby Barry

After about four or three days, I had to be circumcised. Because that is what you have to do if you are born a little Catholic boy.

The Catholics have this law and you better follow it. It states that all boys must be circumcised or else. I never did learn what the "or else" meant. I didn't think I wanted to know bad enough to go around asking grown-ups.

Little Catholic girls don't have to go through that because they don't have, ooooooooh well, aaaaah, they don't got- well because they just don't got to go through that procedure. I came to find out many years later that little girls come in the world looking like everything was cut off already anyway.

When I got the procedure, old Dr. Tomney, he gave me just three drops of wine to knock me out. He should have known that was just not enough wine for a big little Cajun boy to not feel anything. I am gonna toll you something. I believe that I felt the whole thing the whole time that I was under the knife. I think that I kicked old Dr. Tomney so hard that he slipped and took off more than he should have. All my life since that day, I felt like Dr. Tomney short changed me just because he got kicked. He should have known that three drops of wine for an eight plus pound Cajun boy was just not enough to make him don't feel anything. I think a fifth would have been better and done the trick. Then I would not have to be carrying this grudge against old Dr. Tomney around with me all these years.

THE BAPTISM

There come a time when I was a couple of months or weeks old that I had to be baptize. You cannot be a Catholic unless you got baptize. To get baptize, you must have your Momma and Daddy nearby and you got to have a Nan Nan and Paran that will stand in for your Momma and Daddy if something bad happened to them and they don't be around anymore. If something bad like that happen to your parents, your Nan Nan and Paran promised to raise you to be a good little Catholic boy. Make you go to church on Sunday and put money in the collection and everything like that.

After you got a Nan Nan and a Paran all set up, you got to get a name for the baby. Not just any name, but a proper name. If you are a little boy, you got to have a man saint name in your name. Your know like- Peter, Paul, Mark, Anthony, James, etc. If you are a little girl, you got to get a lady saint name in your name like- Mary, Marie, Ann, Elizabeth, Joan, etc., like that.

My Daddy wanted to name me Lawton after the name of one of the owners of the sugar cane plantation that he worked for. My Momma said NO. She did not want my name to be Lawton because the other little children will call me Crawton, which means a turd, and she was not going to have that. Well the name thing became a problem. When they got to the church where my baptism has to take place, they had a name for me. It was Barry Franklin Raffray. At the Church, they ran into a problem with the priest with the name they had picked. My first name Barry, the priest wanted Bartholomew. But again, my Momma said NO. It will be Barry not no Bartholomew. The priest decided to take Barry. My second name "Franklin," after my Daddy's Daddy's Daddy (another way to put this is my Daddy's Grandpa), was not a Saint name and the priest barked at this. I can remember this like it was the day before yesterday because, after all, I was there. The priest, he say that there is no Saint Frank or no Saint Franklin, so they got to come up with another name or they will not be a baptism today. Well, my Momma and Daddy, and my to be Nan Nan and Paran, and some other folks like my big brother Put and my big sister Bobbie Jo (now that is another baptism story) was all there (I think) and they come up with Anthony, which was my Momma's Daddy's name. Since there is a St. Anthony, that name got the approval of the priest. But now, Momma and Daddy did not want to drop my other name and that is how I got baptized as Barry Franklin Anthony Raffray. Now you know why none of my sons are called Junior. I did not want to put this name on them to carry the rest of their life.

This is not the entire story yet. Since my baptism, I got some more names and today, you can call me Barry, Franklin, Frankie, Anthony, Tony, Butch, Rock, Rockbeau, Raff, Peter, Bro, Raffray or any one or a combination of those names will do and that is the rest of this story.

Family picture of Newton, Put, Bobbie Jo, and Barry

VERY YOUNG YEARS: FROM ZERO TO AGE FOUR OR FIVE

I do not remember very much after the Baptism for the next several years. Only a few stories like when I was about two years old, I grabbed a live electric wire in the chicken yard and was shaking all over, which made Mrs. Frieda Henry laugh like crazy. And when I was about three years old, I hit Leon Miller on the head with a water dipper (used for sipping water) so hard that his ears rang, which made everybody in attendance laugh when Leon tried to answer them. I was also a very large little boy. At nine months old, I weighed in at thirty-two pounds or something like that. I could not walk until I was two years old or something like that. I just had too much weight. I have a picture of me at nine months old and I look like a stump with a head on it. I was a fat baby. And I am proud to say that I still have some of that baby fat still attached to me.

I used to get convulsions on a regular basis until the doctor that Mom and Dad would take me to was off of work one time. So in this emergency, they took me to an old doctor in Plaquemine. He told them to take me off Coke and popcorn. This worked out fine since I have not had any convulsions since that time. I know there must be some other stories about me during this time in my life that I just cannot remember at this time. If any thoughts come to me, I will add to this section. If not, well, we will just have to do without.

MOSES (NOT FROM THE BIBLE)

From the time I was about five years old until thirteen, I was afraid of Moses. Not the Moses that led his people out of Egypt but the Moses that lived in our loft/attic in the house we lived in on the Plantation. This Moses was a wolf like man with hair all over his body and very large pointed teeth and claws instead of fingernails. He had big round eyes, a long nose or snout and big pointed ears that stood straight up. If I did not behave, Moses was going to come out of the loft and get me. If I did not do my chores, I had better keep on the lookout for Moses. If I did not take my medicine, Moses would make me take it. And so on, you know, Moses this and Moses that. I was always on the look out for Moses. Moses could show up any where at anytime. But he slept in our loft. My big brother and sister did not seem to be worried about Moses. They did not pay him any mind. He lived in the loft that was above our living room, where in about 1951, our TV was.

All these plantation houses were built on pillars about two to three feet off the ground. They had fourteen feet ceiling and a lot of room between the ceiling and the roof of the house. All the roofs were tin sheets. I used to love to hear the rain hit the roof on our old house. I guess from the ground to the top of the roof was about thirty feet. It was way up there. I refer to this type roof as "rain drop splitters" because they come to a point at the highest part. But this was not a true rain drop splitter. They were really pointed. Much more than the old house on the Plantation that I refer to as ours. Daddy did not own it. Nobody living on the Plantation owned the house that they lived in. It belong to the Plantation owner who lived in Sulphur, Louisiana.

I would only sit in the living room if someone else was in there already. We did not get a TV until I was about ten years old. The living room was a sitting and talking and visiting and just relaxing room until we got that TV.

When momma awoke me in the mornings for school, she usually was back in the kitchen before I made it out of bed. No matter how fast I tried to get out of bed, she was back in the kitchen. I would get up; go to our door which was joining the living room. This door was always closed when we slept. I would peak into the living room to see if my sister or anyone else was in the room. Many times no one was in there so I would fling the door open and make a bee line to the kitchen. I did not spend very much time cutting across this room to get to the kitchen. The kitchen was on one side of the living room, my bedroom was on one side, and momma and daddy's bedroom was on the other side.

Sitting in the living room facing my bedroom, the kitchen was on the right, and momma and daddy's bedroom was on the left. We did not have a room on the other side of the living room. This was the outside of the house. We did have a window on that side.

I do not remember how or why Moses got started, but he made me walk the line. Many times I came flying across the linoleum cover wood floor and sliding and sometimes falling into the kitchen. I caught my momma smiling on several occasions. I never added up two plus two to get four. It just never occurred to me that Moses was a joke to them. I figured it out years later. But if the old house was still standing today, I would have no desire to sit or stand, for that matter, in the living room all by myself. And thats that.

CHAPTER 2

A LITTLE LATER IN MY LIFE: AGES SIX, SEVEN, EIGHT, AND NINE

Me

Playing on the Plantation with Ronald, Sonny, Sister, (later with Mark), Gail, James, Bobbie Jo, Anna May, Gerald, Jimmy,

Rodney, Wayne, Lonnie Ray, Poochie, Leon, Nou Nou and others, was just plain fun.

Doing chores, like shucking, shelling and grinding corn, feeding the chickens, pigs, cows, cats and dogs with corn, slop, hay and table scrapes as a little boy on the farm is something that you did every day. It was just a part of your day. You learn to do chores as soon as you are big enough to do them. When you start in the first grade, you do some chores before the school bus come and again after school when you got back home. Not big jobs but the little things that had to get done. Your bigger brother and sister did some of the harder chores around the house and yard. Being little, I just had to grow into those jobs.

There was still plenty of time to play. And boy did we play. We played- hide and go seek, you are IT, kick the stick (because most of the time we did not have a can), mumbley peg, hop scotch, jump rope, marbles, pitch and catch, throw the cane reeds, base ball and other games. We played in the ditch, played in the canals, played on the levee, played in the shell and gravel roads, played in the yard, played in cow pasture, played in the mule pasture, chewed sugar can during harvesting time, chewed black tar pulled from the water tanks, played in the barn, played in the sun, played in the shade, played under the house, played in the rain, did not play in the house to much. It was fun most of the time. We caught dragonflies, butterflies, and lighting bugs. Put them in a jar at night; let them all go sometime later. We just wanted to see if we could catch them.

I remember the last time I rode in a car with Momma driving. I may have been six or seven years old. It was during grinding/harvesting season and Momma was driving on the Plantation. We were going to Mrs. Olivia Falcon's house in Daddy's black four door flat trunk 1938 (I believe) Plymouth. This is the first car that I can recall that we owned. We had made a right turn off the shell road that the sugar house was on onto a dirt road or should I say mud road because it had been raining and it was now a mud road that lead to Mrs. Olivia's house. The field hands and the tractors and cane loaders were all working in the area. They made large ruts in the road with their heavy equipment. Momma said "I believe I can make it." Well, before I knew what happened, we were sideways in the mud road and the car was facing the large canal which had been on our right after we turned onto this road. I started crying and begged Momma to let me out and I will walk in the mud to Mrs. Olivia's house. We could see it in front of us about a quarter of a mile and I knew that I could walk that distance. Momma said to stay in the car.

Somehow she got the car heading the right way back to the Falcon's house. I do not know how she done it and I do not remember us getting out of the car at all. I guess my Momma was not going to let all the men working nearby say that she cannot drive. Somehow we made it to the house. I do not remember why we went there in the first place and I also do not remember the ride back. I guess nothing out of the ordinary happened on the way back because I would have remembered it. I cannot remember my Momma driving the car anytime after this memory. It may have been about this time that she stopped driving a car. I do remember my sister who is four years older than me, driving Momma everywhere she wanted to go and when I got my driver's license at age fourteen, I started driving Momma around also. My sister got married in my fifteenth year and moved to Plaquemine, so I drove Momma where she needed to go from this time forward, if Daddy could not do it.

I used to get up in the morning, do some house chores, had coffee-milk and bread for breakfast, then caught the bus in front of the house for school. I did this through the first grade, second grade, third grade, and third grade. I liked the third grade so much I spent two years in it. I made all A's my second year. The part about me LIKING the third grade so much that I spent two years in it is not true. A friend of mine, Johnny Martinez, and I made a pact our first year in the third grade. The pact was to fail that year in the third grade as Bootsy Parker was doing in every grade. We supposedly just wanted to see what it felt like. I did not try very hard that year. It came to the end of the year and that little bastard Johnny passed and I failed. I know it was very stupid of me to try something like this and now that I have admitted it for the very first time, anybody who reads this will also know how stupid I was. I was taught several lessons here. One of which was do not take a friends word and another was to be very careful who you consider your friend. Still another lesson here is to never try anything as stupid as this, just to see how Bootsy Parker feels.

I still think that the teacher, after seeing all the A's that I was making in my second year in the third grade, should have pushed me up to the fourth grade. After all, even Bootsy Parker got pushed up to the fourth grade. I do not care if he had already spent two or three years in the third grade, the point is that he got pushed up to the fourth grade. I felt that I was as smart as Bootsy, maybe ever a litter smarter. No offense Boosty. I never failed another grade the rest of my career in the state public school system.

VERY COLD TIMES

When I was about seven years old and living on the plantation, I still remember during the cold winters, standing by the only heater allowed to be on in the house just before bed time. It was in the living room. I would stand so close to it, I almost caught on fire on several occasions. I did this to warm my pajamas before running and getting into my bed in another room. I would run, close the door behind me, jump into bed, get under the quilts and freeze for a while until I warmed up a spot. After I got a spot sort of warm, I did not move because the sheets were ice cold. My flannel pajamas cooled off in a hurry when I left the heater. We used to have home made quilts to cover us. Not blankets, but quilts up to one inch thick and thicker. They are much thicker and heavier than blankets. Blankets would not keep us warm in our raindrop splitting, fourteen-foot ceiling house.

When Momma would call me in the mornings to get up for school, I felt like fifty pounds lay on top of me all night. Sometimes you put your feet on the floor that was covered with linoleum in a water puddle that developed during the night. You were wide-awake in less than a second and made a B-line to the living room where the only heater allowed to be lit was burning. We had propane gas heaters in every room of the house, but Daddy was afraid of the old house burning down or just did not want to burn to much gas or something.

The heater in the living room would stay lit as long as some adult was at home to keep an eye on it. We always kept a little tin can with some water in it on the heater. As the water evaporated, we added more water. This was supposed to help keep the fumes from affecting us too badly.

Daddy always got up early for work, so he went to bed with the chickens each night. What this means is- he went to bed early usually after the six thirty news was over. No heaters were allowed to be on when we were sleeping. Momma would turn it off when she went to bed. If we wanted to stay up later on week ends, no way. When Momma went to bed, everybody else went to bed because the heater was being turned off. Daddy would turn it on and light it when he got up on the mornings.

This was a miserable time, but we did not know that it was a miserable time until we moved to White Castle (town) in 1957. This was just like being poor. You did not know you were poor if everybody in the area was poor also. You cannot judge yourself against what others have if they have as little as you. All of us on the Cedar Grove Plantation did not have much. We did eat well and we had clothes on our backs. In the early years, we went the summers without new shoes, as did everyone else on the plantation. We usually got a pair just before school started up again. I did not have the benefit of hand-me-down clothes or shoes because my big brother was eight years older than I was. By the time his stuff could fit me, either a cousin had it or more than likely; it was worn out and trashed by then.

During these years, the summers weren't too bad. But the winters were just terrible. Sometimes I had so many clothes on that I could not move. And that is the truth.

TRIPS TO NEW ORLEANS

From to time that I was six or seven years old in the late 1940s, I can remember going to New Orleans for over night visits with relatives. We would sleep at my Daddy's sister's house. Nan Maude and Uncle Arthur Richards lived on Napoleon Avenue about two or three blocks from the Napoleon Avenue ferry that crossed the Mississippi River to go over to the West Bank.

Barry Raffray (me), Newton Raffray (Dad), and Cousin Martha Ann Richards in New Orleans

We used Nan Maude's house as a base to make visits to other relatives like Daddy's brother, Uncle Pete. His real name was Sterling, but we knew him as Pete. He lived in New Orleans also with his wife, Aunt Junita and their five kids. Nan Maude and Uncle Arthur had three kids.

While in New Orleans proper, we would make visits to other older folks that I cannot remember their names. They were either relatives or very good friends of our family. Most of these folks on the New Orleans side of the River was on Daddy's side of the family.

Nan Maude and Uncle Arthur lived in a fourplex two story house. Facing the house from the street, they lived on the bottom left side of the house. There were seven rooms in the house, all in a row. From the street, you entered the living room, than a bedroom, another bedroom, the kitchen, a bedroom and another bedroom than a large bathroom was at the end of the house. There was one or two side entrances from the alley also. You had to walk through every room to get to the bathroom. They lived there with the same three other families in the fourplex for over forty years until the late 1970s. They always rented and never did buy a house in New Orleans. When the younger generation took ownership of the two story fourplex and wanted to do something else with the property, all the folks living there had to move out. We thought Nan Maude was going to go to Jackson, which was where they sent people that went coo-coo (crazy) in Louisiana. She went into depression and withdrew from everybody. It took a year or two for her to get over having to move from this location.

Uncle Arthur rented another house; a duplex just two blocks from the old house. He put a lot of his own money into this place to make it more comfortable for them. After about two years, Nan Maude snapped out of her depression state and they went on with their lives.

The very next trip to New Orleans, we would again sleep at Nan Maude's and use their house as the base to go and visit Momma's relatives on the west side of the river. From Nan Maude's, we would take the Napoleon Avenue ferry across the Mississippi River to go to Marrero where we visited with Momma's Aunt Mamie. She married Momma's daddy's brother, Uncle Oscar, who died before I ever knew him. As I grew up, they would say that I looked like Uncle Oscar. Aunt Mamie had three kids.

On other visits on this side of the River, we went to Harvey, Gretna and Westwego to visit Momma's sister, Aunt Tutsie. She was also my Nan Nan. Aunt Tut, as we called her, was married to Uncle Norman Delaune. They had nine or ten kids. They moved around a lot on the west side of the river and sometimes it was hard to find them. There were times that we went where we knew they lived the last time we was there, but they had moved and the folks there did not know where they moved to, so we just could not find them.

I loved it when we went to Nan Maude's. Sometime we went to the Lakefront on Saturday night to eat. The Lakefront was Lake Pontchartrain were some great seafood restaurants were. The older folks had their favorite and that is usually where we ate.

Uncle Arthur used to love Studebaker cars and always owned one until he could not get them anymore. Then he went to the Chevy Nova for a number of years. He kept his cars in impeccable shape. Every one I ever saw was always clean and waxed. They did not have a garage where they lived on Napoleon Avenue, so he rented one several blocks away just to keep his car lock up and out of the weather.

When we arrived at their house in New Orleans, Bobbie Jo or I would go knock on their door, if they were not already outside. Nan Maude or Uncle Arthur would come out and tell Daddy where to park on the street. The people who lived in the Fourplex had a certain area where they parked their cars and we could not park in their spots even if it was empty at the time we arrived. Those spots were reserve for the folks that lived there.

Sometime Uncle Arthur got permission from one of his neighbors to use their spot for a day. We seldom parked in the same spot that we parked in the last trip. Usually after we had a spot, we sued that spot for the two days we would be there.

When Uncle Arthur would take us for a driving tour of Canal Street, or St. Charles Avenue, or the French Quarter, or wherever, we had better keep our eyes peeled and hold on. One time, we saw the sites on Canal Street at fifty miles per hour one afternoon. Uncle Arthur had a heavy foot and timed the red lights just right. We did not stop one time. It would have been nice to catch at least one red light- we might have seen something. As he drove, he pointed here and there and here again while talking the whole time. Daddy said "damn Arthur, I can't see anything, you are going too fast." Uncle Arthur would say back, "Well, Bibby, I have to keep up with the traffic or we will be run over." The New Orleans drivers did go fast. I guess they all knew where they were going.

I went to a Mardi Gras in New Orleans when I was about six or seven years old. A couple of blocks from Uncle Arthur's house was Magazine Street. Each Mardi Gras there was a big parade on Magazine Street. I remember having on a little cowboy outfit. A cowboy hat, a little holster and a cap pistol and little chaps over my pants.

I believe Daddy and Momma was with me in the huge crowd but it could have been my sister and my older cousin Jackie Richards. They told me that I was at the Mardi Gras. I heard a lot of hollowing and yelling but all I could see was behinds. Every where I looked there was a behind in my face. People would bend over to pick things off the sidewalk. They would push and shove. The behinds were really dangerous now, because they were loaded and in the cocked position. I was trying to duck but could not find a position where a behind would not be in my face. I was disgusted, disgruntled, and dismayed by all these behinds in my face.

It could not be proven to me that I went to a Mardi Gras this day. It seemed like a function whereby they knew that Barry the little cowboy was there and they said "let's show him our butts."

I was a sad little boy. It seemed like a very long walk back to Uncle Arthur's house.

To this day, I do not know why no one put me on their shoulders where I could see something. I was not fat any more. I had slimed down pretty well from my two years old size.

All I saw was assholes and elbows. The assholes was in my face every where I looked. The elbows is what I saw when I looked up. I would not go to another Mardi Gras in New Orleans until I was about forty eight years old, when I went with my friends Jordi Alamo and Christian Isonseis of Unimar, International Inspection Company.

MY FIRST WHOLE CAN OF BEER

During the time that I was seven or eight years old, on Saturday nights, Daddy and Momma would drive to White Castle and meet friends at Mr. Emile Shaheens's Bar and Grocery. They would sit and talk and have a few beers to pass the time. It got to be something that I looked forward to. I would see some of my friends there and we played and tried not being a bother to the adults. I would occasionally beg for and get a sip of their beer of choice, which was Goebal in those days. Goebal came in small six-ounce cans. It was the smallest container of beer one could buy so this made it the cheapest also. I kind of liked the taste of beer even at this age.

Sometimes Mr. Emile or some other adult would give me a nickel to play the slot machine there. Gambling was illegal in all of Louisiana. This included slots, dice, cards, pinball, and other type of gaming with the exception of bingo. All the bars had slot machines in them and did not worry about the Law. The Law had their own slot machines. Some of the adults also played cards for high stakes without the worry of being raided. My folks did not get involved with these gambling people.

DIGRESS A LITTLE

The gambling activity stayed like this until sometimes in the early 1960s, when our Sheriff of Iberville Parish warned the Governor (J. J. McKeithen), who was sending State Troopers into other parishes to smash slot machines, to stay our of Iberville Parish. Jessel Ourso, our Sheriff, was a State Trooper for many years before being elected Sheriff, made the mistake of being shown on state wide television shaking his finger at the Governor and warning him to stay away. The next day, there was slot machines in the main street of White Castle being smashed by State Troopers using what looked like fifteen pound malls (large hammers). The Governor had no choice in the matter after the scene on TV.

This happened in every town in the Parish. After the Troopers left, the owners of the businesses who had the slots got in the streets gathering the coins. After all coins were picked up, they then picked up the pieces of the machines so auto traffic could move again. The Sheriff is the most powerful official in any county/parish, but the Governor is more powerful when it come down to a pissing match between the two. Jessel certainly lost this one.

Almost a year leading up to the "Great Slot Machine Bash", we had a nickel slot machine in our house on the plantation. My cousin, J. C. Breaux, had several machines placed about. Most of his machines was in the smaller, black folks bars. The larger operations were all taken by the politicians and their cronies and also some underworld folks that paid the politicians off. Momma used to love to play slots, which is why we ended up with one of

J. C.'s nickel slots in our house. My uncle who lived with us would play it, and my brother and some of our friends from White Castle would come over and play it. When I could find some nickels, I would play it too. J. C. would come over once a month and empty the box and divide it half-and-half with momma. He had the only key to get into the back of the slot where the money box was. He would often say that this was the best slot the he had out. He made more on our slot then the business places where he had his other slots. Momma would put her half right back into the machine. In no time at all, she was broke again, but she knew she would get half of that back, plus half of what everybody else who came by put in. Like my buddies, Davis Callegan, Steve Landry, Bobby Pearce, and others.

One week several strangers came to the house and inquired about wanting to play our slot machine. I talked to a couple of them one time. Our line for strangers was that we do not have the slot machine any more. Mamma got afraid after the third stranger came by and the Governor had started knocking them out of selected places. She had J. C. pick up his machine. We were all sadden to see it go. Some of my friends were disappointed also. It was about two or three weeks later that the shit hit the fan in Iberville Parish. We were really glad that we got rid of that slot machine. J. C. wished that we still had it, because he placed it in a black barroom and it got smashed with some of his other machines. He later told us, that he was out in the road picking up change from his used to be slots.

BACK TO THE EARLY FIFTIES

When I was in the second grade, I had the chance to be in a play as a little elf. I wasn't sure if I wanted to do it or not. I was promised a wish if I did the part by my Daddy. So I played the elf. I had this little elf outfit that momma made and everything.

Momma and Daddy came to the play. I cannot remember if my sister and brother was there or not.

Me Dressed as an Elf

After the play, Daddy said, "all right Barry, what do you want?" I said lets go to Mr. Emile Shaheen's for a beer. Daddy said we will go there but you cannot have a beer.

We got there, showed Mr. Emile my outfit which I still had on. Daddy was going to buy me a soda pop. I said that I wanted a beer. We had a lot of discussion about this. I said but you promised that I could have what I wanted. He relented, and told me if I ordered a beer that I would have to drink the whole thing.

We Raffrays don't believe in waste. I said that I wanted a beer. One little Goebel coming up. I really thought that I was something. After about three sips, I had enough. It was just not as good as the one sip every hour or so. Daddy said, "You wanted it, you will drink it all, we will sit here until you drink every bit of it." I tried my best. After each sip, I would gag. It was just terrible tasting. After about an hour and a half, I still had a little beer to go. It was past hot at this time. I was feeling really bad. I think I was drunk. Daddy said "O K, don't ever ask me for a sip of beer ever again." I threw up, but I don't remember where I was at the time. I even felt bad the next day.

I did not drink or take another sip of beer for another ten years or so after that. Every now and then, momma would offer me a sip of beer at Mr. Emile's place on the weekends. I would say NO, and run to play. A couple times as I looked back, I saw momma and daddy laughing. I used to wonder just what are they laughing at, I did not hear anybody say anything that was funny.

PICNICS

From the time I was very young until I was an older teenager, we went on Picnics and outings on a regular basis. When Nan Maude (Daddy's sister) and Uncle Author came to visit from New Orleans, many times we went on an all day picnic. We went to Grand Bayou, Bayou Corn, Shell Beach and other places. We could fish, crab, play in the water and sometimes, swim. Momma would pack picnic lunches and other times we would bring food and cook out at the picnic area.

We also picnic with the Mabiles and Henrys from the plantation and the Breauxs and Hymels and others.

Anna May Miller and Leon and Gerald Miller lived next door to us and did not get off the plantation very much. Their dad, Mr.

Tan was the caretaker of the plantation's animals and did not have a car. Mr. Tan died when they were still teenagers. Anyway, Anna May was my sisters age and she would come along with us on many occasions. One time we took Gerald and Leon with us on a picnic to Grand Bayou. Leon was the oldest and had never been on a picnic. He really enjoyed himself and so did Gerald. We really enjoyed having Leon with us too.

We were fishing and crabbing and we caught a crab on a chicken neck. We had the crab in the net when Leon said "I'll get it Miss Josie," which was my momma's name. Before anyone could tell him not to just grab a crab, the crab had him. It locked on to one or two of Leon's fingers and he pulled his hand out of the net hollowing and jumping around trying to shake the crab off this fingers. He was twilling around and round waving his arm in and out trying to throw the crab off his hand. All this action seemed like it took several minutes but it was not that long. He finally made another big swing of his arms and the crab let go and flew to within one foot of the other side of the bayou. It was a far piece and a very good throw. The older folks took care of his fingers than we all had a good laugh at Leon expense. He laughed too. He never reached in again to grab a crab. I still do not know if he had ever seen a crab before this one. I still smile when I remember this time in my life. I wonder if Leon remembered it.

Dad and Mr. Joe Mabile

POTTY PANTS
(BAD TIME)

    I went through a period of potty in the pants during these first several years of school. I do not remember in which grade it came to a halt, but I am very happy that it did. I used to have a problem using the toilet/outhouse to do number two. I had to take all my clothes off. I would hop up on the thrown on my feet and crouch down over the hole. I could/would not let my behind touch the seating area at all. I just had this thing about it. After I started going to school, I did not like going to the toilet because they did not have any doors on the stalls and I could not go with the idea that everybody coming into the bathroom could look at me. I surely did not want to take all my clothes off and mount the thrown on my feet in front of anybody. I used to try and hold it until I got back home at about three thirty in the afternoon each day. Sometime, I just could not hold it that long and I pooped in my jeans. I would sit at the back of the bus- by myself on the way home.

Momma and my sister (who road the bus also) would be very upset with me after I arrived home. Momma did not know what she was going to do with me. I wondered about that too. I never did tell my Momma or sister why I did what I did in my pants. This is the first time to tell and I am telling everyone who will read this account of my life.

One time (the last time I remember doing it in my pants), during the second or third grade, I had a case of diarrhea. I had really bad stomach cramps and I just could not hold it back until I got home. I used to be able to make it home many times without doing it in my pants. I also used to have problems getting a bowel movement going after being on the pot for twenty minutes or so. Just after leaving school, it finally all came out while on the bus. Everybody on the bus knew it this time. The high school kids and the grammar school kids- everyone knew. Even Mr. Cleve Callegan the bus driver knew. My sister was really upset.

When we got near our house she told me that Momma will punish me and that I should be ashamed. Which I was. Wouldn't you? It was a long walk up the isle of the bus from the back seat. I had the stuff running down both of my legs. Thank goodness I had on long legged jeans. They held most of it in, but did not help with the smell. I walked this long isle like I was bow legged. During the longer walk from the road up the sidewalk to our house, my sister ran ahead of me to prepare our Momma for the mess that was coming.

Of course Momma was outdone. She put about five or six inches of water in a number 3 wash tub and had me take my clothes off and get in it. This was in a bedroom not the privacy of our bathroom. She helped me clean off and was talking the whole time. I just do not remember what she was saying, but I was being scolded and shamed.

When I got out of the tub, my pant and drawers went in. After drying off, my Momma dressed me in one of my sister's dresses. It dragged the floor. After all she was my Big sister and was bigger than me and four years older. I felt freedom in the dress that I had never felt before. Then Momma said "baby, why don't you go show Mr. Braus how you look with Bobbie Jo's dress on." I said "I will," which really surprised Momma and I think she wished I would not do it. But she could not back down now.

Mr. Braus worked at Cedar Grove Plantation Store, which was across the shell road from our house. So Bobbie Jo and I walked to the store. I do not remember feeling ashamed or embarrassed in the least. I did a twirl for Mr. Braus and Milton (who worked in the store with Mr. Braus (pronance Brossy), for many years until it was shut down in the 1970s or very early 1980s). Mr. Braus smiled and said I would be a pretty little girl and gave me a cookie (which Mr. Burton- the guy who owned the Plantation, paid for I'm sure). I cannot remember if my sister got a cookie or not. Mr. Braus always liked my sister and me. We were polite to him and treated him with respect every time we saw him. He would never give a cookie to most of the other kids on the Plantation because he did not like them.

Sometime after this event, I forced myself to use the toilet in the normal way. I took me some time to get used to it, but I did it. Sometimes, even today, I still wait longer than I should to go to the bathroom. Thus far, I have not had as bad a mess as I did when I was little.

THE HOT WATER BOTTLE

We had this apparatus called "the hot water bottle" that was stationed in the bathroom. It hung on a large nail on the back of our bathroom door and was convenient when someone was on the toilet. This hot water bottle was good to have sometimes and not so good at all other times. It was made out of rubber and was red in color. It was sort of an orange red. It was about twelve inches long and five or six inches wide. It had an opening/mouth over an inch in diameter. I believe it had a screw type stopper or cap that plugged the opening when in use. It also had a hose about six feet long attached to the bottom with a three inch black turned up nozzle at the end of the hose. The nozzle was about a half inch in diameter with a small hole through it for hot water or other liquid to flow. The hose had a small clamp on it to pinch off the flow of water when in use. The neck or top of this object was made so it looked like a collar above the stopper and could be hung on a nail. It was made of thick rubber and fairly strong. This apparatus would expand when liquid was placed into it. It could be used to put ice cubes or cold water into it for burns or bruises or hot water for a stiff neck or aching joints, etc. etc. But the most diabolical thing that it was used for was to give a WASHOUT. I hated washouts. There was a period in my life that I had washouts on a fairly regular basis. Like from six to eight or nine years old.

It you had trouble pooping, it was washout time. As mentioned earlier, I did not like to use public bathrooms. After I started the first grade I would hold my poop all day until I got back home. A lot of the time when I did this, I would stay plugged up. When that happened, the fight was on. Momma would have to corner me somewhere in the house and drag me to the bathroom for a good washout. She usually had to tell me "I'll wait until your Daddy get home and tell him" to get me to not run away any more. She would put hot/warm water and something else in the bottle that would help to unplug poop. I had to bend over and the insertion was made into my you know where. The hot water bottle was loaded and hanging on a large nail above the heads of anyone who sat on the toilet. She would release the little clamp on the hose and the liquid would flow into my stomach. I got so big I thought I would pop each time I went through this procedure. I would beg and holler - but to no avail. Momma knew where my full mark was.

I can still remember my Momma telling me over and over that if I cannot poop on my own and continue this constant constipation, I would have to get my piles cut out by Old Doctor Tomeny before I was fourteen years old. I did not like that prospect. This made me think of the red rubber doughnut that Daddy and Momma had to use for weeks after they each had their piles cut out by that same old doc Tomeny. I did not want to come face to face with that possibility. And I didn't. After I started using the toilets to poop at school, I did not have to get washouts anymore. It was great relief to me to not poop in my pants anymore and to not have to go through any more washouts. I was very delighted the morning that I got out of bed on my fourteenth birthday and I still had my own original PILES.

It took me another ten years or so to learn the other use for the "hot water bottle." The washouts for me were not its primary use or why it was invented in the first place. Go figure. Who would have thought it.

LEARNING TO RIDE A BICYCLE

After one of our trips to New Orleans to visit with Nan Maude and Uncle Arthur, we brought back a little two wheel bicycle. This bicycle had what they called "training wheels" on it. These are small wheels that attached to the rear wheel of the bicycle. When these small wheels were attached, the bicycle would stand up without a kick stand. In fact, as I recall, this bicycle did not have a kick stand.

As soon as we arrived home that Sunday afternoon, Daddy took the bicycle out of the trunk of the car. I tried to ride it. My sister held it up straight and I got on it. When I started peddling, it would lean over to one side or another and I would fall over. I was not used to keeping my weight balanced and even with the training wheels; I would lean to one side to much and cause the bicycle to tip over.

I practiced with the training wheels on for a number of days and learned to ride pretty good. My sister or daddy took them off. This created another problem.

My sister would push the bicycle with me on it. I would concentrate on keeping it upright. I had trouble peddling and keeping the bicycle upright at the same time. Chewing gum during this time was really out of the question. When my sister stopped pushing, I would fall over. We worked on this for maybe four or five days, I do not know.

It came to pass, one day my sister was pushing the bicycle and me and I was peddling in front of Anna Maye Miller's house. I kept peddling. I yelled to my sister to stop pushing. I kept going and I was still peddling. I yelled again to stop pushing and looked back to give her that look that meant business. By now, I was in front of the water pump shed. When I saw her standing in the road still in front of Anna Maye's house, I promptly fell over. She came running to check on me saying you were riding it by yourself. I was not hurt. I took a deep breath, dusted myself off and got back on. I rode past Mr. Granier house then stop peddling so I could slow down and put my feet down on the shell road to keep me from falling over. I now could ride a bicycle without any help. Now I had to learn how to turn around while still riding it.

   I do not remember any big ordeal of turning while the bicycle was still moving. I know that I fell down a number of times. But I got the hang of it fairly quickly and been riding ever since.

SMOKING CIGARETTES AND WATCHING THE GRASS GROW (DON'T TELL ME I'VE NOTHING TO DO)

From the time I was about eight years old to about eleven we rolled and try to smoke home made cigarettes. We were about eleven years old when we figured out how nasty what we were doing was and stopped doing it.

About forty yards from our house was the gathering spot where the laborers (field hands) waited to be picked up by the Overseers to go to work in the fields. Every morning, six days a week, seven during cane planting and harvesting time, and again at one p. m. for some of the workers, the field hands and tractor drivers and others would gather before the designated time to depart for work at this spot. It was near the entrance to the small mule lot where the mule equipment was located and where the mules were rigged up for there work day also.

The workers would sit or stand or lean on the fence or large cotton ball tree rolling their early morning smokes. All of the cigarettes were rolled by hand in 1949 and the early 1950s. None of the field hands could afford packaged cigarettes anyway. Filter tip cigarettes had not been invented yet either. In front of the small mule lot had been the gathering point for many years.

Me, Sonny, and Ronald Mabile

When the bright idea came to Ronald, Sonny and me, that there were thousands of cigarette butts all about this area and we could use them to make smokes, we jumped into action. I got an old empty Prince Albert tobacco can with a pop up lid. On Saturdays after our Daddy's picked up the hands to deliver them to their working spots for the day, we collected the butts, tour off the paper and put the tobacco in my Prince Albert can. We collected hundreds of butts as some of the butts was not even a quarter inch long. These black folks got all the tobacco they could out of a rolled cigarette. I used to watch some of them smoke before being picked up at one p. m. to go back into the field and their lips were blistered from the heat of the cigarette butts. They really got all that can be gotten out of their smokes. I had to be very careful because several times I almost blurted out "save some for us, gee wiz." As soon as they would leave, we would get some fresh tobacco.

The first time collecting the butts took us two hours or so and we only got about a quarter of my Prince Albert can full of tobacco. This was enough to roll several cigarettes but really not that much for the time and efforts we were putting in.

We decided to go to Ronald and Sonny Mabile's house and try em out. We did not have any roll paper and if we would have had the nickel to buy a booklet, we could not do it for four good reasons. First, a nickel was hard to come by and if any one of us had one, we would buy candy or five soda crackers. Second and third, Mr. Braus, if he waited on us, or Milton, if he waited on us, would have told our Dads. Not that they were rat finks or anything like that, but they would tell to protect us and for our own good. And our behinds would have hurt for several days. But this is the way that adults protect little kids. By whipping our asses, they are teaching us a lesson that we were not going to forget any time soon. I got protected several times that this when I was little. And fourth, well, I do not know what the fourth reason is. So we found some newspaper.

We now had the tobacco and the wrapping. We now had to find a place to do the deed and not be seen or get caught. The spot under the Mabile's house where we used to play when it rained looked to be a good spot. We were far enough under there that we could hide behind some brick pillars that held the house off the ground and we had a good view of legs from our spot. It was hard to sneak up on us. From the other three sides of the house, we could not be seen.

One of us got some kitchen matches, I do not remember who. We were now ready for the smokes. I tore a small piece of paper from the newspaper sheet and started trying to roll a cigarette. I did alright. I did not have any glue to get the rolled up cigarette to stick, so I just wet the paper slightly with my tongue and it stuck o k. Time to light er up. But before we could light it, some of the tobacco was falling out of each end. We had seen how the smokers packed their cigs, so I tried it and most of the tobacco came out. I added more tobacco and re-rolled my smoke. I used a match stick to poke some extra tobacco in each end to try and make it a full and firm smoke. By the way, it was a real match stick that I used. We did not have those paper matches then or any bic lighters. The bic ball point pen had not even been invented yet.

I lit it up. It burned fairly quick and tasted like shit. Well maybe not like shit, but it tasted bad. It had some blackish smoke that we never seen come from a regular cigarette. Some time latter we figured out that the really bad taste and blackish smoke came from the inks and dyes that was in the newspaper.

We met like this a number of times over the next several years but did not make a habitat of smoking because the tobacco was just too hard to come by. After picking the work area clean, we did not have another great location like that to go to. We just kept going to the mule lot but would not fine but five or six butts and it took us a month or longer to get enough tobacco for a couple smokes. None of our dads smoked so that eliminated a possible supply there. We just finally gave up on trying to smoke smokes.

CHAPTER 3

DOCTOR/DENTIST VISITS: AGES EIGHT AND NINE

I really did not want to ever go to the medical doctor or dentist. I did not even like to visit people in the hospital because sometimes the doctor came in while you were visiting. The very first thing a doctor or dentist wanted to do as soon as you get in there is to give you one of their shots and some awful tasting medicine.

I had a problem swallowing pills. I could swallow bubble gum the size of a golf ball but I just could not swallow an aspirin or a pill even smaller than an aspirin. This meant that whenever medicine was prescribed for me, it had to be in liquid form. This also meant that even if the pill tasted good or sweet, the liquid would be black, thick and just taste terrible and would leave this awful after taste in your mouth for hours. I hated taking medicine.

I also had problem putting eye drops in my eyes. I just could not make myself do it. From the time I was a little kid until my sister got married and moved away, she would put the drops in my eyes. I would sit in a chair in the kitchen with my head leaned way back. I closed my eyes. She would have the eye dropped full and ready to go over the eye that needed the drops. Sometimes this ordeal took fifteen to twenty minutes to get a couple of drops in my eye. She would wait very quiet and patiently and when I opened my eyes to see if she was still there, BAM- she would squirt the stuff into my eye. She had the patience of Job is what the older folks in our household would remark. This guy, Job, was from the Bible and apparently had a lot of patience during his time for people to still be talking about him during the late 1940s and 1950s.

Thanks to my sister, my eyes got the treatment they needed when it was prescribed by old Dr. Tomney.

Doctor Foley and his Nurse, Doris was the dentist and his helper in town. Almost every tooth in my head was filled by Doc Foley. I did not like going to the Dentist. I did not like being stuck in my mouth by the needles they used. I did not like the grinding of my teeth and still don't when the dentist is making it ready for a filling. It give me the chills. I did not even like it when he cleaned my teeth.

One time when I was about eight years old, Aunt Connie and Uncle Granue (John Ourso) was visiting us and I had a dentist appointment. They drove Momma and me to town to see Dr. Foley. I believe this was just for a check up or something. Dr. Foley used to like to play jokes on people. Being there was not a joking matter to me. He would come out into the waiting room to look around and see who was there. They did not have a receptionist in those days to announce you. Then he would go back to the person he was working on and have them hollow and yell for mercy just to affect the folks there waiting to see him. That worked on me. After looking in his waiting room and noticing that I was waiting, and he knew that I did not like needles and shots, he come out with a big needle and motioned that it was for me. My thought was 'THAT'S YOUR ASS' I am out of here and I took off. I made it out the door and down the steps before anyone knew what happened. Uncle Granue caught me on the railroad track heading for downtown White Castle. I made it about one hundred yards or so before he caught up with me and dragged me back. I guess I stirred up everybody and interrupted the routine for a while because from that day forward, Dr. Foley didn't try to be funny or tease me with this needle business. If

Uncle Granue would not have caught me, I would still be running like Forrest Gump did in that movie.

DEAD MAN'S MONEY

One time when I was about eight or nine years old, Daddy was told that one of his field hands did not come home during the weekend. This was not unusual for this fellow. He was known to do this from time to time. He was the best ditch and drain digger on the plantation. This was when the ditches and field drains were dug by hand with shovels. He as so good, he got paid by the foot because he covered so much more ground than the other diggers who got paid by the hour. But he had this drinking problem and sometimes, after payday on Saturdays, he would ride his horse to White Castle and stay there for several days until his money ran out even if it meant missing a day or two of work. When he was broke, he came back, slept it off for a day than showed up ready to work. I guess since the plantation paid off every two weeks, this fellow probably did this every other week.

Well, Monday or Tuesday, while putting the other field hands to work in the back of the plantation, someone noticed his horse standing on the headland near the White Castle boundary line. One of the other Overseers came and got Daddy, who happened to be home drinking a cup of coffee. I asked Daddy if I could go and he said yes. So off we went.

We lived on the River road and had to go three quarters through the plantation to get to where the horse was. When we got there, there was seven or eight black men and the other two Overseers (Mr. Joe and Jules Mabile), looking in this big ditch. The Sheriff had been called. They all recognized the man even though he was face down in the ditch. This ditch had about six inches of water in it at this time. Over the weekend, it had much more than that because it had been raining. Everyone figured that he was riding his horse back as usual and for some reason fell off into the ditch and drown because he was to drunk to get out. The Mabiles, had not checked the body out, so Daddy jumped into the ditch and went through the pants and jacket pockets. He found about eighty cents. He offered it to all the black men there. One by one to a man, they did not want the money of a dead man. He could not force anyone to take it. Daddy tried to approach several men saying you need the money and they backed away. They all needed the money, but was not going to take money off a dead man. Boy have things and times really changed since then, huh?

The Sheriff and a team of men showed up and after Daddy gave out the name and other information, he took me home eighty cents richer. You damn right I took the money. This was the most money I ever had. I needed this money and put it to good use with Mr. Brase at the plantation store.

THE BLACKSMITH SHOP

Mr. Bolotte was the blacksmith for the Plantation. He was the go-to guy for horseshoes and all the equipment and tools used for cultivating and harvesting the crops. He made and molded horseshoes from rods of iron. He also repaired all plow shears and chopper disc and made replacement parts for such. He made items to repair the mule drawn carts and the tractors, loaders, sugarcane cutters, the field loading derricks and other equipment used on the plantation and for tenant farmers who rented land from the plantation.

The blacksmith on any plantation was a very important person. He kept the equipment and mules working. The blacksmith worked long, hard hours every day. This was hard and hot work. The blacksmith had to be in good shape to do this work and handle the heavy iron and tools used to beat this iron into the shapes needed to do a job.

Among other duties, he had to keep the hearth hot at all times. The hearth was near the middle of the shop on our plantation. It was made of old fireproof bricks is what I recall. It had a chimney going up through the top of the roof to let out smoke and heat. Sometimes even sparks from the coals came out of the top when Mr. Bolotte was stoking the coals to get them hotter for the iron he was getting ready to work on.

I do not remember what Mr. Bolotte burned to keep the supply of cinders/coals, but his hearth was always hot and ready to go after just a stirring stick and some air from an apparatus that was a windbag. It had a sort of V or funnel shape and looked like an accordion laying flat. It had two wooden handles on it. When you pulled the handles away from each other, it sucked in air. When you squeezed them together, it flew air on the coals and really heated them up. This apparatus was narrow at the nose end and about a foot or more, wide at the end with the handles. As I mentioned before, it looked like a squeeze box/accordion – except it lay flat most of the time. You could use it in a stationary position or move it around the hearth to blow air on the coals to get them hot. As an eight or nine year old, I had the privilege to watch Mr. Bolotte take a flat iron bar and heat it up and beat on it after hot, on an anvil with a large ball peen hammer. He would heat the iron, beat it after it was red hot, soaked it in water and heat it up again. This process was done over and over until he beat the shape he wanted and it was complete.

I watched as he made plow shares and chopper blades out of sheet iron using the same technique. It was hot, heavy, manual labor with not short cuts.

THE NOT SO GREAT ROCK THROWING CONTEST

When I was about eight or nine years old, I was playing with Ronald and Sonny Mabile at their house. We were playing on their shell driveway just off the gravel River road under the large Mulberry tree. They had two large Mulberry trees and both were near their house. One would bare huge purple Mulberry and the other huge white Mulberrys. These fruits would grow over an inch long and over a half inch in diameter. They both were very sweet and tasty. But if you got any Mulberry juice on you clothes, it was not coming off. You had a stain on your clothes for life. We often played around and in these trees, as we did the China berry (ball) trees and the pink and red flowered Crepe Myrtle trees. They were not bushes, they were trees.

Someone got the idea to throw a rock at the wheel of a passing vehicle. It sounded alright to me because I knew that I could throw a rock with the best of them. It would not be a problem to hit a wheel passing by at forty miles per hour. I guess we knew that Mr. Clarence Martinez would be passing by in his school bus from bringing the high school teenagers back to Bayou Goula. Us grammar kids were usually on the first bus trip to go home. Then the older kids made the second trip. I believe this is the way it was for the first three or four grades.

We saw the bus coming. It was passing by Dorseyville which was a half mile down the River road from us. We each got a rock from the gravel road and backed up to the shell driveway. We all planned to throw our rocks at the same time when the bus past in front of us. We would go for the rear wheel on the bus because Mr. Clarence would be in the front of the bus and would not know what hit him. With all the gravel that flew when something as big as a bus drove on it, on one could tell if a rock was thrown or not.

We all cocked our arms, the bus was passing by. BAM-I heard this rock hit. Then all of a sudden, dust and gravel started flying everywhere. Mr. Clarence had kit the brakes and the bus was stopping. I said "RUN" and took off. I thought Ronald and Sonny was running also. I ran past the Mabile's house and through two gates and into a chicken coup/house. I was hiding under the chicken roost in the chicken poop. In less than a minute here came Sonny and Ronald pointing my hiding place out to Mr. Clarence. He told me to come out, which I did. He wanted me to see what I did to his bus. He was very upset. I said that it was not my rock, that I hit the tire. This is when Ronald and Sonny said that they did not throw a rock. They just made like they did. I did not buy this story on bit, but Mr. Clarence Martinez did.

There was a good size dent in his fender over the wheel. I guess I started crying and said that I was sorry, still not believing my two accomplices had not thrown a rock

Mr. Clarence asked where my daddy was. In the field working, say I. Mr. Clarence knew who we were and said he would contact my dad when Mr. Joe Mabile turned into the driveway. He talked with Mr. Joe. Showed him what I done and said he would contact the police. I really started crying now. I was told how dangerous this was and damaging other people's property could land me in jail and so on. I kept saying that I would never do this again, still pissed at Ronald and Sonny for me taking the rap by myself. Mr. Joe said that he would notify Newton (my dad) of this situation. Mr. Clarence finally left.

I do not remember being punished by Daddy. I don't think Mr. Joe ever told him. I do not remember if Mr. Joe whipped his boys or not. I know that I did not catch a whipping.

I still do not believe that it was my rock that hit the bus. I also still do not believe that Ronald and Sonny did not throw a rock. They just could not hide good enough and got caught first and blamed the whole thing on me. Those little bastards, I bet that is what they did.

As I grew up, I became close to Mr. Clarence Martinez. He owned the store across from the high school and when I was in high school saw him quite often. After high school, when I was a parts man for J & L Engineering Company in White Castle, several time Mr. Clarence came to our house on Sunday mornings to get me out of bed to go open our parts department up to sell hem a part that he needed for a tractor. He did this on holidays too, until I got married and moved to Baton Rouge. Pay back is hell. I guess he figured that I still owed him for the dent I put in his bus many years earlier. He did not have any problem coming to get me a any hour to go open up the parts department so he could get what he needed.

By the way, I never did throw another rock or anything else at a vehicle after this one time experience. Once, like this was enough for me.

CAUGHT UP A TREE

I was play with Ronald and Sonny Mabile at their house one day. We were playing in their front yard in a big tree. This tree was close to the fence that divided their yard from our yard. I do not remember the game we were playing but it included climbing in the tree and going out on a limb.

I had short pants on and a button down short sleeve shirt and no shoes, so it must have been during the summer. Somehow, I got out on this branch and I was going to jump down to the ground, maybe to get away from one of the Mabiles. We may have been playing "Tag, you're IT," or something like that. I was higher up in the tree than I thought I was and when I looked down, I changed my mind about just jumping from this spot. So I leaned forward and put my arms around the branch that I was on. I was going to just ease myself over the branch and hang by my hands then let go of the branch. This way I was much closer to the ground. I though I could drop from this height and not hurt myself.

Well, unbeknown to me, when I was leaning over to put my arms around the branch, my shirt collar got caught on a broken off part of what used to be another limb. It stuck out about eight inches from the branch it grew from. When I let go to drop to the ground, this stub of a limb had me by the collar. My shirt pulled up to my neck and my arms were locked in the air. I could not move my arms enough to grab the nearest branch. I was just hanging there by the collar of my shirt. I started chocking a bit because my shirt had pulled up around my neck.

Ronald and Sonny climbed down the tree. They could not reach enough of me from the ground and did not have the strength to pull me up from in the tree. I was hanging and starting trying to holler for help. I could not even wiggle loose. The old shirt I was wearing would not tear away. It was much stronger that it looked. So here I was hanging in the Mabile's tree. I thought that I was a goner for sure. I thought that I was up about nine or ten feet and my feet were seven foot from the ground. I did not think I could last that much longer. I was trying to cough but was having trouble even doing that.

One of the Mabile boys ran to get Miss Violet. She was a good sized woman; much bigger (taller) than my Momma. She came running out to where I was. She was tall enough and strong enough to rap her arms around my lower legs and lift me up to loosen the chock hold that my collar had on me.

On her second lift my arms became free enough to lift my collar over the broken off limb and she let me down easy. I was really happy. My arms were numb and just hanging to my sides. The

Mabiles rubbed them to try and get the blood circulating again and in a few minutes, I was ready to play some more. But not in that damn tree.

I had a red mark around my neck and under both arms that lasted for a couple of days. If it wasn't for my arms, I guess I would have hung myself. I can see how these things happen. I survived that experience without having to go see old Dr. Tomney.

WALKING THE FENCE

It had rained earlier in the day and I was bored and looking for someone to play with. I went to the Mabile's house to look for a playing partner and had another problem.

This is starting to sound like the Mabile's house was bad luck to me. I had never given this any thought until now.

We had the cypress picket fence between our side and back yards. The yard areas were large. Well over an acre each. The fence for the front yard was made of two by fours and hog wire, you know the square or rectangular shaped wire. There would be a four by four post in the ground every so many feet and a two by four runner from each four by four nailed on top. This was when a two by four was a two inch thick by four inches wide board and not a one and a half inch by three and a half inch board. These were really two by fours.

The full four inch width made it great for walking on top of the fence. This type fence started from the side of our house on the shell road. It went to the gravel road in front of our house then made a left turn and went all the way to where the Mabile's yard started. This was over one hundred fifty feet from the corner near the shell road. Where it intersected with the Mabile's fence, it went straight in front of their house and also went left and divided our yard from theirs. Going left where it divided our yards, it passed the big tree that I got hung up on and went about another thirty feet to where the cypress picket fence started. At this point it turned right and went to the Mabile's porch. The part of the fence that went straight in front of their house turned left before it got to their shell driveway and went to the other end of their porch. It had a two section gate that a large truck could drive through about half way from the gravel road to the porch on this side.

The fence from our house has a large two section gate on it also that was near the shell road and across from the plantation store's porch.

When we walked the top of this fence, we could not walk any gate area because the wood on the gates was too narrow. The gates did not have any two by fours on the top of them. They were used in the framing as cross sections. We would straddle the gate or otherwise scoot sideways across it and did not ever touch the ground as that would be against the rules of fence walking.

I would climb our gate across from the store and walk on the top of the fence to the gravel road about sixty feet. Then go left on top of the fence about one hundred fifty feet to the boundary fence between us and the Mabiles. Sometime, I made the left there and walk the seventy five or so feet to the cypress picket fence then right the thirty feet to the porch. All of this without ever touching the ground.

Other times I would go straight at the boundary line onto the Mabile's fence and walk the one hundred plus feet in front of their house than go left before the shell driveway to the gate. I would straddle the gate and scoot until I made it across and get back on top the fence for the rest of the twenty five feet journey to their porch. This section from the gravel road including the gate was about sixty feet long. The Mabile's porch was about sixty feet or more long. It was all under roof and we played on it when it rain and did not get wet, unless the wind was blowing in from the River.

This day I was at the Mabile's house coming from their driveway. It was after a rain and I came to play with Ronald and/or Sonny. I had knocked on the two back side doors. One on the side our house was on and the other back door on the side that Thomas Pansono's house was on. No one answered. This was a very large ten room house, so it was not unusual for them inside the house to not hear me. It depended upon where they were in the house. I went to the driveway and parking area and Mr. Joe's old field truck was there. So I went to check their garage where they kept the car at. It was closer to the gravel road and to Thomas Pansano's house. Before I got all the way there, I noticed that the garage double doors were opened, which meant that the car was gone. The doors were always closed when their car was in the garage.

They had all went somewhere. So instead of back tracing my steps all around the big house to the other side where we always went, I decided to take a short cut and climb two fences and I was in my yard in only one hundred feet or so and not the two hundred feet it would take me to go all around this house.

I started climbing the gate near their driveway which always stayed lock closed. I was about half way up it when I started to raise one leg to go over the top to place on this diagonal two by four when my foot with all my weight on it slipped on the wet wood. The wood was slippery from the rain, which is why we never tried to walk a fence after a rain. I was not intending to walk the fence, I was just trying to cross the gate and walk across the yard, then climb our fence.

I fell on the same side of the gate that I started the climb on. I fell on my left arm. It snapped, and started to hurt really bad. I got up crying. This time Miss Violet was not at home to help me. I had to go the long way around anyway. Trying to hold my arm in place and hurting every step of the way and crying each step also. I made it home and Daddy was there, thank goodness. When it rained, the field hands could not work so the Overseers usually came home from the fields early.

Daddy put me in the truck and off to see old Dr. Tomney we went. When I came home, I had a cast over my arm. It stayed on my arm for several weeks; I could not play any climbing games for a while. I did not feel like climbing very much at this time anyway.

THE CURE-ALLS (CASTER AND MINERAL OIL AND MILK OF MAGNESIA, ETC)

There was a home cure for almost everything. If you got any kind of stomach ache or cramps or anything to do with the area around the belly, and for other symptoms, after the Hot Water Bottle treatment came the Caster oil or Mineral oil or Milk of Magnesia treatment. These items were used a lot. A couple table spoons of this stuff and you would be as good as new in a day or two or three or.

I cannot recall the taste of the Caster oil but the mineral oil I remember all to well. It was a thick water color liquid that did not have any specific taste but was very hard to swallow. I guess it tasted thick. The thickness almost made you have to chew it to get it down. It made me gag and beg not to have any more. I really did not like the taste either - whatever the taste was. Daddy continued to take mineral oil late in his life. He believed in it and always has some on hand. I may still have some put away in a box some place here that I have had for forty years or so. I will not use it, but used to give some to my sons when they were little. No, they did not like it either. I liked the taste of milk of magnesia. I still don't know what is was or how it helped me, but it tasted okay. It seemed we never had any at home to treat me when I needed it. I remember the caster and mineral oils being at home all the time. Nan Noon and Paran Charlie had the milk of magnesia at their house on Richland. I took it many times when visiting with them. I think it came in a pretty blue bottle and was whitish in color. They used it an awful lot at their house. I saw their empty bottle graveyard and it was what seemed like hundreds of used up milk of magnesia bottles in it. Yea, good ole milk of magnesia for what ails ya.

As a kid, we always seam to have these items in our medicine cabinet along with the merthiolate, which burned like the dickens when applied to a cut or scratch. It was reddish in color and must have been 90 percent alcohol by the way it burned. There was another reddish substance called Mercurochrome which we called monkey blood for what reason I know not. It did not burn when applies to cut and scratches. I always wanted the monkey blood applied to any cuts, scrapes and scratches that I got. But as fate would have it, we seemed to be out of it if an adult was applying it to my sore. When I treated myself, I could often find the monkey blood and always applied it. As an adult, I always had, and still have, both products. I must admit that I use the merthiolate with the 90 percent alcohol most of the time. I figured out a long time ago, if it burns, it must be doing something good. I guess this is what my parents figured out those many years ago also.

No pain, no gain or should I say - cure.

HEAT STROKE

One summer when I was about eight or nine, I played in the hot sun to long. That afternoon, I was feeling hot and ill. I was running a low grade fever and could not seam to shake it. When Daddy came home after work, Momma told him that she thought I had heat stroke. Right away dad told me to get in the truck that we were going to town. I sighed and said that I feel better now. We took off for White Castle and when daddy passed the doctors office I did not know what to think. We went to his daddy's house- my grandpa. Grandpa was on the porch in his rocking chair when we arrived. Daddy told him what he thought I had. Grandpa had me kneel down in front of hem. He then placed his hands on my head. Starting with the forehead, he went all around my head pressing with his fingers and thumbs as he went. His diagnosis- heat stroke. Now for the treatment. He told dad what things he needed and sent him after them. I stayed there on the porch with grandpa and sat in the shadows on the porch. About a half hour passed and daddy returned with some stuff in a paper bag. Grandpa called me over again and fingered and thumbed my head again. He then opened a bottle of salve and spread it over my forehead and just over my ears and the back of my head. He applied this stuff liberally. He sort of massaged it in. While he was doing this, daddy was pulling leaves off some branches that he freshly cut from some elderberry bushes. Grandpa took the leaves and stuck them to the salve/grease he place all around my head. I had white salve and green leaves on my head. He than cut a length of gauze and wrapped it around my head over the salve and leaves a couple times. Somehow he than tied it off in the back of my head. I did not like this at all. I felt like a bozo and a fool. I did not want anybody to see me looking like this. As grandpa was doing the work on my head, he kept massaging and saying some hokus pookus words that I could not understand. He told dad and me to don't take this off for a couple of days. I was pissed. Although I did not want to go to the doctor, now I wish we had. I did not think that old Dr. Tomney would tie me up in a contraption like this. I would have rather take medicine knowing that it was hard for them to give me medicine. All my medicine had to be liquid because I could not swallow a pill. I have taken some awful tasting medicine because of this problem. I learn to swallow pills as a teenager and had a better time of it when I had to take medicine. On the way home, I slouched down low in the truck hoping that nobody could see me. After arriving home, I hurried into the house and did not come out for a day or two. The next day I felt better but I had to ware that damn headdress for another day before I was free of it. After this episode, I played mostly under a tree or in the shadows of the house or barn. I even played under the house. I did not spend much time in the sun getting from shade to shadow for a very long time. I never got a heat stroke since - that I ever got this treatment for.

CHAPTER 4

WART TREATMENT: AGES NINE AND TEN

Ever since I can remember, I had a wart on the little finger of my left hand. I tried picking at it with my fingernail and would remove some of it. It was a bloody mess for a while and would heel up and the wart was back. I was too afraid to try and cut it off with a knife. That would be more than I could stand. The wart was not that noticeable but I just did not like it. Daddy used to get on me for picking at it at dinner. Our dinner was always at twelve noon at our house. This is the one meal that we had together as a family. We all had breakfast on the run and supper when you felt like heating the leftovers from dinner.

About my wart. Daddy talked with Mr. Grainier about it. He worked in the sugar house and lived just up the shell road from us. He lived near the big mule pasture where the black and white kids would sometimes play baseball. One afternoon daddy asked me if I wanted to get rid of the wart. I responded "of course I do." He told me to come with him. We walked to Mr. Grainer's house. Mr. Grainier came out. Daddy told him what this visit was all about. Mr. Grainer said "no problem" and pulled out his pocket knife. I started to make a break for it but daddy had one of my arms. Mr. Grainier said not to worry, that he would not cut me and that this was not a trick. I really liked Mr. Grainier. He was always good and nice to all the kids on the plantation. I did not have any reason to distrust him. After all, he and his wife were raising Jackie Grainer their grandson. Jackie's mom lived in New Orleans with her husband and two other kids. I never did know for sure why Jackie was raised with us and not in New Orleans with his half brother and sister. I will not speculate about it.

Mr. Grainer opened his pocket knife blade and placed the sharp part at the base of my wart. He mumbled some hokus pookus words and proceeded to place the blade all around my wart. He did this several times all the while chanting something. I was very afraid that at any time he would just cut the wart out. He and daddy had a hold on me so I would not be able to run or jerk my hand back even if I wanted to. After a minute or so, he closed his blade and put the knife back into his pocket. There was no pain and no blood at all and the wart was still there. He said that it may take several days for it to go away. I thought - yea- sure. How can that be- he did not do anything. He and dad went on with some small talk while I went to play. Well, I do not remember how long it took for the wart to disappear but disappear it did. I forgot about the treatment of the wart for several days. When I remembered to check it - it was gone. It is the damnest thing. Yes, it is still gone.

DOMESTIC HELP (MRS. IDA WASHINGTON AND MRS. SISTER LINK)

From the time that I can remember anything, Momma used to have domestic help in the house. During my time on the plantation, there were two black ladies who helped my momma do shores in the house. I think momma was sickly a lot of the time is the reason for the helpers. The ladies lived in the black quarters on the plantation. They both had their own houses to care for also.

(Note: On the plantation, Mr. William T. Burton owned all the buildings and land, and store, etc. Whenever I refer to our house or their home when talking about someone on the plantation, I am referring to the house that they were currently living in.)

Their husbands (Bolo Washington and Abe Link) were field hands and worked for my daddy and the two other overseers on the plantation.

Mrs. Ida Washington - was a good natured black woman. She was kind and a gentleperson and she was firm and fair. She was about five feet five inches in height and close to 180 pounds. She was on the heavy side but not big and fat at all. She did all sorts of chores inside the house, like mopping floors, doing the dishes, washing and hanging out clothes on the line, ironing clothes, sometimes cooking, general house cleaning, and the hardest part of her job - giving me a bath.

I did not like taking my clothes off in front of anybody. I may have felt different if old Dr. Tomney had not taken off more than was necessary at the circumcision - but I believed he did and it affected me then and still does now. Anyway - It was always a circus when it was time for Ida to see to it that I was bathed. I would stall and stall, hide, make like I was on the toilet and lock everybody out of the bathroom. Ida coped with this each time she was to bathe me. All the baths that she gave me was accomplished in this manner. O K, Mr. Barra, we will just wait until Mr. Newton get home. I will tell him that you did not want to bathe. Well - that did it every time. I was out of my clothes and into the tub in no time at all. I am not sure why I was so afraid of my daddy when I was a youngster. He never beat or hit me except for that little pop behind the head for burning down the corn crib some years later. But if you wanted me to do something that I did not want to do - you just mention - NEWTON and I was on it. Newton and Moses could make me walk on water if I had to.

Ida worked for momma into my mid teenage years. She got sick when I was about sixteen or seventeen and had to quit doing domestic work. All the time she worked at our house she had her own large family to care for. Besides Bolo (her husband), she had a bunch of kids. I cannot remember all of their names but the oldest were: George, Blanchard, Bobbie Gene, and Herman. Herman was younger than me. The oldest daughter, Bobbie Gene, was about my age and named after my sister, Bobbie Jo.

We had a lot of fun during my teenage years with Ida and my best friend Davis Callegan. Davis could borrow his dad or one of his brother's cars every weekend. We would go to the Youth Center dances in Plaquemine almost every Saturday night. Davis would come to pick me up early just to talk with and tease Ida. When he pulled up and parked on the road by our gate, Ida would call out "Barra, ole po ass Davis is here." Sometime it was ole skinny ass Davis is here. Davis was very thin all during high school. You would never know that to look at him now. After the Army he really filled out well. He went into the Army as ole skinny ass Davis - he came out much a man and soon after was over two hundred pounds and stayed there.

Ida really enjoyed the teasing back and forth also, as did my momma, Davis and me. Sometimes, this was the highlight of our Saturday evenings. When Ida could not work anymore, Sister Link took over.

Mrs. Sister Link was a more serious black woman than Ida. She was all business. She was about five feet seven inches tall and maybe one hundred and sixty pounds. She was not fat. She was solid and looked strong. Both of these ladies had dark complexions. When Sister Link came to work, she got to it. There was no B S ing around. She did not cut up with Davis and I very much.

She had a family also, but at this time in my life, all her kids were grown. Two of them (Blue and a brother) worked as tractor drivers for the Plantation. They were good workers just like their dad and mom.

When Davis came over, he tried to tease Sister Link but she was not having none of it. She was a serious woman and wanted respect from all youngsters. I believe she came to realize that Davis and I were not disrespecting her when we made fun remarks. Occasionally she would participate in some playful antics. On one occasion, she was ironing my slacks that I was waiting for to put on and go to Plaquemine with Davis. Davis had not arrived yet. I had one other pair that I could have worn but I wanted to ware this black one to go with my red and black shirt. I sort of chided her about taking to much time to iron my slacks. She got hot and pissed. She ask me what I was going to do if she did not iron them - all the while working on them. I told her that she was going to iron them or ELSE. In one motion, she placed the iron on its back, point up, jumped back with her arms folded across her chess and shouted "OR ELSE WHAT?" I just looked at her, with my arms outstretched from my sides and said, "or else don't iron them." Her facial expression really changed. She looked at momma, than back at me, than grabbed the iron and started laughing. She told me that my pants would be ready shortly. She then said to momma "Miss Josie, that boy is something else," all the while shaking her head back and forth and smiling. Davis missed all this because he was not coming over as early as he used to when Ida worked on Saturdays.

RIDING MY BICYCLE

I got really good at riding a bike. At about nine or ten years old, I was at the Mabiles house sitting on my bike. It was another used bike but bigger then the one that came with training wheels. Sonny was sitting on the steps that faced the driveway and I was sitting on my bike with both bare feet on the ground. Mr. Joe had a dump truck load of fresh new shells put down and spread in the driveway just a day or two before. New shell is very sharp. After the tires of the truck and cars drove over them several times, they crumbled to where we could walk on them bare footed without cutting our feet. We were very careful around fresh shell because of this reason.

I had on long blue jeans, a short sleeve button down shirt, and no shoes, since it was summer time and we did not wear shoes when we were not in school to just mess around in. I moved my left foot because it was on a sharp shell and lost my balance. I fell over to the left and my left knee hit the shells. It was not a hard fall. It seemed like I was falling in slow motion. Before I could get up, I felt something warm running down my leg. I stood up. Sonny had come down the steps to help me up. He saw the blood running off my left foot before I did. He put his hands to his mouth and hollowed, then took off to find his momma, Miss Violet. I now saw the blood on my foot. I could also see that my jeans was cut clean through in a half moon shape over my left knee. Oh, shit. I wanted to cry now. It never really hurt. The blood felt warm as I tried to roll up my pant leg above the knee, which I should not have done. I saw my knee bone sticking out. I started to hollow now. Even thought it was not hurting, I was hollowing.

Miss Violet was there and walked me around the side of the house and into the yard on the other side of their house. This was the side that faced the back of our house. We only had the cypress picket fence and gate between the Mabile's yard and our house. This was our main passage way to go back and fourth between the houses.

She took me to the cesspool area and went inside to get a towel and something for me to drink. I was kind of feeling dizzy now. Seeing all that blood. My blood!

The cesspool area was a ten by ten slab of cement about ten inches high that covered the cesspool. We played on it all the time. It was our home base for many games.

While in the house, Miss Violet called momma and told her what was going on. Daddy happened to be home. He walked over at the time Miss Violet came out with the wet towel and started wiping some blood from my leg and told me to drink the stuff in the glass she carried from the house that it would be good for me. It tasted awful and after the first sip I said so. Daddy knew what it was and ordered me to drink all of it, which I did.

After the drink and my leg being washed a bit, the towel was wrapped around my knee to hold back the blood. Daddy picked me up and carried me through the gate and our yard to our steps and porch and down our side steps to this old truck. He told momma that we were going to the hospital. I really started hollowing now. This is not a place that I wanted to go to. I told daddy that it would heal alright. He said not a cut where the bone is showing. This is not something that I wanted to hear.

I whimpered all the way to town. It was still not really hurting. We parked in front of the hospital. Daddy came around and carried me inside. As soon as we got into the waiting room, the nurse said to take him right to the back, Newton (which is my daddy's name).

Old Dr. Tomney looked at my wound, told a nurse to clean it up and get it ready. They then gave me this same awful stuff to drink that Miss Violet had just fifteen minutes before. I told them that I already had that medicine. It did not make them any difference they said drink it. I said "but," then Daddy said "drink it," which I did. This stuff was making me sicker than my opened up knee.

Dr. Tomney put some shots into my knee area which I felt more than the cut itself. They had to cut my blue jeans with scissors to make enough room for the doctor to work. He sowed up my knee. It took eight stitches to close the gap. After a couple more shots and a prescription for medicine, daddy carried my back to the truck and sat me in the seat. He then went into Mr. Lester Hebert's drug store attached to the hospital and got the prescription filled. I think some of the medicine was to stop any infection before it started and some was pain pills.

I really needed the pain pills for the next several days. I had a hard time swallowing them, but I got em down after drinking plenty water with each pill. I was laid up for several days and could not go out and play for about a week or so.

In due time, Dr. Tomney took out the stitches. It never occurred to me to kick the old fart for the circumcision job he did on me right after I was born. I had other things on my mind, I guess. I was just happy that I would not have to see him again.

He did a pretty good job on stitching my knee up. I can hardly see the scar. Of course, at fifty-eight plus years old, I do not see as well as I used to when I was little.

MY FIRST DRIVE-IN MOVIE

When I was about nine or ten, the Joe Mabile family went to a drive-in movie in Plaquemine which was ten miles north of White Castle. Ronald and Sonny could not stop telling me how great it was. It was a movie outside. You could sit in the car or truck, or on the fender or on the ground and watch the movie. This was almost unbelievable but sound great to me. I guess Daddy could not afford to take us because when I asked him to, he did not seam too interested.

The first time I went was with the Mabiles. We got there while it was still daylight, found a place to park and settled down. We parked by what looked to be a parking meter but it had these speakers attached to it. Mr. Joe rolled us his window (driver's side) about three inches and hung one of the speakers on it inside the car. It had a volume knob that the driver of the car could put up or down. I did not know it when we arrived, but we had to wait until it got dark enough before they would run the movie.

Ronald, Sonny and I was sitting outside on the ground. Then we sat on the fender, then the ground, then the fender, then leaned on the car, then the ground as the movie started.

I do not remember the name of the movie, but the folks were in some old town in what seemed to be another country where Gypsies live. They looked Italian. They had a dark complexion. The girl had some sort of problem. She was pretty enough, alright, but she had problems. Guys would call on her during the day which was O.K., but she could not stay out late at night. Her momma was scary, and reminded me of the old Gypsy lady that was in the Lon Chaney Jr. movie about the Werewolf. Anyway, her momma made them take her home early, which they did not like to do. The guys wanted to keep this girl out late and shake a leg and have a few drinks and such. One time (because I did not see much of the movie after this one time, so it may have happen again), this guy kept her out too late and it was a full moon, and it started to get spooky. The music got spooky and I got spooky and started looking all around. If Mr. Joe would have blown the horn, I would have shit all over the drive-in movie grounds. All of a sudden, this pretty woman turned into a black Panther and killed the guy she was with and I almost died too. It may not have happened like this, but this is what I remember of it. I wanted into the car in a hurry. I could not get in fast enough. There was some laughter in the Mabile car and it was not me doing the laughing. I wondered what they was laughing at because that sure in hell was not a funny movie. As mentioned, I do not remember seeing very much of the movie after the first time she turned into that black Panther. I just lost interest, I guess.

During the year, Daddy took us to several drive-in movies. No spooky ones. I did not care for scary movies. I had my hands full with Moses at the House. I did not need this spooky stuff on the road too.

This was the early fifties and TV had been out for a number of years. We did not have one of course. My sister and I begged Daddy to buy a TV. He asked "if I get a TV, will you not want to go to the drive-in any more." We said "yes," we would not ask to go to the drive-in movie any more. Well, he got the TV. I think it took him years to pay it off. After about one month, we were asking Daddy to take us to the movies. He was PEE OOD. He told us that we promised not to ask to go to the movies if he got the TV. Now he could not take it back, which we did not want him to do. His answer was a resounding NO, go watch that TV. That is your movies.

Uncle Miltie (Milton Berle) is the only show that I can remember from the first year that we got a TV. Then The Peoples Choice with Jackie Cooper, The Life of Riley with William Bendix, Walt Disney, Amos and Andy (my favorite), The Ozzie and Harriet Show was just great, Ernie Kovax, and Sid Ceaser's "Show of Shows." Later I remember watching December Bride, starring Spring Bindington and Frances Rafferty played her TV daughter. This name Rafferty brings back a memory. When I was in Sister (Catholic) School, in about the fourth grade, after Daddy purchased the television, I wanted to be identified with some one of notoriety. So I started spelling my name Rafferty. I took it from Francis. I pretended she was family. I used to sign my homework and turn in test papers with my name spelled this way. I did this for several weeks. The nuns (teachers) scolded me several times for not using my correct name. I did not care; I continued to spell it this way until a nun said she would notify my daddy. This got my attention and I stopped spelling it Frances's way and went back to the original way. I was disappointed that I could not change the spelling of my name. But, life goes on. It was just great watching the old black and white in a more innocent time.

FIRST (AND ONLY) TRAIN RIDE

One summer vacation from school, when I was about nine or ten years old, I went on a passenger train ride. The old Texas and Pacific Railroad tracks cut across the plantation and ran along the side of Louisiana Highway # 1. We would sometimes watch the trains go by and a lot of the time have to wait for them to pass before going over the tracks toward the sugar mill and tractor sheds. Daddy and Mr. Joe Mabile and most of the laborers had to cross La 1 and the railroad tracks every day to go into the field to work.

We, Ronald and Sonny Mabile and me, had been asking our daddies to let us ride the train for a couple of years. This one summer, they said yes. So one day, I do not remember what day of the week it was, Daddy, Mr. Joe, Ronald, Sonny, and I, got in Daddy's pickup truck and we drove north on La.1, went through Plaquemine to the little town of Addis, Louisiana. It was about fifteen miles from Cedar Grove/White Castle. We all got out and went into the depot where Daddy and Mr. Joe bought four tickets to ride the train from the Addis station to Donaldsonville, Louisiana which was ten miles south of White Castle. This trip was to be about twenty-five miles. Mr. Joe would ride with us boys and Daddy would drive to Donaldsonville and be there to pick us up upon arrival.

We boarded the train and all sat in the same area. Soon the conductor came by and Mr. Joe handed him our tickets which he punched with this puncher thing and handed them back. We settled into our seats. We really enjoyed the ride to Plaquemine which was about four miles. We crossed Bayou Plaquemine. This bayou lead to the Plaquemine Locks which we could see from the train. This Lock kept the Mississippi River from coming into the bayou and flooding out Plaquemine and killing everybody. The

Locks was for barge traffic coming to and from the Mississippi River. The Bayou Plaquemine route was the passage to other bayous that led to Morgan City, Louisiana, where the barges and push boats connected to the Intercoastal Canal and could transit east to Mississippi, Alabama, etc. or west to Texas.

After passing through Plaquemine, there was nothing, but sugar cane fields and very little woods for the next ten miles to White Castle. Highway La1 was on our left the whole way. The train stopped at the White Castle Depot to pick up freight or something. Passenger could not board the train at this stop, but packages/freight could be put on the train or delivered by the train to this depot.

Many years later, when I was working for J & L Engineering, we received a box car load of Alice Charmers parts and farm implements. The train would place the car on a siding at the White Castle Depot. I was in charge of empting the box car as soon as possible so we would not have to pay any detention charges. Detention is a certain dollar amount that you pay if the car is not unloaded in the "free time allowed." Free time is the hours you are allowed based on the tonnage in the car and the amount of freight you paid.

While stopped in White Castle, I could see cousin Mattie or Margie's (they were twins and I could not tell them apart) house. She lived along the railroad tracks less than a rock throw away. Either Mattie or Margie was on the porch talking with cousin Jessie Doiron.

I was hollowing and waving my arms inside the train passenger compartment and much to my chagrin, they never did see me.

We left from White Castle heading for Donaldsonville which was about ten more miles south. We still had La 1 on our left. There was nothing but sugar cane fields and woods between White Castle and Donaldsonville. I mean nothing until we started coming into Donaldsonville. Then there was some houses and small business places until we stopped at the Depot where daddy was waiting for us. I was really excited telling Daddy about the trip and what all I saw and our cousins that I saw who did not see me back. I was pissed that they did not see me back while I was in "all my glory."

On this twenty five mile trip we could see and passed through five plantations and sugar mills. At Plaquemine, just before we crossed Bayou Plaquemine, was the Wilbert's Plantation. Before getting into White Castle, we could see and passed through Catherine's Plantation and their sugar mill also known as Supple's Plantation because they owned it. Where Supple's property ended was Cedar Grove Plantation and sugar mill. Cedar Grove Plantation was owned by W. T. Burton Industries an absentee owner who lived in Lake Charles, Louisiana. All these mills were on our right hand side as we came south. Where Cedar Grove ended, started the town of White Castle. On the south side of White Castle was Cora Texas Plantation and sugar mill. This property was owned by the Paul Kessler family and the mill was to our left this time between La1 and the Mississippi River. The next Plantation and sugar mill we passed through was Evan Hall. This plantation was owned by the Thibeauts. The mill was on our right again and the closest to the railroad tracks and La1 and about four miles before we got into Donaldsonville.

At one time in the 1940s and 50s, there were over thirty sugar mills in Iberville Parrish alone. Today in the year 2001, there is one. The Cora Texas Mill stilled owned by the Paul Kessler family. It is tremendously larger in tonnage handled than it was when I was little.

THE CATHOLIC SCHOOL EXPERIENCE AGES TEN, ELEVEN, TWELVE, AND THIRTEEN

My photo from Catholic School (1955-'56)

    I went to Sister School for the fourth, fifth, sixth, and seventh grades. The proper school name was Our Lady of Prompt Succor Catholic School. While there, I was forced to eat food that I did not like, and punished for not eating certain foods, and hit harder, in the back, by a nun than I ever been hit before or since. This was for drinking water after the first bell, which was a warning bell to get in line because the second bell was about to ring. It hurt so much that I let out a yell. I almost punched her. Until this day, I do not know why I didn't.

I wore a uniform to school, which consisted of a white button down shirt with a collar or a white tee shirt and khaki pants. It was O K. Every boy wore the same outfit. Rich and poor alike. I was neither rich nor poor. I figured that our family was right in the between. The girls had to ware a white blouse and navy blue skirts.

Nothing exceptional happened except the knife fight between Quinn Falcon and Ronnie Dunn. Sister Anglia (the head Nun) intervened and no blood was spilled. Everybody liked and respected Sister Anglia. Also, one time I hit a softball into the back seat of a car that was passing by the school playground. The lady stopped and threw our ball back and we continued the game. And, it was during my time there that I got sick and threw up all over myself and a classroom. I ended up going to Dr. Tomney and he took out my appendix. That year was a very hard year on the family and Daddy's pocketbook. Between Momma, Daddy, Bobbie Jo and me, we had nine major operations. Bobbie, Daddy and I had two each and Momma had three. It was a bad year and took Daddy a number of years to pay off Dr. Tomney and Hebert Drugs.

When we played at recess, sometime Mr. Olley Hebert would stop by. He loved to bat out flies to us. Whenever he saw us, he would stop and ask if he could hit the soft ball to us. We all enjoyed it. This gave us a chance to practice catching the ball. Mr. Olley was in the well digging business and would have his big safari hat and rubber boots on. But he could hit that ball. I used to think that he was in his sixties during this time.

Davis Callegan was in all my classes at Sister School. We all watch him get popped by every teacher he ever had. This is not a correct statement. Every teacher he ever had issued out the number of time he was popped but they all got that bitch Sister Mary Charles (who hit me in the back at the water fountain) to give out the paddling. She had this thirty six inch long three inch wide paddle with a half inch in diameter hole drilled every three inches or so in it for less wind resistance. She would make Davis bend over with his hands on his knees or around his ankles and hit his behind. If he raised up, he got an extra one. I believe he got ten of these one time. I still do not know how his little pointed ass could take the pounding. But he did and the next day or two, he was ready for some more.

Sister Mary Charles was the meanest Nun I ever knew. She was the enforcer. She did the whippings. I know that someone had to do it, and maybe she was ordered to do it. It was her job to do it. But she just looked like she enjoyed it to much. Perhaps she did. This may have been her way to get back at society for her giving up so much to become a Nun. I don't know. What I do know is, any person who is in a position to hand out punishment, does not have to enjoy is as much as Sister Mary Charles seemed to. Just being hit by her in the back that one time made a non-believer out of me. I think I starting drifting away from the Catholic faith then. It also made a believer out of me. I did not ever want to be hit by her again. I truly believed that.

If you go through the history of the World and see what/how the so-called Catholic Priests and Nuns treated people, you will come to the same conclusions as I did. Many of these mean and terrible people will burn in hell forever with the Hitlers of the world for their sins against humanity and the wars and atrocities they committed in the name of Catholicism. May GOD have mercy on their miserable souls. Please remember that this is just the opinion of one man, me. I pray for all the Catholics who have been mislead by this cult and I pray for myself also. Catholics please pick up a Bible and read it from cover to cover. Then read it again, please do this in remembrance of Jesus Christ.

This punishment thing stayed with Davis throughout our school career. If four guys were talking in a group and Davis was not doing anything, he would get called out for punishment.

It was at Sister School that we named Francis Canella, Frog and Louise Bouque, Buck. These nicknames stuck with these girls all through high school. Ladies, I am sorry that I participated in this and hope that it did not affect you all your life. If it did, well, you can call me "ole potty pants" for the rest of my life and longer if you want to.

Many times the priest, Father Wisehoft, would come and teach us catechism and also had us go to confession at the school. I hated this. I did not have anything to hide behind. Every few confessions, he would get up from behind his little slide door and walk into the room where we were lined up against the wall to see him and size up who was next in line. He did this one time right when I was next to see him. I fixed his ass. As soon as he got ready to start hearing confessions again, I switch places with Johnny Latino and several other boys moved around also. We went in the turn that he did not know about and for the rest of his life; he had all of our sins mixed up in his head. He did not know what he thought he knew about my sins. So, it just shows to go you.

CHAPTER 5

MY COMMUNION AND OTHER THINGS

Barry and Ronald Mabile

When you are raised a Catholic, you must eventually have your Communion. I had mine when I was about ten years old. You have to study your religion and go to classes that the priest and nuns teach. You must learn the Catholic Catechism that have stories about Jesus and God and others in it.

Your have classes for a year or more and know some stuff before being allowed to have your Communion. I guess I had a test but do not remember any written test. Maybe they were all oral.

When the Communion day finally comes, there is a big to do at the church. Usually a bunch of kids have their Communion at the same time. I guess it is too much of a to-do to have just one person have their Communion at a time. This is an important part of being a Catholic, so it was a big deal. So your whole class have their Communion together. Everybody dresses up as best they can. Usually the little girls wore all white dresses. Some little boys wore suits but many little boys could not afford to buy suits so they wore pants and white button down shirt (if they had or could borrow one) and the small neck tie. All the kids and their families and friends of the families and on lookers and gawkers, were all in the church.

I think all of us Communion kids sat together in the front rows of the church. The priest went through the Communion service. There is a service for every occasion in the Catholic Church. We all went to confession to tell the priest our sins sometime before the Communion Service started.

The Catholic Priest is the go-between, between us and God. We could not talk direct to God. You have to be a priest to do that. We tell our sins to the priest, he give us so many Our Fathers, Hail Marys, Act of Contritions, to do based on how bad our sins were. (When I was a teenager, I saw some folks saying the whole rosary for confession. They had some really big sins to get rid of when you have the pray the whole rosary for penance). Then the priest tell God our sins when we are not looking. I guess he took the flack from God for us. During the time in the confessional box, the priest had to wear a certain outfit or he would not be able to communicate with God. He had to wear the Confession Outfit for this to work. You have to go to confession to confess your sins before receiving communion or you committed another sin. There were sins everywhere just waiting for you to commit them. Sometimes, you made a sin and did not even know it.

Communion is this little piece of bread, that they call a wafer about the size of a quarter but much thinner. It is referred to as the Host. It represents the body of Jesus Christ Our Lord and Savoir. The wine represents the blood of Jesus but when I was little, regular Catholics did/could not drink wine at Church Services. Only the priest could do that, and boy, could some of the priest put this wine away.

The Host (the little wafer) was hidden in the little Tabernacle on the altar where the priest did the service form. We were told that is where God lives. My first thought was that it was a very small house, but God did not need a lot of space. He could take up the whole universe it he wanted to, but on Sundays he lived in the Our Lady of Prompt Succur Catholic Church in White Castle, Louisiana in the Tabernacle.

During my Communion Service, at a certain time, a Nun or someone gave a signal to the first person on the front row to get up. As this person got up so did the rest of us. We walked up to the Communion Rail and would all knell down as soon as you got there all in a row to get ready for the Host. We all made the sign of the cross. You Know. Where you use the right hand to touch your forehead, than your right shoulder, than your left shoulder and then clasp your hands together like you was praying. When you made the first motion to your forehead, you said "in the name of the Father (forehead), the Son (right shoulder), and the Holly Ghost/Spirit (left shoulder), Amen (clasp hand together)."

After everybody was settled in, on our knees, hands clasped, faces forward, chins up, and mouths opened, we were ready for the Communion Host. The priest and his helper (altar boy) would come by each one of us.

The altar boy would either be in front or behind the priest. He had this little golden saucier that he put under our chin. This was to catch the Host if it fell before it got to your tongue. You could not let the Host hit the floor. That would have been really bad. I guess the Catholic had another rule that said don't let the Host hit the floor. Maybe a mortal sin or something like that.

When it was my turn, I stuck out my tongue; the plate was under my chin usually touching skin. (If you knew the altar boy, he might bump you with the saucier). The priest would mumble some words while putting the wafer on the tongue. He mumbled the same words for every wafer that he put in every person's mouth.

It the altar boy was in front of the priest, he had to be fast and move very quickly or the priest would run over him. The priest like to do this job in a hurry. There was usually many people standing in line waiting for the place you occupied to get to the Communion Rail so they can get their Host on the priest's return trip. So as soon as you got yours, you mumbled Amen, like you said a prayer, did the sign of the cross again, got up and went back to the same seat that you was sitting in.

All Catholics were instructed to place the Host with your tongue on your upper palate and let it stick there until in dissolved. Above all, DO NOT CHEW IT. It was against all Catholic rules to chew your Host. I do not know what the penalty for chewing was, but they instilled in our minds to never chew the Host.

Kenneth Hebert (now he was a work of art), was hard headed and seemed to chew his Host whenever I saw him at Sunday services. I never did learn what penalty he may have paid for that.

Before entering and exiting a pew, we usually genuflected and made the sign of the cross while facing the altar. It was another rule that the Catholics had. To genuflect meant to go down on one knee and make the sign of the cross while on that one knee. You also bowed your head and always, always, faced toward the Altar and Tabernacle where God lived.

After receiving Communion and back in our seat, we would kneel and was suppose to pray while the Priest was still giving out Communion to others. After a while, you make the sign of the cross again than sat back in the pew until the next instruction to rise, kneel or sit back. There are parts in the Service that you did all these things plus many other gestures, sayings, and motions. After you've been a Catholic for some time, you learned these things and did them automatically.

When anyone entered the church from the front or sides, there was always containers about waist high on adults with holey water in them. (What made the water holy was that it was blessed by the priest in a Holy Water Blessing Service). So from every entrance into the church, you could/should dip your fingers of your right hand into the holey water, face the altar and make the sign of the cross. You did this on the way into the church and when you left after the service.

After my Communion service was over, we stood outside in front of the church congratulating each other for what we did not have the slightest idea for. But our parents were doing it so we did also. Then folks either went home or to friends of the family for dinner and desert celebration of Communion.

Life got more serious after Communion. I knew now, if I made a sin, I had better get to the priest quickly before I died or it was hell for me-forever. I tried to keep count of all my venial (small) sins and had trouble remembering how many venial sins equal to one MORTAL sin. With venial sins on your soul, you could still make it to heaven or at least Purgatory. But a MORTAL sin, even only one MORTAL sin and you are a gone pecan; into the fires of HELL for an eternity or longer. This mortal sin business just ate me up. I could not get to confession quick enough. I lived out in the country. The priest was four miles away. It could have been a hundred miles. I would not be able to fine him at my age. The mortal sins was so easy to commit. You use God's name in vein and WHAM-O- you got a MORTAL sin on your soul. You could commit one of the big sins just by touching yourself, or looking at dirty pictures, just even thinking of some things. I did a lot of praying because of a slip of the tongue. Why did they make a mortal sin so easy to do? If you repeated something that you overheard, you may commit a mortal sin and did not even know it yet.

Even saying shit is a sin. If it is not a sin when you do it, why should it be a sin to say it? If you refuse to do it, you would die. It has to come out. That is the way that God made us. And if you die because you refused to shit, that was a sin. You killed yourself and therefore could not make it to heaven because you died with murder on your soul.

It was very hard being a good Catholic. I do not know if I ever was a good Catholic or not. I tried to be, BUT

When I was a kid, eating meat on every Friday was a mortal sin that sent you straight to hell if you died without confessing and being forgiven by the priest acting for God. My friends that were Baptist could eat meat on Friday and it was not a sin at all. How could that be? How come I am not a Baptist? Oh, I remember now, they do not drink beer. Many of the best Catholic families in town were great beer drinkers and did a lot to support that industry. The Catholic's not only loved beer, but wine, gin, whiskey, etc., etc.

After I was all grown up and married and attending Lutheran Church, I found out that eating meat on every Friday was not a sin anymore for Catholics. What is that all about? What happened to all those poor hungry souls who ate meat on a Friday because they did not have any other food and died before confession and went to hell? Huh? What became of them? Did they get pushed up to Purgatory? Or what?

Purgatory, that brings on a thought. The Catholics did have more of a choice. They had Heaven, Hell and a third place for souls call Purgatory, the halfway house for souls. If you died without a mortal sin on your soul, say a bunch of venial sins, you can make it to Purgatory instead of Hell. This is not a bad deal. Also, as I understand it, if you are sitting in Purgatory, and your family said a lot of prayers for you, you may get pushed up to Heaven. Your family could light/burn candles for you at the church. You must pay for each candle you burn. Or they could pay the priest and he would say a prayer in church services and even dedicate a Mass on Sunday if the money was right. He would even put it in the bulletin and everything and try and get other folks to pray for your soul but the money had to be right. I do not know if this worked or not, but there are many folks praying and paying to try and get family member's soul from Purgatory to Heaven.

I do not know of any other religion that have a halfway house for souls to go like the Catholics got.

I still have my Mamma's Catholic bible. As a Catholic, you are always asked to purchase a bible from the church. But the Catholics never used the bible for church services. We always left the bible home. The services were performed using the

Catholic missals and other rewritten books. We also had the Catholic Catechism, and other Catholic writing to go by.

Oh, I forgot to mention about Saint Christopher, the Saint of Safety. I, along with many other Catholics for many, many years, prayed to St. Christopher for safety in travel. What happened to all the prayers when the Pope un-sainted St. Christopher? There was such a strong outpouring of the people that they remade St. Christopher a Saint in good standing again, I think. What was that all about, huh?

THE BAJON BOYS (FROM MRS. BARLOW'S CLASS WINDOW)

Mrs. Roger Barlow was our teacher while in the sixth grade at Sister School. She was what they call a Lay Teacher because she was not a Nun. There may have been one or two more Lay Teachers there for the eight grades. I know that Mrs. Olivia Falcon (Quinn's Mom) taught there for a while. I do not remember if she was a substitute Lay Teacher or not.

Mrs. Barlow's room was on the side of the River Road and across the street from the Bajon's house. The Bajon brothers were druggist who owned and ran a drug store in town. There were three drug stores in town. The Bajon brothers, Mr. Lester Hebert that was attached to Dr. Tomney's hospital, and the Vialon brothers who ran the Rexal drug store. They all made a good living. We had two hospitals in town. Dr. Tomney that later became Doctors Major, and Dr. Musso owned the other. The Majors were a husband and wife team that came to town when the Tomney family sold their hospital. We had a lot of drugs in our little town.

The Bajon brother that lived across the street from the school had at least three little boys. At the time that I was in the sixth grade, their ages seemed to be about four, three and one years old. Every day those boys got into something. They must have driven their Momma crazy. I spent a lot of my time looking out of the window from my desk at them carrying on. Mrs. Barlow would catch others gazing out the window and issue punishment work, but never caught me. This was like chewing gum in class. There is a art to it. What I mean is not getting caught by the teacher doing it; peeking out the window or chewing gum- that is. The thirteen years I spent in formal education, I can remember being caught only one time chewing gum. And I chew gum every day, in every class I ever had. My buddies and a lot of the girls would get caught all the time and get punished. But they chewed like a cow. I could chew and my lips, cheeks, ears and anything else would not move. I had it down pat. In the eighth grade, Mr. Elliott looked everywhere in my mouth on suspicion that I was chewing gum. He could not find any gum in my mouth. But I had some in there. I have to admit, I laid low a couple of days after that because he was paying special attention to me. After that time off, I went back to chewing full time again.

I did get yelled at several times in school for this habit I have. When sitting I move my right or left foot and leg very rapidly up and down. Using the ball of either foot to push up in rapid succession, my leg would bounce up and down. This would cause the room to vibrate and the windows to rattle. It I was really concentrating on work, I would not notice how badly it disturbed the other folks. I still do it today. On a cement slab and carpeted floor, it does not disturb anybody.

The Bajon boys would fight in their yard, in the street and in the house. We could hear their Momma try to correct them from our classroom. We also heard them crying when she whipped their behinds. Less than five minutes later, they was back doing things that they should not be doing.

They played with the water hose a lot. They liked to make water puddles and get and roll in it. Their Mom would come out and drag them inside screaming. Twenty minutes later they were back outside, in clean clothes and rolling in the mud puddle again.

One time, the two older boys was outside playing with the water hose. They were fighting for control of it. When a car passed by, they would spray water at it. The youngest son was in a baby crib inside the house under an open window. It was during the warm months, all the windows on the house were opened. We could see well into the house from the classroom when Mrs. Bajon opened the windows and pushed the curtain aside. On several occasions, I saw Mrs. Bajon chasing those boys inside the house trying to issue out punishment. Those guys really could run.

This time the two oldest were outside, the one year old in the crib looking outside at his brothers fighting for control of the water hose and the water was shooting out of the nozzle. As they struggled with each other, the water spray would go through the open window and hit the baby and down he would go. I watched his little hands grab the side of the crib and lift himself up standing again and laughing. He would get hit with another spray and down he go again. After the second time, the boys outside decided to take turns sharing the water hose and spraying their little brother with water when they saw his head above the crib.

They were having so much fun, on several occasions, I almost lost it. I had to stick my handkerchief in my mouth to smother my laughter. Some of my classmates got caught again. If you saw this, even if you were a sourpuss, you had to laugh.

The baby was having fun to. He knew when he showed his face that he was going to get some water sprayed in it. After about twenty minutes of this, I could see the Momma coming to see what all the noise and laughter was about. When she got to that bedroom, I saw her hands go up to her hair and heard her screams.

There must have been a really bad mess in the house by now with all that water they were spraying in there. She checked the baby real quick like and ran out of the room to get to the front door. When she hit the door and through it open hollowing, the yard boys scattered into two directions. She did not know which one to chase first. She cut the water off and started chasing the one that ran behind the house. She circled the house twice trying to catch him, while the other boy ran to Mr. Rodester's house and was hiding over there.

Mrs. Barlow was really upset with the class now because everybody was laughing. She came and stood in front of the windows and facing us and just daring someone to look that way.

I never saw if the Momma caught the boys or just what happened. About an hour later, I snuck a peek and the Momma was in the baby's bedroom still cleaning it. It was a good thing that Mr. Bajon was a druggist. I bet she took a lot of them before these boys were grown.

MY FIRST HIGH SCHOOL BASKETBALL GAME - ALMOST

When I was about ten or eleven years old, my sister offered to take me with her girlfriends to a White Castle High basketball game. I do not know why she offered, but it sounded great to me.

Daddy gave me just enough change to pay at the door to get in, I had one penny extra.

I do not remember who picked us up, but I was with my sister and her best friends, Pot Tee Rushing and Butsy Landry.

Before going to the gym, we went to Mr. Martinez's store to get something. While in the store, I saw this penny gumball machine. I had this extra penny, so I stuck it in the machine, pushed the knob sideways and out came the gumball. I popped it into my mouth and started to run after my sister who was leaving the store, when Mrs. Martinez ask me if I had put a dime into the penny machine. I assured her that in no way would I put a dime in a penny machine.

I ran back across Bowie Street to catch up with my sister at the gym. The girls were in front of me; they paid and got lost in the crowd in a hurry. I gave all the money that I had but was nine cents short and they would not let me in. I could not see where my sister went. The door guys told me to back out of the way. Which I did. I looked through the small window with the bars on it.

All the windows and doors on the gym had bars on them. I looked through them all and I still could not see or find her or her friends.

I then went back across the street to the Martinez's store to the gumball machine. The gum did not taste very sweet now. I told

Mrs. Martinez that it was my dime that I put into the machine and not a penny and could I get it back. She just said "NO." I looked around. I knew that if Mr. Clarence was there he would give me my dime back for the penny I had in my pocket. I shook the machine but nothing came out.

I did not have the sense to ask her for nine cents which is the difference that the gumball machine owed me and the exact amount I need to get into the basketball game. She knew that I had put the dime in this damn machine. She should have offered me the nine cents. She did nothing.

She may be the reason that so many tricks were played on them during Halloween and at other times during the year. I don't know. I do know that I liked Mr. Clarence but did not care very much for his wife.

I went back across Bowie Street to the gym without my nine cents. I looked through the doors and the little window again and again. My sister should have been out here looking for me. There were many folks at the game and they were now playing basketball. But this was not on my mind at this time. I did not know what to do. All kinds of thoughts went through my mind.

It came to me. I am not going to stand out here all night. I will just walk home to Cedar Grove. This was not an easy decision for me to make. After all, it was night time and I did not like the dark. But I did not like it here by myself either. I felt more afraid outside the gym than the thought of walking back to Cedar Grove three miles or so. Nobody was outside the gym but me. I made another look through the window and the doors. No sister in sight.

I started walking toward down town White Castle. There were street light for as long as I was in town. I do not remember if we had a telephone or not during this time. I guess we did. I just do not remember.

As I got out of White Castle and away from the street lights, I was thankful that there was a full moon out. It was dark but not near as dark as it would have been if not for the full moon.

As I walked, I tried to whistle. I learned to whistle at a very early age. Then I thought about Cannonball's house. Cannonball was an old black man that walked the gravel road and on the top of the levee. He never worked that I know of, but he apparently made out O K. He would scavenge in the trash piles and get enough money for the stuff he found and sold to make out alright. Sometime he slept in the old house that was on Cedar Grove property just as you came out of town on the gravel road. It had a two story frame but was really gutted out. It was not in livable condition, but hobos and vagrants slept in it.

I refer to it as Cannonball's house. I found out some years later from my daddy, that it was part of the much larger house that was known as the White Castle and for which the town got its name. The old Family tomb behind this house and almost on top of highway La 1 had the name Vaughn on it. It is an above ground tomb and have the birth and death dates of a number of the Vaughns still on it. There were no bodies or skeletons there when I was little. I do not know what happened to the dead or alive Vaughns. This tomb was restored in the 1980s by folks of White Castle. I believe some of the dates on it goes back to the late 1700s.

This old house was moved from its original site in the early 1900s when the Corp of Engineers built the levee to hold the Mississippi River in its banks. The rest of the original huge White Castle was gone long before the time they built the levee. It would be where part of the River flows today. I believe the old gutted out house is where the servants cooked the meals and maybe even lived. In the seventeen and eighteen hundreds, the large house that the rich folks live in did not have a kitchen. All the cooking and preparing of the meals was done in another nearby house and delivered to the main house at mealtime.

This is the case with the Nottoway Home about two miles North of White Castle on the River Road near Bayou Goula. This antebellum house is opened to the public for tours and sleepovers. Many rooms have been restored to the way they were when the Randolph family built and lived in the house.

If you ever visit the home, be aware of the facts. They may say that Nottoway is the largest antebellum home built in the South, and I believe this to be true. But the last time that I visited there, they told the story of how White Castle got its name and they said it was because of Nottoway. This is not true.

The story told for generations is that a rich plantation owner went to New Orleans to pick up his new to be bride who had never been to this part of Louisiana before. As they rounded the bend coming up River from New Orleans via barge, the young bride to be exclaimed "Oh what a Beautiful White Castle," when see saw the large White House. The large white house she was talking about has been gone for over one hundred and fifty years and was in what is part of the Mississippi River today. It is how the town of White Castle got its name. It bordered the town's property. The property is part of Cedar Grove Plantation.

Cannonball's house that was part of the original White Castle got in really bad shape and my daddy had it torn down in 1962 because too many teenagers and other folks were trespassing on the property and it was not safe. He was afraid that somebody would get hurt really bad and sue W. T. Burton Industries who owned Cedar Grove Plantation; all thirty five hundred acres of it including some surrounding property.

There is a funeral home on that property today.

Back to my walk.

Just before I got to the old dilapidated house, I crossed the gravel road and started walking up the levee. I did not want to walk to close in front of this old house. I thought that Cannonball might get me.

I soon remembered that Cannonball was not a bad man. When us kids would see him walking and hollow out "hey Cannonball," he would always wave to us. He was not a bad guy to be afraid of. Not like that Lon Chaney Jr. (the Werewolf), or Raymond Massey (the Frankenstein Monster), or Bella LeGosse (the Vampire), or whomever it was that was The Mummy.

Now here I was walking on top of the levee in a full moon lit night thinking about the very last things that I should be thinking about. I was absolutely sure that Moses from our attic would team up with them to get me. What the hell am I doing walking up here away from any help that I might need near the gravel road. Where is Cannonball when I need him? He is always around when not needed. Where in the hell is he now.

I was several hundred yards from being in front of Mr. Luban Caillet (Poochie's house) and Mr. Norman Brown (Norma Ann, Jackie and Dianne's house). But I was still way up here on the levee. I cannot see into their yards from way over here. Damn, nobody outside, no outside light on either. What will I do?

I was a half mile from my house. I know what, I will run and I did; all the rest of the way home.

Near our house, I started running down the levee. I almost fell down several times. I was going down hill way too fast. I was able to maintain my balance and keep going. I tried to jump the ditch between the levee and the gravel road. Thump, I am in the ditch. It is alright. There is not water/mud in it and I am much too fast for a snake to bite me. I am out the ditch in no time at all. Across the gravel road I go. Now I am on the shell road. I was sure that I was kicking up dust and shell behind me, but was not about to look back to see because something or somebody might be gaining on me.

Through the fence and up the walk I ran. Up the steps. I think I skipped two of them. Bang, bang, bang, on the door, let me in, out of breath. Mamma opened the door. Baby, what are you doing here she asked? I could not answer right away. I ran all the way home I said after catching my breath. Where is Bobbie Jo? I don't know. At the game at school, I guess. Then I told her the whole story. Daddy was in bed sleeping. Momma was wondering about Bobbie Jo and how to get word to her when a car pulled up. It was my sister and her friends coming to tell momma that she lost me.

When she saw me, she was happy and mad. I ruined her whole night. My night was not a picnic either I thought. She said that she and her friends looked all over the place for me and got really worried. She promised never to take me to a game again and she kept her promise. I understood very well. I did not want to go through this again either. Her promise was alright with me. I rather stay home with the old folks- and I did until I was about fourteen or fifteen year old.

THE 4440 WINCHESTER

We played softball in a vacant lot across a street from Sister School. It used to house a big wooden Catholic Church that we all went to when I was younger. One day an old man set fire to the church and burned it down. Something about his wife had left him or died or something, and since he got married in that Church, be blamed the church for his loss. After the area was all cleaned up, the Sister School used the land for a playground. It took years to build another church in town. In the mean time, we went to church on Sundays in Mr. Pete Gauthier's White Castle

Movie Theater. It was really odd going to a movie on Saturday afternoon and the next morning going to Sunday services there as a church.

One day we were playing softball at recess and a black man, Mr. Clarence Prevoist called me over. He worked for the Chevy dealership that was next door to the playground. He asked "aren't you Mr. Newton's boy." I said "yes sir" and he said "when you get home today, tell you Daddy to come see me. I have something for him." I could not figure what it could be. Later that day, when Dad got in from the field, I gave him the message. I rode with him to Mr. Clarence's house in Dorseyville. It was about one mile from where we lived on the Plantation. We went upon the porch where the two adults talked. Mr. Clarence had a rifle that he bought some forty years before from my Daddy's Grandpa for ten dollars. He offered it to Daddy for a lot more than that. Mr. Clarence needed some money for something. Daddy told him that he did not need a rifle but would give him what he paid for it to help him out. Mr. Clarence said "No." As we were getting back into the truck, I was really sad. Even as a little kid, I appreciated something that old that had belonged to someone in our family. I was about to ask Dad about this when Mr. Clarence said "hold on," and brought the rifle to Daddy and took the ten dollars. This made me very happy. This was in the early 1950s.

Sterling Raffray (Uncle Pete) and my dad, Newton

Sometime after we brought the old 4440 Winchester home, my big brother got a hold of the rifle. It was in fair shape. It got in worse shape over the next forty years. In the early 1990s, my brother traded the 4440 with me for a small German game rifle because I told him that I would have the Winchester restored. Which I did. The rifle is locked up in my gun cabinet now. I take it out every so often and re-oil and clean it and just admire it.

The rifle that I gave to my brother is a double barrel German made small game rifle. It has a 22 caliber on the left side and a 9-mm on the right side. Our Uncle Pete, my Daddy's brother, sent it home during the latter part of WW II when the Allies invaded Germany. It was packed in a crate from the manufacturing plant there. He send a number of weapons home, but this is one of the very few to get to the USA all the way from Germany. The others got stolen in the Post Offices is what the adults used to say.

This rifle should not be shot. The barrel is ringed, which means that it was shot while the barrel was plugged with mud or something. I have not idea when or how this happened, but it is very dangerous to shoot it in this condition. The barrel could be replaced and the rifle would be fine to shoot. But it would not be the same gun that has been with our family for five generations. This is a keepsake rifle and not a hunting rifle any more. It has served it time as a hunting rifle. My grandpa and Daddy both told me many years ago the Franklin used to hunt deer with it.

HI-LIFE (SOME HOT STUFF)

During the pre-teenage years of my life and later for that matter, folks from town would drive out to the plantation and drop off their unwanted pets. Stray dogs and cats were showing up on our porch on a regular basis. This upset my daddy very much. Every time he saw a new animal in the yard, he would raise hell. He wished that those damn people in White Castle would dump their unwanted pets someplace else and he was damn tired of feeding strays. What he meant was that he did not want to pay anything to feed them. We never paid for dog food in those days. We fed them table scraps but we hardly had enough to feed our dogs and cats.

Daddy was not a bad man but he did not like stray animals nor allow us to own more than a couple of each. Like maybe two dogs and two cats. When our pets had a litter, we would give away the pups or kittens to friends or neighbors. If we were not successful in giving them all away, daddy would dispose of the rest. We tried extra hard to find the animals a home.

Daddy had a way of getting rid of adult dogs. There was a liquid water white product he called HI-LIFE. I do not know what it was or is. But when daddy poured a cup full on stray dogs, they would howl and howl and run and flip all around the yard and then head on down the road and never come back to our house. This is what daddy liked about that stuff. The other overseers and managers on the plantation used this product for the same purposes.

I remember this one time when this adult male dog stayed around the house for a couple of days. Daddy had run him out of the yard several times by just chasing after him but he kept coming back. When daddy came in from work, me and Ronald was on the porch swing. Momma and Bobbie Jo were in the kitchen. Daddy saw the dog again and retorted "you still here huh, well I will fix your ass." He went back to his truck to get some of this stuff. Momma and my sister came out onto the porch. Momma mentioned to dad that he should not pour that stuff on the dog. She never did approve of that. Daddy came back from the truck with a small container of hi-life. He went up the steps onto the porch. He called the stray dog over. As the dog neared the steps, he poured the stuff on its back. That dog did some howling, spinning around and around than started growling and barking at daddy. The dog then started up the steps after daddy. Daddy ran to the screen door and got into the kitchen and quickly closed the screen door behind him as he was shouting "look at this son of a bitch." This dog was madder than any dog that I ever seen in my life. I guess the dog weighed about twenty-five to thirty pounds. Not a big dog by any means. The dog had only one thing on his mind, and that was to get at daddy.

The dog chewed and scratched at the screen door until he broke the wooden slats on the bottom part of the door. He tore through the screen door. We were all watching in awe. This was a well constructed and strong screen door. The dog was now in the kitchen with daddy. Daddy grabbed a chair at the kitchen table and was fending the dog off with it. They were both going around and around the table. Daddy was hollowing and yelling and the dog was growling and barking. There was a big commotion going on in the kitchen. The dog broke the bottom part of the chair. Daddy was hollering for help but we were afraid and did not know what to do. It seemed like this went on for several minutes. Finally Daddy was able to use the broken chair to push the dog out of the kitchen through the broken screen door onto the porch. He pushed him down the steps. When the dog got to the walkway, he high tailed it out of the yard. He never did bite daddy. Daddy was sweating profusely and trying to catch his breath. He mumbled something like, "can you believe what that damn dog done?" Yea, we could all believe it. We saw it.

During the melee, the dog had only one thing on his mind and that was to get at Daddy. He did not even look at the rest of us. I guess he knew who did the bad thing to him, and it was not any of us bystanders. Daddy had gotten rid of the dog, but now he had a screen door and kitchen chair to repair/replace. He was pissing and moaning about this for some time.

I do not ever remember my Daddy using hi-life to run off a stray again after this event. As I think about this it sure was an exciting time, but I would not want this to happen to me as a dog or as the person.

STILL RIDING MY BICYCLE

By eleven or twelve year of age, I could ride my bike without any hands. And this was on the shell and gravel roads. I could go on the shell road a good quarter of mile if no cars were coming, without touching the handlebars. I was good at this. I would crisscross my hands on the handlebars and fell down several times trying to make this work. I would never try this today.

We would ride two to a bike. If they sat on the handlebars or the cross bar between the handlebar and the seat, I could ride them up and down the shell road.

We would ride up the ramp to the top of the levee and ride on top of the levee. We could have ridden behind the levee but if we did, our parents would ware our behinds out if they found out. And with nosey Mr. Braus always looking out of a window at the store, we would not chance it. We would not do it, because they had spies out and about and every time I ever went behind the levee on the River side, my dad found out about it and his belt would come off. I would not take that chance at this age. You don't think that it was Mr. Braus, my good friend that was the rat fink, do you?

When we rode down the ramp, we had to be careful of traffic on the gravel road because we built up great speed coming down hill and sometime would hit the loose gravel and fall down in the road, which I did a number of times. I came out with just scratches and bruises and not serious injury, thanks be to God.

Sometimes, I tried to come straight down the levee by not using the ramp. The levee was much steeper going up and down when not on the ramp. I always ended up standing on my brakes to stop the bike before I would get to the second hump in the levee and abandon this madness except for this one time.

This one time was when I was about thirteen. I got the bright idea that I would ride my bike straight down the levee in front of the Mabile's driveway. I picked this spot because it look like the bottom of the levee came back up a bit right where the ditch started. I thought that this would give me the up lift that I needed to get over the ditch and into the middle of the gravel road.

It was not a smart thing to do, but I had been thinking about this jump since I was ten or eleven years old. Nobody had ever tried it that I was aware of and if I made it once, I could do it again later. Anyway, good or bad, I was smart enough to try it when nobody else was around.

I rode my bike up the ramp which was in front of the Plantation store. I rode it on top of the levee past our house and past the Mabile's house intil I got to the area across from the driveway, just before you get to Thomas Ponsano's little shotgun house. From the top of the levee, I could see a long way on the gravel road. I could almost see all the way to White Castle to my left and past Dorseyville to my right. It was all clear for as far as I could see. On the side roads, I could not see any traffic either.

I mounted my trusty bike, aimed it down the patch that I eyeballed, looked again for traffic and took off. I did not peddle on the first hump or section of the levee. I built up good speed coming straight down like this without peddling.

I started down the second hump/section. I tried to peddle but don't think I did any good. I came to the end and tried to lift my handlebars up to sail over the ditch to no avail. The slight rise that I though would lift me up, did not. I went straight out. I did make it over the ditch, barely, but hit the gravel road and sprawled out in the gravel. I hit hard. I was out of breath. I was hurting all over. I laid in the road for what seemed like minutes but it was not more like thirty or forty seconds. I was trying to look from side to side to be sure no cars were coming. There is a slight curve in the road here and it was possible that I would not be seen by a car coming from Dorseyville in the position that I was in.

I made it to my feet, looked around again. My back tire was on the edge of the ditch. I walked my bike to the big Mulberry tree near the driveway. I checked my bike over. It looked to be in good shape except for some additional scratches.

I sat there a long while rubbing my arms and legs where I had some bruises just thinking about what went wrong. I should have cleared the ditch much more than I did. I do not know if I put on my brakes or not. I just did not know. I was happy that nobody saw me. I never again tried this jump, but still think that today's kids could do it without the slightest problem. This I believe.

CHAPTER 6

MORE DOCTOR STUFF: AGES TWELVE AND THIRTEEN

Several years after the running from the dentist ordeal, our family had nine major operations. I lost my tonsils and appendix during this one year period. The tonsil operation was a big deal in the early 50s. I stayed in the hospital two days or so; and stayed in bed after going home for another day or so. I did not want to eat because I had to swallow and it hurt for a week after the operation. Momma fed me soft things to eat. I remember when I swallowed the scab from the sore in my throat. I almost choked, but this meant that I was all healed.

My appendix operation was a much bigger ordeal than my tonsil operation. I had thrown up at school the day before and just was not feeling good. Bobbie Jo had taken Momma to work at Supple's Sugarhouse and was back at home trying to get me ready for school. I was feeling awful. My left side was hurting really bad. My sister went back to Supple's to get Momma. When Momma got home, she helped me dress to go to see Dr. Tomney. I was willing to go this time. We sat (I lied down) in his waiting room for several hours before it was my turn to see him. After he saw me, he canceled the other patience still waiting to see him because he said that he needed to operate on me right away before my appendix burst. I was not ready for this. I did not want to be cut on.

The nurse was Mrs. Olivia Falcon (Quinn the knife fighters Mom) and a good friend of our family. She got the operating room ready and was preparing me for the slaughter- I mean operation. I had just this little white gown on and nothing underneath. They strapped both arms and each leg to the operating table and was trying to put this mask over my face to give me ether. I was fighting it and not keeping my head still. Mrs. Olivia said "if you don't quit fighting, we will have to do this the hard way." Well even at eleven or twelve years of age, that statement made me think about it. If this is not the hard way, I do not want to find out what the hard way is. I settled down and they put me to sleep. I can still remember the feeling like a circle that was not all the way completed, going around and around with the section not complete trying to catch the other section to make a complete circle. It was weird and frustrating. I never could make the two get together. I awoke some hours later in a hospital bed.

Later, I overheard the nurses talking and saying that I was lucky because while I was knocked out during the operation, I threw up and they had to be sure that I did not choke with the vomit in my throat. They cleaned it out some way and I lived. They also said that Dr. Tomney took out hands full of growing glands from inside me to find where my appendix was. Until this day, I still blame him for my short penis and for me not being over six foot two inches tall. He should have put all my growing glands back in after he took the appendix out. That's what I think.

I stayed in the hospital for two or three days. It really hurt to pass gas until a nurse placed a rubber hose in my behind. Somehow this worked wonderfully. The only problem I had in the hospital after this was with that asshole, Kenneth Hebert. His Dad, Mr. Lester Hebert, owned and operated Hebert Drug Store on the hospital property. Kenneth would come by my window several times a day and make all kinds of monkey shines to make me laugh which I did and that made me hurt. When I laughed, it hurt and Kenneth could see the pain in my face from outside through the window and he would laugh at me which made me want to laugh more. I got the nurses to run him off almost every time he came by. This was just too much fun for him at my expense.

After going home, I stayed in bed for several more days. I liked it now, because some adults that came by to visit would give me money for all my troubles. This was just great.

Mrs. Frieda Henry gave a dollar to momma for me. I saw her give it to momma. They talked as Mrs. Frieda was leaving and momma followed her outside. When momma came back in to check on me, I ask her where my dollar was. She did not know. She looked and looked and could not find it. A dollar was big bucks in those days. This was the most money I had since the poor ole dead man's money. Momma retraced her steps but still could not find my dollar. I got out of bed even though momma said not to. I said that I don't come by a dollar to often and we needed to find it. I went on the back porch were momma and Mrs. Frieda was talking. I looked on the porch. I looked on the steps. I looked in the yard. Low, what is this I see? I went down the steps, softly and into the yard near the porch. There was the dollar crumpled up in a little ball like it was a small rolled up piece of paper. Momma had forgot that it was a dollar while she was talking and crumpled it up and threw it in the yard as trash as Mrs. Frieda was leaving and just did not remember doing it. I was so happy, I farted without the hose and felt no pain at all.

THE GLOVE

Between the ages of fifteen and sixteen, I played American Legion Softball. We had a fair team. Our win/loss record was about fifty/fifty I guess. We would play a short inning game before the adults played their game. The American Legion adults were our coaches and managers. We had the same names on our team as our adult sponsor. We all had a good time except when the adults was ready to play ball. If our game was still going on, they would have us try to steal bases knowing we would get thrown out or tell us to swing at everything and do not take a walk. We know what they were doing and it certainly was not teaching us honesty and sportsmanship.

When I was about twelve or thirteen years old, Leon Miller gave an old fielders glove to me. Leon loved baseball. This was a hardball glove. He usually kept a glove for four or five years then went to Western Auto in town and purchased another. This time he purchased a first baseman mitt then gave me this infielder's glove. We did not have much money; heck nobody on the plantation had any money except Mr. Joulett the office manager of the plantation. And he did not ever live on the plantation. He lived in White Castle. I would not have had a glove at this age if it had not been for Leon. He had given away gloves to different folks before when he got a new one. Leon worked hard for his money in the cane field. He save up for a long time and pay off the company store bill before he could buy a new glove. I was very grateful to Leon and still am. He promised to give me the first baseman mitt when he bought a new glove. About three or four years later, he purchase a new glove but gave his first baseman mitt to Dicky Barbier. He must have forgot that he promised it to me. I did not forget. It was a fine mitt, but Dicky and Leon was close and Dicky was playing first base for an adult team and a pretty good player. He was four years older than me.

I still have my four finger infielder's glove today. It is over fifty years old and I've owned it for the last forty five years or there abouts. I use my glove when playing softball and ruined my pocket, but I still can catch a hardball with it and I take it to every Astros game that I go to just in case a ball is hit my way. I want to have protection. I may not be able to catch it, but I believe that I can knock it down and jump on it. It make for great conversation with the younger generations who have never seen a real four finger glove. My glove is less than half the size of baseball gloves made today. You really had to have a bead on the ball in the old days. Today, you can miss it by three or four inches and still catch the ball. Know what I mean Vern. There are baseball players with hands larger than my glove. I love it. It don't smell too good any more, but I still love it.

NOU NOU IN THE CORN CRIB-SMOKING

Several years after my cigarette smoking experience, I was shucking corn in our old corn crib. Nou Nou Pansano came over to the house. Not to help me with my chores but to show me how to smoke some dried corn silk.

Nou Nou was about three years older than me and said that he could smoke corn silk. I did not believe him. He took some dried corn silk and rolled it in some newspaper. He done a better job at rolling it than I could do. He also said that he could make a corn cob pipe and use it to smoke with. This gave me an idea for later.

Nou Nou was smoking this here corn silk and we were talking while I kept on shucking my corn. After a minute or two, he did not look to good to me. Then he said that he was not feeling to good. He started getting dizzy. He really looked pale now. He started dry heaving then went to wet heaving and throwing up. He threw up all over the place and all over himself. He started crawling in his puke to get to the door because he needed more air. Nou Nou was sick as a dog. He made it outside the crib and I helped him get to our water facet where he cleaned himself off as best he could. I just watched. I did not want to get his puke on me. If he would have gotten worse off, I would have ran to get Momma. But he soon stopped throwing up and his color was coming back. After sitting a long time in our yard, he went home. I never saw or even heard anything else from him about smoking corn silk. And I certainly never did try it. I may not be to smart, but I sure in hell was not stupid. I did the stupid thing my first year in the third grade. I was trying to grow out of the stupid era of my life.

SLED-RIDING DOWN THE LEVEE

We loved to play on the Mississippi River levee in front of our house. Where we lived the river started to bend to the left, so the levee was very high. Standing on the road on top of the levee and looking back at our house, I always felt that the levee was higher than the top of our roof. We lived in a very high pitched roof house.

We hunted red wing blackbirds and Robin Red Breast on the levee. When we killed one with our bee-bee guns, we would have a cookout. We normally did not shoot a bird for no reason, especially Robin Red Breast. If the Game Warden caught you with on of those birds, they would take your bee-bee gun and you to jail. It was against the law, or so we were told to shoot a Robin Red Breast. But they was such good eating. We just took the chance anyway. I killed a couple small birds by accident. Birds that I did not mean to shoot. They were not the eating kind. You just know that you cannot hit it, so you shoot anyway and dang it you don't kill it. It make you feel bad for a little while, then you give the little bird to the cat and it does not go to waste. The cats love them. Sometimes you try a shot that is just impossible, like holding the bee-bee gun upside down and shooting left handed, when you are right handed, and hit the poor bird. You could never do it again to save your life. If no one saw you, you may as well not tell because nobody will believe you. If someone did see you, you let him or her brag for you because you still will not try it again because you could not do it in a hundred years. So you just save the bee bees for something else.

When anyone on the River front of the Plantation purchased a washing machine, or ice box or any big appliance, we usually found out about it pretty quick. We wanted the cardboard box to play with and sometimes in. Many times we could cut an ice box

box into about four large pieces of cardboard. We would cut it at the corners and end up with four large pieces. We use this to slide down the levee. The best part of the year to do this was the early Spring when the clover would start to sprout out. After we mashed down the clover, it became slippery. So we would get on the cardboard on the edge of the road on top of the levee. We hold onto the cardboard in front of our feet and pull it back toward us about ten inches or so. This would lift the front part of the sled upwards a bit. We took turns pushing and riding down the levee. Sometime a good push to get you started would send you more than half the way down the levee. After we mashed the grass and clover down, we tried to stay on the same pathway. Sometimes we got off the pathway into a clump of grass and the sled would come to an abrupt halt and send whoever was riding tumbling down the levee without the cardboard.

All this was fun with one exception. We kept our cows in a pasture near our house. The black folks who owned cows did not have a pasture so they tied their cows on the levee to eat fresh grass. They would walk their cows every morning after milking from the quarters where they lived pass our house on the shell road and stake then out on a fifty foot chain on the levee. They came and get them in the afternoon each day to milk them before dark. After a day or two, they rotated the spots where they chained the cows, until the grass grew back in the original spot. So every several weeks the cows were chained in the same area. During the really cold winter months, they kept them chained at their houses or in small pens in their yards and fed them corn feed that the Plantation supplied. There was not much grass on the levee during the winter months.

During the Spring time with all the grass and clover growing, we could not always see the cow patties just under the clover. A cow patty will stop a sled on a dime. And off you go into another fresh cow patty. It is common knowledge on a farm that if you find one cow patty, there will be several more within a few feet. This was the drawback. And a cow patty would put an abrupt end to a sledding party in a hurry. I always felt like cow do-do should make the sled slide better. But I am here to tell you that it does not. If it was someone else that slid through the cow do-do, it was very funny. But if it happened to you, well that was a different story. I had a different story to tell a number of times during my levee sledding career.

MY FIRST NEW (USED) BIG BICYCLE

I do not remember exactly how old I was. Somewhere between twelve and thirteen I believe. It came for Christmas. Santa Clause delivered it from Mr. Joe Mobile's house. I actually saw it by mistake at Mr. Joe's house about four or five days before Christmas. They live in the ten room house (that we would move into when we moved back from White Castle in 1959) next to ours and there were several bicycles in one of the empty rooms that we used to make kites in. We were ushered out of the house without getting a good look at the bikes. But I did see them. I was not sure that one would be for me at the time. I believe that Santa got the bikes from Mr. LeBlanc who could find anything you want to buy. That Christmas Eve, I went to work with Momma. When you make your living in the agriculture business you work every day until the crop is in. She worked at Supple's Sugarhouse (Catherine Plantation) during the sugar cane harvesting/grinding season. In the early afternoon, I was bored and Momma said that I could go visit Nan Noon and Paran Charlie at Richland. They lived about a mile or two from the sugar mill if I took the short cut through the cane fields and woods. I had made this journey several times before and the only part that bothered me was the "woods" part. I was really bored, so I took off. I had planned for Momma and Daddy to come and pick me up after Daddy picked up Momma about five p.m. that evening. I did not share may plan with Momma.

I made it to Nan Noon's about two in the afternoon. Paran Charlie was in the cane field working to get his crop to the mill. I played and had fun until Paran came in from the field. We had supper and waited for Daddy to come get me. After all, this was Christmas Eve. It got dark and no Momma and Daddy. Nan Noon did not have that modern devise called a telephone, so I could not call them and Paran was tired and did not feel like driving me home to Cedar Grove. They said you could sleep here like you done before. But this was Christmas Eve. I was pissed. Nan Noon and Paran Charlie never had any children and did not buy Christmas gifts as I remember, so on Christmas morning, I got my coffee-milk for breakfast and that was it. I started waiting for Momma and Daddy again. I figured that they would come get me early; after all, it was Christmas Day.

It was customary on Christmas Day and New Years Day for friends and family members to visit each other and offer greeting and best wishes. On Christmas Day they may exchange gifts and on New Years Day have a drink or two. I am not sure how the adults worked out the schedule of who would visit and who would stay home to be visited, but this is what used to take place. Folks started out early in the morning, as they would visit several homes to pass best wishes on.

At seven a.m., Momma and Daddy hadn't arrived. Neither at 8 a.m. They were not there at 9 a.m. Come 10 a.m., and no word from them. They had not arrived yet. I was hopping mad. It was around 11 a.m. when they showed up like it was all normal and everything. I saw the bicycle in the back of the pickup truck. I got really happy in a hurry. Daddy Got the bike out of the truck and I road it all around the yard and road while they visited with Nan Noon and Paran Charlie. In about an hour they were ready to leave for our house. I wanted to ride my new (used) bike home. It was about three or four miles. Daddy agreed because there was no traffic at all in the country. He said to be careful. I took off on Richland road. Daddy followed behind me. From Richland road, I went to Hwy 992 and took a left on it. All the roads were gravel back then except the road on Cedar Grove between our house and the Store. It was a shell road. It was also a private road and belonged to the Plantation. I road on Hwy 992 coming toward the Mississippi River. I crossed the Texas and Pacific Railroad track and came to Louisiana Highway 1. It was a state highway and it was paved. I went across it to another section of gravel road. At this point, Dad turned left onto highway 1. About one half mile up the highway was the shell road to our house. Dad would take a right on it to get back to the River road and our house. As I mentioned, I went straight and got to River Road, Which was also graveled. I took a left and in about one half mile, I came to the Company Store and the shell road and our house.

Our house was on the corner of the River Road and the Plantation shell road. Across the shell road from us was one side of the Company store. The front of the store faced the River Road. The front of our house faced the River Road also. Across the River Road is the levee that hold in the Mississippi River. This is the levee that I played on throughout the year. The top of the levee was higher than the highest point of our very high, raindrop splitter roof house.

On the ride from Nan Noon's house, I noticed a scratch in the new paint on my new (used) bike. When I got to the house, Dad had already parked and was waiting on the porch. I showed him the scratch and asked if he knew what happened to it. I was informed that the Henry's had came over that morning to wish Merry Christmas and Wayne Henry had ridden MY bike and fell down and scratched it. I got so mad that I could have bitten the heads off ten-penny nails. Damn him. Wayne Henry rode my bike before I did. How could they let this happen? Mr. Lulu and Mrs. Frieda Henry's only boy, Wayne, rode my bike. This was the same Wayne Henry that in 1962, when he was in the Army, his Mom and Dad bought for him a 1962 white two door hard top Chevy 409. A very sharp, good looking, powerful, and fast car to surprise him when he came home on leave. Although I begged, Frieda Henry would NOT let me drive the car before Wayne drove it. She pissed me off again. I did ride in it a number of times when Wayne was driving, but I NEVER drove that damn car.

Wayne Henry still owe ME for being the first to ride my bike and the first to put a scratch on the new re-paint job on it.

THE CORNCRIB FIRE

The corncrib was a one room building about twenty feet by twenty feet with a floor off the ground and a good roof and one window and one door for entry.

When I was about nine or ten years old, I used to like to burn trash. I liked to burn anything that would burn. Every chance I got, I put a match to debris in the yard at the designated burning area. My daddy used to say that I liked to play with fire.

One Saturday I was working in the corncrib shucking corn for the chickens. I used to try and shuck enough corn to feed the chickens all week. This way, in the afternoons I only needed to shell the ears of corn in the hand shell hopper and throw it out to the chickens. The shelling part of this job was much easier and cleaner than the shucking part. When shucking, I would accumulate a large pile of dried corn shucks. When I stop shucking, I carrier the shucks to the burning area that was some distance from the corn crib and placed all that I could get into a 55 gallon drum that we sued to burn trash. The drum had holes cut in the sides towards the bottom of the drum so that air could get into it and this would make the burning easier and faster. We always had a stick to stir and poke the fire with. After about one half-hour of burning the shucks, the fire was really down and about burnt out. My fire poking stick had caught fire and I waived it around thinking that this would blow out the flame, which it did. I left the area. Instead of leaving the poking stick near the drum, I dragged it on the ground behind me on the way back to the house. I walked through more shucks near the corncrib on the way back to the house. I did not realize that my stick was still very hot or had a flame on it.

After about a half-hour in the house, I heard all kinds of commotions outside. I ran out to the end of the porch and saw some people throwing water on our corncrib that was on fire. Before long, many people from the plantation was standing around looking or trying to throw water on the crib. We had a water facet nearby and someone connected the hose onto it and started spraying water on the side of our house, which was really getting hot. We lost a lot of corn and some tools and leather hardware that the mules used to be fitted with when they worked the field. I think we lost some things that would be very valuable today.

Then the White Castle fire truck showed up. The crib was just about gone by this time. After finding out what was going on, The Chief of Police came to me and said that he heard that I was a "firebug," and firebugs usually go to jail. He asked if I was ready to go to jail. Of course I was not. I promised that I would not play with fire ever again. He then talked to my Daddy and Daddy said to not take me to jail- this time. I was so scared and became so happy that I must have smiled. The Chief, Mr. Eddie Boudreaux, said all right I will not take him this time. Daddy popped me behind the head and told me to go in the house and get on my knees in a corner. Which I did post haste.

After everybody left the scene outside, I was still kneeling down in Momma and Daddy's bedroom. Nan Noon and Paran Charlie was still there. I was still crying and afraid of what might happen next. I used to really like money although I never saw it often as a kid. Nan Noon try to give me about seven cents and I would not take it. They knew then that I was really perturbed. She left the money on the floor, which is where it stayed for an hour or more until I was told to get off my knees and go to my room- which was also my big brother's and my Uncle Nolan's room. We all slept in the same room. This was a five room house plus a bathroom.

All the time that I was on my knees, I was hearing about how bad being a "firebug" is, and I promised several times that I would not ever play with fire again. I just knew that Mr. Eddie Boudreaux was watching every move I made and would like nothing better than to hand cuff me and lock me up forever with all the other fire bugs. After this, I never burned up or down anything that I did not want to- thus far.

JESSY'S CANAL (ON THE PLANTATION)

Cedar Grove Plantation was divided in two by Highway 992, also called Brickla Lane. The side of the Plantation that bordered the Supple's Plantation, which we live on, was named "Cedar Grove Plantation." The section on the other side of Brickla Lane that bordered the town of White Castle was called White Castle Plantation. Both sides started at the River and went toward the back for a couple of miles.

The sugar mill was on the front part of Cedar Grove and the airplane landing strip was on the back part of White Castle.

There were three major shell roads in addition to Brickla Lane that ran the length of the Plantation from the River to the back. They had names as did certain sections of the Plantation. I cannot remember the ten or so other names beside White Castle and Cedar Grove Plantations.

On the White Castle side was a canal that ran over a mile long. It was the main drainage ditch for White Castle Plantation. It was larger than the other ditches or canals on this side of Brickla Lane. It usually had more water in it than the other ditches/canals. This meant it was good for craw fishing. When I was eleven, twelve and thirteen years old, this was the best craw fishing location on the whole Plantation.

On the other side of the canal, coming from Brickla Lane, and toward the front part of the plantation was two frame houses for workers to live. Cousin John Alabardo and his family lived in one of them. The youngest son was named Jessy. Jessy Alabardo-Chroshe. Jessy may have changed his last name from Alabardo to Chroshe later because he really was a Chroche and not a Alabardo, so I overheard a number of times. He was cousin John's wife's son. When we were kids, he went by Alabardo.

Jessy was a couple years older than Ronald and me and therefore was a foot or so taller or it seemed that he was a foot or so taller to us at the time.

During summer vacations, we loved to go crawfishing in this canal because it yielded the best results. It had larger and more crawfish than the other canals/ditches on the place.

Either Daddy or Mr. Joe Mabile would take Ronald, Sonny and me and drop us off near cousin John's house, then leave and pick us up there or four hours later. We learned the first time that we crawfished there that Jessy did not want us to crawfish in his canal. After the adult would leave, Jessy would come out of hiding with a stick and run us further down the canal. We did not run to a particular location, we ran until Jessy stopped chasing us cussing and waving his big stick.

Jessy did not like anybody crawfishing in what he called "his canal." Especially near his house. He ran off the black kids and other white kids if he was home when they tried to crawfish there.

For the several years we tried to crawfish there, he was only gone a couple of time and we enjoyed our time there. There were a number of times when one of our dads' would drop us off; we would wait a while before setting up to see if Jessy was coming out or not. We learned our lesson the hard way. One time we place several of our poles with string and chicken necks (bait) out about ten feet apart. Before we made a pass, Jessy and his stick came out. He was ready to fight as always. We could only grab about three of our baited poles and run. Running is bad enough, but running with poles, string, a bucket, a bag of bait, a crawfish net and water jug (for drinking) and whatever else, was not easy. After we departed, Jessy would get a crawfish net and use our setup to catch crawfish for himself. He could never afford to buy bait. So he used to get his crawfishing equipment for free when his timing was right.

It got to a point when our driver left; we just started walking down the canal instead of waiting to see if Jessy was coming out. If our driver was going to stay with us a while, we would crawfish right there. Jessy still came out sometimes, but without his stick. He would not try anything when an adult was there but he would give each of us that look; and whispered that he would get us later. He never did.

We usually caught a water bucket of crawfish or more. When we got back home, we would purge the crawfish. This meant we rinse them in fresh water several time and fill the bucket again with water and put some table salt in it. We let them sit for five or ten minutes while we collect wood to build a fire. The salt in the water made the crawfish burp up all the mud that was inside of them. This cleaned their insides out. If you don't purge them, they would have a musty taste. We get the fire going.

Then we pour off the salt water. It would have a dark color because of the burping of the crawfish. We pour off the water in an area that did not have grass because this water with salt will kill grass.

We hold the crawfish in a bucket without water while partly filling another bucket with fresh water to do the boiling in. We get seasoning from Momma or Miss Violet. Put it in the bucket of water on the fire with some more salt. A lot of salt is used when boiling crawfish. When the water came to a boil, we poured in the crawfish. Stir them with a stick, bring it back to a boil for six or seven minutes, than with a pole placed under the bucket handle, move it from the fire. We let them soak for a couple of minutes than dip them out of the bucket with a strainer or sifter used for flower and place them on our cesspool cement cover.

We then just had a boil crawfish feast among ourselves. We usually pour the boiling water with all the seasoning in it, in the ditch along the shell road or any place where Daddy did not want grass to grow. This stuff still had a lot of salt and other stuff in it that would kill grass for a very long time.

Jessy also chase us from picking pecans anywhere on White Castle Plantation. So again, whenever picking pecans, we had to keep an eye out for Jessy. We could not afford for him to catch us picking his pecans. He would take them away for us. Picking pecans is a back breaking chore and it would have been hard to loose them without a fight.

Many years later, after I married and moved from the Plantation and had my own family, we went to visit Momma and Daddy. Daddy would take me riding in the field to show me the crop. We made a turn on the shell road where we used to crawfish and I made the comment about Jessy's Canal. Daddy said "what did you say?" So I repeated that we called this Jessy's Canal and why. He was outdone. He had never heard it before. It was really something else canal, but Daddy said if he had known that we had all that trouble, he would have kicked young Jessy's ass. We never thought to tell our dads about Jessy the bully. Hell, Jessy never had a lot going for him anyway. So this was something that if it made him feel good, that was alright by us kids. We did not tell on Jessy.

By the time I was fourteen, I was what they refer to as big for my age. I was as big as Jessy and most of the seniors in high school. I was not afraid of any of then either. If Jessy or any of the older boys would have started something then, I would have just kicked their asses. If I could not and any one of them whipped me, he would have to do it every day until the day I whipped him. This was the kind of kid I was. I did not ever go looking for trouble, but I never ran after fourteen years of age.

I can remember being in the eight grade. We would have to stand in line to enter the lunch room or for other functions. On many occasions, the juniors and seniors in high school would walk by us and a number of them would hit each boy in line. When they got to me, I turned and face each one. As if to say "go ahead and see what will happen." In every incident, they skipped me and hit the guys next to me. I was not going to take the shit from an eighteen year old. Maybe any number of them could have wipped my ass. We never got the opportunity to find out.

I had made up my mind that year that I grew over a foot taller, that I was not going to take what the older boys always did to the younger ones. If one of them whipped my ass, he would had to do it every day until the day came when I would beat the living shit out of him. I figured from an early age that you learned from your mistakes and that should apply in fights also. Improve yourself each time out and don't make the same mistake twice and everyone will do just fine.

I was never a bad ass. I was always and still am, a want-to-be bad ass.

CHAPTER 7

CRAWFISHING AS A YOUNGSTER WITH MOMMA AGES SIX THROUGH SEVENTEEN

We used to go craw fishing in the spillway at Bayou Pigeon when I was a little kid. Momma, cousin Jessie Doiron, Put, Pocko, Ronald, me and sometimes Sonny, would all go along for the day. The older folks did all the work of baiting and setting the nets and gathering the crawdads with the set nets by using either beef melt or chicken necks or both as bate.

We would catch nine or ten sacks of crawfish and then buy five or six more sacks to take home. This was for putting up in the freezer to enjoy during the winter months when they were not available. When we got back from crawfishing all day, we would put all the sacks of crawfish under cousin Jessie's house where it was sort of cool. The crawfish must be alive to start processing them. Cousin Jessie's house was built off the ground high up on pillars and we could get under it rather easy. The next day, however many families involved in catching and buying the crawfish would gather early in the morning at her house and start working on processing the crawfish.

We would bring a large kettle and put water in it to boil. Most of the dirty work was done outside in the yard. We gathered wood and logs to burn for heating the water. The bigger boys would empty the sacks, one at a time into a number 3 tub and put fresh water in it to clean off the crawfish. This was done to each sack load.

The cleaned crawfish was placed in tubs or large buckets and when the large kettle of water cane to a boil, we used a regular size cooking pot from cousin Jessie's kitchen, to dip the hot boiling water from the kettle and pour over the crawfish. This would scald them to death. We did NOT boil them. You do not want to boil them for putting up/processing for the freezer because they would get over cooked before you cooked them. After scalding, we dipped them out with a fishing net and otherwise drained off the water and placed on a table where they could cool down a bit and we could get at them. The processing consisted of twisting the heads off, squeezing the head over a bowl or pan to get the fat out, and then throw the heads in a trash can unless it was big enough to be used for a bisque. The fat was used to cook the several different dishes with. The larger claws of the crawfish was also broken off and would be used in several of the gravies that was cooked. The heads that we saved for a bisque was placed to the side where we could get back to them later in the processing. We squeezed the tail from the shell into another pan. This action usually left the vain with the tail end and not in the meat. If the vein broke off in the tail meat, you had to get it out before placing the meat into the pan. The empty tail shell went into the trash with the heads to be thrown away later.

One of my main jobs was to clean the heads and make them ready for the bisque. The women that was peeling the crawfish decided which heads to keep and which to dispose of. I would strip off the legs, and body parts still on, eyes, whiskers, etc. from it and rinsed them off by dipping into a pan of water. I cleaned the head inside and out and place it into another bucket or pan to be used latter. They had better be cleaned well because from here they would be used to stuff with the bisque mixture. They did get a final inspection by the women that was making the bisque before being filled.

We put up crawfish for stews, gumbo, bisque (which was the hardest to make), etouffee, crawfish balls, stuff bell peppers, soups, and stuffed whatever. From morning into night usually for two days we worked processing these crawdads.

There were always several families involved in an operation this large. When we did this for just our family, three to five sacks of crawfish is all we would do at one processing.

When the crawfish was being processed, someone else was getting the onions, shallots, celery, garlic, bell peppers, etc. cleaned and cut up to grind up with some tails in a meat grinder to make the stuffing to put in the bisque (heads) or patties or the other things that was stuffed. As mentioned before, the bisque was a very tedious and time consuming job and I never did like doing it. I won't go into how this was done except to say after a day and most of the time, two days, of working, we would be very happy it was over and wanted to start eating some on rice right away.

As stated earlier, this was done during the crawfish season to have crawfish in the freezer during the winter months. In the late 1940s and 1950s, crawfish was not readily available as they are now. There weren't any pond growers yet. That came later and became a very large cash crop for many of the families that had low/marshy land. Many sugarcane growers also went into the crawfish raising business. They done come a long way baby - I am gonna told you that.

THE BOUCHERIE/PIG PROCESSING

During my preteen years we butchered pigs each year. I remember this well. Most of the time we did it at Nan Noon and Paran Charlie's house. Sometimes two pigs was slaughtered.

After you raised a pig and it was big enough to butcher, you would pen it up for a couple weeks and feed it corn and clean slop. You could not take a chance by leaving in out to roam its living area and eat wild onions or something else that would ruin the taste of the meat.

The Boucherie was another multiple family gathering. You must remember that I am talking about fifty or so years ago. In those days, you grew your pigs to 500 to 800 pounds or more. You wanted them really fat. This fat/oil/lard is what you had to cook with for the next year. The Boucherie was during the winter months when the weather was cool. Usually after September for sure. Again, it took those big black iron kettles and lots of boiling water. You set the kettles up on bricks and place sticks/log and anything that would burn around it. It was best to have two big kettles when it was time to cook the fat to make cracklin and lard/oil.

The slaughter went like this. Shoot the hog in the head or hit it between his eyes with a large hammer or blunt instrument. Drag it to the entrance door of the pen. Slit its throat with a very sharp knife and catch the blood with a pan. I usually covered my eyes when the gun was fired or the hammer was used and then covered my ears when the pig's throat was slit because of the noise it would make. I did not like this at all. It is just something you had to do if you wanted food. The men would then grab a hold of the pigs legs to carry it to a wide board. It usually took six good men to carry it. The wide board could be an old door placed across two carpenter's horses to make a table. Of course all of this is done outside. We always hoped for good weather for a Boucherie.

The boiling water would be dipped out of the black kettle with a small pot and poured over a small section of the pig. The men, with large butcher knives, would place the blade on the carcass and scrape the hair off. This was not skinning a pig. It was removing all the hair from the animal. When completed, the pig would not have any hair from his mouth to the tip of his tail. Yes even the hair from the tail and the feet, the ears, and the head, was scrapped off. Pour hot water on an area then scrape then pour more hot water then scrape. Turn the pig over and do it again until all the hair is removed. Then the pig is gutted and the internals emptied into one or two number 3 tubs or washtub which is bigger than a number 3 tub. Almost everything on a hog is used. The bladder, tongue, feet, tail, lips, head, brains, blood, etc. Maybe not the eyes. I am not sure about the eyes. From the internals, you kept the liver, kidneys, heart, bladder, intestines, and other stuff. My job was to clean/scrape/wash the intestines to be used for casings for the boudin/sausage. After getting the stuff out of them, I had to rinse them in fresh water and go through the whole intestine. I would blow into it and gather it up with my fingers and blow in it again and again and again. If I found a hole in it, I would cut it there and tie the end in a knot. Then start blowing again until I did the complete length of it. I believe that my sister did this job also.

Some of the food we made was: Hogs head cheese (I have never eaten this), red boudin (blood sausage), white boudin, boudin with cooked rice, cracklin, lard/oil, pickle pigs feet, pickle pig tail and ears- I believe and all the other cuts of meat that come from pigs. At a very early age, I can remember seeing salt pork in what we call a pork barrel. It was a large crock jar. This is where cuts of pork meat was placed and salts added in top of it and then more pork and more salt and so on until you filled the container. This was before having a freezer to store our food stuff. Paran Charlie had a smoke house where he cured sausage and the back upper portion of the pig's legs to make smoked ham. In later years, we carried this stuff to a company that cured them for us. It was a business where they also made hot dogs and other pork products.

When everything was done, the families divided up the goodies. If you was just helping out then you got a roast and some cracklin and lard or something else. We would wrap the cuts of pork in freezer paper. We would mark the package with a black marker that stated the cut of meat, and date it was put up. We stop raising pigs when I was about nine or ten year old. Over the years, into the 60s and 70s, the raising of pigs to 700 pounds or more stopped. With the invention of vegetable oil and other type of cooking oils, the folks that lived off the land did not need the lard/oil any more and a pig was considered to be full-grown at 300 pounds. Seemed pretty skinny to me.

BEEF BUTCHERING

We also butchered for beef. Mostly, steers, when we had one. We had several cows to milk each day. When they dropped a calf, sometimes Daddy purchased another calf to raise with the calf, for the freezer. We would take a little male calf and make him a steer by cutting off his balls. This was supposed to make the calf grow quicker and make the meat tender when it was grown. I always felt sorry for the little calf. He did not have any say so in the matter. The adults said that they did not feel it. Well, if it happened to me, I think that I would feel it as I am sure I felt it when old Dr. Tomeny circumcised me some years earlier and that was not removing my balls. Thank God. My sons, Kent, Lane and Todd should thank God too. There was several men on the Plantation who were experts at removing balls from little calves and the calves be without a lot of distress. Daddy did not do this that I can recall.

When the animal was large enough to butcher, Daddy would get the Mabiles to help with the butchering. We helped them do their butchering when Mr. Joe or Mr. Jules (they are brothers) needed help. They worked on the Plantation also. Mr. Joe was the Head Overseer or Field Manager and Daddy and Mr. Jules worked as Overseers for Mr. Joe.

When beef was butchered, we got Mr. Shirley Dennis, a black man, to skin and gut the animal. He was very good at doing this.

He was a butcher on the side. He was always given the hide and head and some meat for his help. This was his pay.

Usually, somebody shot the animal in the brain to kill it. After Mr. Dennis did the skinning and gutting and cleaning out the innards, we would use a hack saw to cut it in half. The two halves were taken to the Ice House in White Castle to hang in cold storage for a week or so to tenderize the meat. This made the meat better tasting. In later years, the beef would be taken to large coolers that was made cold by electric refrigeration. After a week or so, we pickup the beef up and delivered it to a butcher and told them how to cut the steaks, and roasts, and ribs, and ground meat, etc. The cuts were placed into large boxes which we brought home and had a meat wrapping party. It was not a party, we wrapped and labeled the cuts and dated the packages before placing into our home deep freezer. The beef butchering was not nearly as much work as the butchering pigs.

CHICKEN PROCESSING

We raised chickens for eggs and also hatched little chicks to raise and to butcher. The females would not be butchered unless we had more than we wanted to keep on the yard. We raised the males to about four pounds net and then butchered them and put in the freezer. Sometimes, Daddy would mail order 25 or 50 male chicks or so to raise just for the freezer. Like the pigs and crawfish which usually took two days to process and the beef which took one day to get it ready for the cooler and another day to cut and wrap up, the chickens took two days unless you only did ten to fifteen of them. We usually did more than that.

When they were big enough, Daddy and Momma would start ringing the necks of each chicken. They would reach into the cage and catch one, ring its neck and throw it on the ground. After they were all dead, we started the processing. This meant picking all the feathers off the chickens. Sometimes the little pen feathers had to be burned off because we could not grab enough of the feather to pluck it from the chicken. Then it had to be gutted. Momma usually did this. All the innards were removed. The good stuff put aside and the other stuff thrown in the waste can to be buried or thrown behind the levee later. Then Momma or my sister would cut the chicken up into the pieces we usually wanted it to be in when cooked. Then we wrapped it in freezer paper labeled and dated the package and placed into the freezer for later use. Sometimes we left some chickens whole and wrapped them that way. Momma cut them up before she cooked them.

Our neighbor, Mr. Joe Mabile, would tie the chicken's feet together and hang them on the picket fence upside down then walk by and cut off the heads with a very sharp butcher knife. I did not like this at all. The chickens would flop all around on the fence spraying blood everywhere. This was a good way to drain the blood out of them though.

One time Daddy made me ring a rooster's neck. His neck did not break and he flopped and flopped around all over the yard than got back on his feet with his head all bent over to one side and ran and flopped toward under the house. Daddy hollered for me to grab him before he got under the house. I was not quick enough. When he flopped, I would jump back. So there was the rooster with a cracked neck, flopping under the house. This was my kill, so I had to crawl under the house to get him. Of course I did not want to go, but it would teach me a lesson to do a better job of ringing necks in the future, and I did not have a choice in this matter. Every time I got close to the rooster, he would jump or flop over and I would jump back and hit my head on the two by six frames under the house. I am sure happy that I did not bump my head into a nail from the flooring above my head. I would be getting encouragement from my Dad to catch that rooster. I believe that he may have done a little laughing but can not be sure of that because I was occupied with the job at hand. Beside the tone of his encouragement did not lead me to believe that he was having a good time at my expense. I had done a bad job and I need to fix it. Dad kept urging me to hurry up. After what seemed like fifteen or ten minutes, I came out with that damn rooster. It was still kicking. I was ready to let him go, you know, like the criminal that the electricity did not kill. With all that this rooster went through, I thought that he should have a stay of execution. But Daddy said that I had to finish the job. I think that Momma would have let me go inside, but Daddy was in charge-this time.

So I rung his neck again this time until I felt it pop and threw him to the ground. He flopped a couple of times and died like he should have done the first time. I do not remember my Daddy having me ring any more chicken necks after this one although we processed many a chickens in the years to come. I did not and do not feel any resentment toward my Dad for making me learn how to ring a chicken's neck. It is just something you do on a farm and if you want to eat, you better learn how to do certain things that you may not want to do. You never know when you may need to know how to do something such as this to feed your family.

Now back to the chicken processing.

After the chickens were dead, you had to pluck all the feathers off them. Even the very small pen feathers and some time when you got all that you can get with your fingers, you had to burn some of them off over an open flame, without burning or otherwise harming the meat. After all the feathers were off, then someone gutted the chicken. The innards were cleaned out. The gizzards, heart, liver and I don't know what all, was placed on the side. This is great giblets for dirty rice and stuffing and other meals. The chicken was cut up into serving pieces. The head was thrown away with the guts and feet. Sometimes the feet was kept and boiled in seasoned water or pickled so my sister could knaw on them later. She liked knawing on pigs and chicken feet.

The whole cut up chicken was wrapped in freezer paper, labeled, dated (everything processed and put in the freezer or canned was dated) before being placed in the freezer.

When the female chickens got too old to lay eggs, they was processed also. When placed in the freezer, the package would be labeled HEN. A hen is an older chicken and is to be used for stews and other dishes that took a very long time to cook. Something like fried chicken would use chickens that was processed when they were young. Cooking a hen a long time made them tender and tastier.

PROCESSING VEGETABLES

We also put up vegetables, like snap beans, butter beans (lima), all different kinds of peas such as field, black eye, crowder, etc., white beans, okra, corn, and tomatoes. Some of the processing was hard work and very time consuming. All the different peas and beans had to be shelled by hand while still "green" before processing could began. Processing was accomplished by placing the product into boiling water for some length of time and quickly transferring the product into a container filled with ice and very cold water for a length of time. This action cooled the product off very quickly which is what you needed to do before placing it in a container and into the freezer. When you see the word "blanched" it means the vegetables went through the process mentioned above.

The snap beans were picked green and we snapped off the tips on both ends and most of the time had to slice the bean with a knife to make it smaller. All this before boiling the water to start processing. We also left some of the beans and peas to nature and dry on the stalk before picking/harvesting them. Some were picked before completely dry and were shelled and blanched and placed in the freezer. Some of the beans and peas were picked after completely drying on the stalk and were shelled by hand and put up in jars as dried beans/peas. We used these later to plant for the crop the next year. We did this with okra too. I believe we put black pepper in the jars which helped to kill or keep insects from developing in them. After shelling, we hand picked them to process only the good beans. You always had to be on the watch for bugs or half eaten beans, etc. We picked out the ones that did not look good and fed them to the chickens.

The corn mixed with tomatoes was the hardest work to process and took all day to accomplish. The corn had to be harvested from the field by hand. Each ear was checked for tenderness before being taken from the stark. Daddy and some field workers did this. After delivery to our house, we shucked the corn and had to pull off all the corn silk from each ear. Then we washed and rinsed them. Each ear had to be cut and scrapped to get the kernels from the cob. We gave these green cobs to the cows and chickens and they loved them. This was very time consuming. The tomatoes had to be picked from our garden nearby, washed and checked for bad spots and bugs than placed in a ban of boiling water to blanch them. After they were blanched, the skins cracked and we peeled them off. This left the tomatoes looking whole, but soft and mushy.

The corn kernels was blanched in boiling water also. After draining off as much water as possible, the blanched corn was placed into a large pan with sided about five inches high. Some of the whole blanched tomatoes was placed into the pan with the corn and the stirring/mixing began. It seemed like Momma stirred for hours to get the corn and tomatoes thoroughly mixed and to cool off the mixture also before it could be placed in bags and put in the freezer. When processing this mixture, we did/could not run the corn and tomatoes through ice water to cool them down before placing in containers and putting in the freezer as we did with all the other vegetables. I never did learn how many tomatoes was added to how much corn to make this come out just right. All I know is that when cooked, this mixture of whole kernel corn and tomatoes was great tasting and one of my favorite dishes. We all enjoyed eating it except Daddy. He did not like corn and said that corn was for horses. When Momma cooked corn soup, Daddy must have become a horse because he sure liked it.

GROWING POTATOES

We also raised potatoes in the field. Usually Daddy went on half with some else. They shared the cost of seed potatoes and planted them when the time was right. Come harvest time, we worked all day and sometimes two or more days in the field gathering them. We stored them under our house in a section that was built for them. There was an all wooded structure with a swinging door that had a latch on it. It had to be enclosed to keep the chickens and varmints from getting at the potatoes and eating and otherwise ruining them. Our house was up on pillars about two to three feet off the ground. I was the youngest and smallest so I fetched a lot of potatoes during my early years.

During the winter time, we covered them with hay so that they would not freeze. It they froze, they would rotten very fast and that was a stinky and sticky mess. As it was, some of them would just rot over time anyway. If we had a big rain and it seeped into the storage pen and the potatoes was not used or moved, it/they would rotten. When fetching them, since there was no light under the house, you just had to search around with your hands to find them. Many times I poked my fingers into rotten potatoes. When you found one, you had to remove it because it would make all the potatoes touching it rotten also. So you throw it out into the yard where the chickens would fight over it. In a few minutes it would be gone. Chickens will eat anything that don't eat them first. They are very nasty animals. But what gooooooooood eating when someone that knows how to cook, cooks them.

Years later, for some reason, we stopped storing potatoes under the house and built an area in the corn crib and stored them there until I left the Plantation. I'm just thinking, maybe I got to big to get under the house to fetch them. I just do not know.

GROWING CORN/TENDING TO COWS

Earlier I mentioned that corn was grown on the Plantation. A lot of corn was grown each year, several hundred acres of it. When I was little, we had mules to pull plows and open drains and pull the water cart and other jobs. Each Overseer and some other workers was allowed to have a certain number of cow/cattle or horses for themselves. The limit was two or three for each family. We had over one hundred people working on the Plantation in the 50s. So this added up to being quite a few head of cattle all together. The Plantation owner would buy the seed corn to be planted to supply the mules and cattle with feed. When we put corn up for the freezer, we would harvest it "green", not matured. The corn kernels was still soft. The vast majority of the corn was harvested in late August after it had matured. The stalks and shucks on the corn would be brownish and dried. The kernels would be hard and yellow and orange colored. All this corn was picked by hand by the field hands when I was a little kid, and stored in a large storage shed on the plantation near the big corn grinder where the mules were housed/pastured.

Each overseer or boss that had cows/houses, chickens, guinea hens, ducks, etc. would get a wagon load of corn free. Generally the wagon load was delivered to your house from the field while harvesting was going on so as to not handle the corn twice, and from the storage shed during the rest of the year. When you ran out, you go to the shed and pick up more corn after arrangements were made with the Overseer in charge. At home we would shuck, shell and grind (for baby chicks) the corn. We fed the shucks to our cows. They loved it. This left us with the cob to get rid of.

At the storage shed where the bulk of the corn was stored was this big grinder. You would place the whole ear of corn, shuck and all, as is, in it and it would ground the shucks, corn, cob, and silk to smithereens and it became cattle feed. We all got to share the feed for our cow/horses also. When we milked our cows, we would place this feed in their feeding trough and pour molasses on it. The plantation produced molasses during the harvesting/grinding season at the sugar house where we made the brown sugar. Molasses it one of the products produced from sugar cane as is syrup and other type sweet products.

The cows enjoyed the sweet taste of molasses on the feed and kept very still when eating while we were milking them. We had to learn how fast each cow would eat to judge how much feed to pour in her trough. Some cows, when finish eating what was there, will come out of the milking pen whether we had it boarded up or not. Daddy had one cow that tore the shirt off my back with her horns trying to hook me and get out of the milking pen after she was done eating. It did not make her and difference that I still had a lot of milking to do. I was nervous when milking her and when she finished eating, I was finished milking regardless of where I was in the milking process. I got out of the pen as quickly as I could and slide back to the rails that we used to enclose me and the cows in the milking pen. We had this cow for years and she never did settle down. She stayed a wild one. She kicked me on several occasions, she stepped in my pail of milk a number of times when I almost had it full. She went to the bathroom in my milk pail on several occasions as well. She was just a bad cow. I did not like milking her. I would even give her extra feed and molasses but sometimes she just get a while hair and would not eat it all and did not want to be milked anymore. I threw away many, many gallons of milk from the cow that she ruined. Daddy did not like to milk this cow either, so when she dropped a calf, Daddy would buy a feeder calf and we would raise two calves on her. We would stop milking her and let the two calves have the milk in the morning and evening times. We kept the calves locked up in a pen all day long. The cows roamed around in a several acre pasture. We could not leave a calf with the mother all day long because they would nurse all day long and get diarrhea and could die. We still had to watch this cow close at feeding time when I put both calves on her. She would not want the strange calf to nurse. It was a job trying to protect the little calf but it was still better then me trying to milk that bitch. I wish we would have but her in the freezer many times. I am just lucky that she did not kill me.

For most of the time that I was little, we had two or three cows to milk each morning and evening. We made a lot of home made butter and it was a good thing that my brother liked butter milk because after butter making time, he had a lot of it to drink. It was an odd thing, but my dad and I did not like or drink white milk. I would drink it if I could mix in some Bosco or Ovaltene in it which made it sweet and gave it a chocolate taste.

THE PROCESS OF MAKING BUTTER

We made butter buy putting the fresh milk into a pan and placing in the refrigerator. When the milk chilled, the cream would raise to the top of the milk. The next day to two, Momma would skim off the cream with a large spoon and kept the cream in a large container in the refrigerator until we had enough to make butter.

After skimming off the cream, Momma poured the milk into quart and gallon jugs which we gave to family and friends who drank milk.

On butter making days, several of us would get quart jars filled two-thirds full with cream. We got bath towels and folded them into as small as possible and placed over a leg and started bouncing the jar of cream on our towel covered leg. The towel was to help absorbed the shock. We would continue to do this until the contents of the jar became butter and butter milk. Than you grabbed another jar and switched legs and started the process all over again. After all the jars had butter in them, Momma would strain the butter milk into larger milk containers and pour the butter into a large pan. At that time she would add salt and stir the butter over and over until the salt was mixed well into the butter. She added salt according to her taste. When she was satisfied, she scooped the butter into plastic containers and labeled and dated each carton and placed into the freezer.

When I got married, Momma gave me five containers of butter to take with me when I moved to Baton Rouge in 1967.

I continued to process snap beans and butter beans from my own garden when I lived in Baton Rouge and Seabrook, Texas for many years. We did not do much hunting or fishing when I was growing up on the Plantation so we did not eat much game. From time to time we did eat fish when my Uncle Nolan would give some to us. He went fishing every Sunday but seldom did he give the fish to us. He also did not like to clean fish. We grew much of what we ate and worked hard to do it. It is amazing to me that I still had as much time to play as I did.

TAKING ADVANTAGE OF FOOD STUFF

As kids living on the Plantation, we took advantage of food stuff that was available to us. Besides crawfishing in the canals/ditches and eating Red Wing Blackbirds and an occasional Robin Red Breast, we had many other food stuff that grew nearby. You know about the potatoes, corn, peas, beans and other vegetables from the gardens. We also had three Mulberry trees that was in the Mabiles's yard. One purple Mulberry and two white Mulberry trees that grew Mulberries about the size of a kids thumb. They were sweet and juicy. We also had fig trees and picked and ate figs during the spring and early summer. There were two persimmon trees in the mule lot. When we could not wait for them to fall, we threw sticks into the trees to knock them down. These were over two inches in diameter and sweet also. We had many pecans trees available to us and ate a lot of pecans in September. We also sold some.

I used to pick the flower from a honeysuckle vine and pull the little stem for one drop of honey from the flower. You had to do a lot of these for very little liquid. When I had a craving for something sweet and did not have a penny, to the honeysuckle vine I went. We also had thistles growing wild in the cow pasture. Thistle is a prickly plant that grew straight up. It had a main trunk and prickly leaves sprouted from the trunk. When we had an envey for thistle, we would find one about a foot and a half high and still tender. Cut it off at the bottom. Cut all the leaves off. Cut up and peel the stalk and put salt and pepper and sometimes, vinegar on it. We ate it as salad. We never ate poke salad. Don't know what it is.

We also picked and ate many dewberrys/blackberrys during the spring and early summer. There was also a small fruit that grew wild on a vine. It reminded me of very small watermelons. I cannot remember its name, but we ate it. We chewed sugar cane for the juice during the winter months. We chewed black tar that was used to coat our water tanks or cisterns to help insulate the tank from the weather- I guess.

Only several occasions a local farmer tried to grow peanuts that we got our hands on. The weather in South Louisiana is not conducive to growing peanuts or watermelons. Only occasionally did these type crops do well. That was in a exceptional dry season for us.

There also were plum trees and pear trees within reach, but I did not care for either, so I never partook of these fruits.

We also had opportunity to fish and hunt for rabbits, squirrels, turtles, frogs, alligators, etc., but we very seldom did this when I was little. We did catch a few shrimp from the Mississippi River during high water a couple of times that I remember. Daddy would tie a rope around my waist and I would start out about fifty feet upriver from where he wanted the shrimp box/trap to be placed. We had to do it this way because the current would take me to the top of the tree that I used to tie the trap onto. Without the rope tied to me, I would have never made it back to land. Daddy had to pull me in after I tied the trap to the tree with the hole in the trap facing the current flowing against it.

I caught a few crawfish from the River during high water also. This is how I found out that River crawfish were whitish and spillway crawfish were redish. They both taste soooooo gooooooooood. The food supply was abundant.

MY BIG BROTHER'S OLD RADIO PROGRAMS

From the time I was two year old (I guess) until about twelve, when my brother graduated from high school, we shared a room and a bed together. Our Uncle Nolan (momma's brother), who lived with us all our lives at that time, shared the bedroom also. He had his own bed to sleep in.

My brother liked the Grand Old Oprey and the Louisiana Hayride radio programs, so we listened to this whenever they came on at night. We used to catch sports like the Red Sticks baseball team playing other Minor League teams. They were a Baton Rouge team. In fact Baton Rouge (French) means Red Stick (English). It seem to me that it should be stick red, but the French say thing backwards. That may be where I get it from. We listened to everything that LSU had on the radio. We also listened to the St. Louis Hawks, a professional basketball team when they had Bob Pettit playing for them. Pettit played college basketball at LSU and was a local hero. We also could get Ohio State games because we got good reception from their station and Oklahoma City Basketball games when coach Hank Iba was there. Again because we could get good signals from their station. We caught several other sports programs as well. We also listened to programs like "Mr. and Mrs. North"-detectives, "The Shadow" - a do-gooder detective. If you don't know nothing, the Shadow do. The Squeaking Door, The Intersankdom, Fiber McGee and Molly Too, Mystery Theater, Red Ryder, The Lone Ranger, and others that I just cannot remember. They were all just great.

These programs put me to sleep every night. I had this habit of shaking my foot while laying in bed waiting for sleep to slip up on me and sometimes I would wake up or otherwise aggravate my brother and he would throw me on the floor to break me of this habit. I never did get broken of the habit. I did my best to try and not do it when we were in bed together. I still have the habit. When I am in bed and on my back, my foot just goes from side to side for no good reason. This is just the way it is.

After my brother moved out of the house, my uncle and I shared a room until I moved out when I was twenty-four years old.

As far as our family is concern, our uncle was like a much older brother who lived with us, except he did not milk cows or do any yard work or other chores around the house/yard whatsoever. He would work on our cars for nothing. We buy the parts, he put them on. He paid momma ten dollars a week for living with us. This was momma's mad money to get things for her, but I know she spent in on us and later on her grand kids from my brother and sister and later on my kids. I do not have any grand kids- yet. Hopefully, if God say the same, I will have some one day.

CHAPTER 8

MY FIRST AIRPLANE RIDE: AGES THIRTEEN AND FOURTEEN

My first airplane ride was when I was about thirteen or so. One Sunday, Daddy's boss from Lake Charles flew to Cedar Grove Plantation, which had their own air strip for small planes. He was meeting with someone else in the area. We drove to the air strip to see if anyone needed a ride to the company car which was located near the sugar mill. When we got there, the boss was already gone but the pilot was there. He also worked for W. T. Burton Industries and was told to just wait until the boss got back. He had a couple of hours to kill and asked if we wanted to go for a ride while he was waiting. Right away daddy said no. I begged to go and momma wanted to go also. Momma and I climbed into the seats behind the front two seats. This was a Sunday afternoon and I was suppose to serve as alter boy for the Catholic afternoon services at church. I sort of forgot about my alter boy duties for the time being. I was serving with Pat Tomney and he never showed up anyway. Today I decided to quit being an alter boy. This was not a smart thing to do at this time. I would miss church service and it is a MORTAL SIN to miss church services on Sundays. If we would have crashed and I died, I would have gone straight to HELL. Even Purgatory would have been out of the question. When a Catholic die with a big sin on their soul, they were a sure shot for hell. And all the praying by the family afterwards was not going to get them to that half-way house called Purgatory. I would have to hurry up and go to confession for missing Sunday service the first chance I got.

This four to six passenger plane had pontoons on it. It could land on land or water. We took off. We flew over our house then over the Mississippi River. Mr. Bob, the pilot, ask daddy if he could see any ducks flying around. Daddy said that he was not looking for any damn ducks. Mr. Bob said how about landing in the river. I said sure. Daddy said no. Momma did not say anything. So he asked Daddy to look out his window an see if the wheel on the right side of the airplane was locked in the up position. Daddy could not give an intelligent answer. I look out and after being told again what to look for, I confirmed that the wheel was up into the pontoons where it must be to land into the water. Mr. Bob had already checked the wheel on his side of the plane. Down we came. We had to land against the current to keep the airplane from tipping over. Which we did. It was very bumpy because the river was choppy. We did not stay floating very long. Mr. Bob gave it the gas and we took off again. At this time I think I was having fun. I had to check the wheel on my side again to be sure that it was locked in the land landing position. It was and we then came back to the Cedar Grove landing strip and landed after circling over White Castle several times. I thanked Mr. Bob as did daddy and momma and we were off. I then told Daddy and Momma that I had missed my alter boy assignment for the day and that I wanted to quit. They did not like it very much but honored my wishes. I think that I went to confession within the next several days. I did not want to take a chance and go a long time with this mortal sin on my soul. I did not have to worry about dying in an airplane anymore but there are many other ways that death can sneak up on you.

1955 A VERY IMPORTANT YEAR

My brother graduated from White Castle High School in 1955. He took a job with the state of Louisiana in the Department of

Highways Division. This job took him on the road for five days a week. They called it roustabout work when you traveled all over the state like that. I was twelve years old when my brother started his job and had to be on the road. This meant that he could not milk the cows in the mornings or evenings or do any of the other chores that needed to be done. I took over many of these chores full time. Like milking, shucking, shelling and grinding corn, and feeding the chickens, gathering eggs (when my sister did not do it). By this time, we had stopped raising pigs, thank God. When my brother came in on week ends, he would milk the cows and do some of the other chores.

From this time until I moved away from home at age twenty-four, I did these chores, plus cut the grass and other yard work. I also worked in the garden planting, picking, spraying, watering, and later harvesting the different crops. We put up corn, snap beans, shell beans, and several varieties of peas, butter beans, tomatoes, squash, bell peppers, cucumbers and other vegetables. We also made butter from the cream that we skimmed off the cow milk. With all this milking of cows all these years, I did not even drink white milk and still don't today. If I put some chocolate in it, I could drink a quart at a time and did on numerous occasions. I don't ever remember seeing Momma or Daddy drink milk or my sister either for that matter. My brother and Uncle Nolan (who lived with us) did drink it. They could not drink enough to keep it from piling up on us. We had so much milk; we had to give most of it away to some of your friends and cousins. After a little while, they got so trifling that they would not come and pickup the milk and garden vegetables that we GAVE to them. Daddy would deliver to their houses on the plantation and to town. When I got my driving license at the age of fourteen, I started delivering to these trifling folks. Although I like to drive the old car, this really pissed me off.

When I moved from the plantation at age twenty-four (because I got married), I took about six containers of home made butter with me because half came from my cow and I helped make it according to my Momma. The funny part about this butter was that my wife would not eat any of it. She was a city girl and purchased Borden's butter at the super market. It took me years to use up all that butter. But use it up I did.

I have more to come of putting up/processing food for the freezer later.

MY EARLY TEENAGE YEARS: AGES FOURTEEN THROUGH SIXTEEN - EIGHTH, NINTH AND TENTH GRADES

Playing baseball and the other games mentioned earlier with the same folks on the plantation. Shooting/hunting red-wing black birds, robins red breast, pigeons, then cleaning (picking feathers and gutting) and cooking them outside over a fire made with dead grass and sticks - boy this was the life.

At age fourteen, I was old enough to get a social security card and work eight hours a day in the sugar cane fields. I remember it all to well. I made forty-three cents an hour. This was back in 1957. I worked on week ends, holidays and summer vacation when I had a break from school. I worked six days a week, made no overtime and was paid every two weeks in cash. I got my pay at the office which was in the old store. They issued a lot of two dollar bills in those days. For instance, if you have an amount that included five dollars, they would pay the five dollars with a one dollar bill and two, two dollar bills. I still have several two dollar bills dated 1957 in my safety deposit box at the bank. I had to spend some of them along the way but I still have some.

When I made sixteen years old, I became a man under farm labor laws. I had the right to work nine hours a day, which I did. It was not my choice. That is just the way it was. One extra hour a day made me another forty-three cents richer for that day.

I this day, the plantation stores had everything you needed from groceries, hardware, tools, clothes, oil, gas, cookies, candy, salt pork (which was kept with luncheon meat cold cuts in an ice box). Yes, an ice box, not a refrigerator. The Ice Man would deliver ice each day and deliver extra ice on Saturday because the store was closed on Sundays. The store carried as much different supplies as possible so the folks living and working on the plantation would not go somewhere else to make purchases. Most folks did not have the transportation needed to go somewhere else and you could "charge it" to your account at the store. The office would deduct from your pay each two weeks. This is how they kept the poorer folks in servitude. The prices at the store were high. Sometimes your store bill was higher than your pay, so you had to keep working there just to try and catch up on your store bills. They did not charge any interest on the goods or money owed. They did not have to. The prices were very high as I mentioned before. If a man made fifty dollars for the two weeks work and owed the store sixty dollars, they would keep forty dollars of his pay toward his bill and give him ten dollars as pay. We went into the new pay period owning money. It was very hard to get ahead in those days, just as it is today for way to many folks.

Starting in September each year, the plantation had to have a certain amount of sugar cane planted for future crops. And in October the harvesting/grinding season started. It was during this four month period that the workers could work seven days a week and make more money to pay off the company store. Remember, this is farm labor, so no overtime is ever made or paid, but if you worked all seven days a week, you could pay off your store bills and have a little extra for Christmas. This was the labor intensive part of the year. The Plantation always needed extra workers for sugar cane planting and harvesting time. This is when a lot of the women worked in the fields. I worked with them cutting cane by hand, scraping behind the cane loaders, walking the rows and keeping the cane straight in the row during cane planting time. Sowing (planting) peas after freshly planted sugar cane is covered up. I did this type work on my days out of school.

HEAD LIGHTING FOR RABBIT

When I was a young teenager, daddy used to take me into the sugar cane field to hunt rabbit at night. This was called "head lighting" and was illegal. This is the only times that my daddy ever hunted for any game although he never shot the gun to my knowledge. He just drove the old truck all over the plantation. Daddy used to say that we were looking for poachers who were trespassing on Mr. Burton's property. The whole plantation was posted. There were "No Trespassing" signs at all the entrance roads onto the place. The owners did not want anyone coming on the property that did not live on it unless you were visiting or had business to do there.

There were trespassers who dumped their garbage and trash on the plantation. There were also poachers who hunted deer and rabbits and birds and fired guns on the plantation. There were also thieves who stole fresh corn and peas and other vegetables from the fields and equipment and tools.

If Daddy heard a shot at night, he got dressed and headed for the field. Sometimes I went with him. He would search the area where he thought the sound of the shot came from. Sometimes he would find who it was. The times that I was with him, it was someone from the plantation that forgot to let the overseers know.

This was alright. If it was a stranger or someone not from the plantation, daddy would stop them and give them one warning to get off the plantation or he would call the High Sheriff. This one warning was all it took for them to leave. They were well warned that there would not be another warning for them. No one ever got smart or sassy with my dad as far as I ever heard about.

Daddy was a big man. He was almost six feet tall and well over two hundred pounds. He had really wide shoulders which made him look ever larger than he was. I believe he wore a size fifty-two dress coat.

On many occasions we took a shotgun when I went with him to look for hunters, head-

lighters, poachers, or thieves. I would sit on the right fender near the headlight of the old truck with the shotgun ready while daddy drove slowly on the headlands through the cane fields. Occasionally rabbits would dart across the grass road in front of us. They were fast. I would hurry and shoot. I missed more than I got the first several trips but I got better and started to pick my shots better. What I mean is I only shot at the ones that I had a chance to hit. This way, I did not waste shotgun shells, which cost money, for nothing. Daddy liked it better this way since he was the one buying the shells.

One time when I was about fifteen, we were following the normal procedure. I was on the right fender so Dad could see where he was going better. I was not too happy with the sitting arrangements. But Daddy would drive really slow and I could lean to my left on the hood which was about a foot higher than the fender for support. I also had this large right truck headlight that I sort of leaned on and could grab a hold of when we hit a bump. I believe the old pickup was a late nineteen thirties model. All the overseers had old trucks like this to drive on the plantation. All the trucks on the plantation were over twenty years old, faded red in color, and always needed painting. They really looked as old as they were, but was in tip top running condition. Mr. Lu Lu Henry saw to that. He was the head of the repair shop on the plantation and kept the old vehicles and tractors and field machines in excellent repair order. The owner of the plantation would rather spent four thousand dollars in parts to repair equipment then spend that much on something new. I found out why that was many years later. The reason was- if you purchase a brand new truck, tractor or piece of equipment, you had to amortize it over the expected life of the item. This could be twenty or thirty years that you could only deduct one twentieth or one thirtieth of the cost each tax year. If you repaired old equipment or vehicles with new parts you could deduct the whole amount in that tax year. The plantation owners look at this as a way to save money. They use the plantation for write offs every chance they got. Losing money in certain years made the owners a lot of money by reducing taxes on other business they owned. They had it figured out.

Back to hunting for rabbit: I was in my position. We were coming to another headland intersection. By the way the headland is the area of ground just in front of or just behind the cultivated area. It is the pathway for the truck and tractors or harvesters, etc., to get into the crop area. Old dirt or shell or gravel roads led to the headlands. Sometimes you could turn from a black top highway onto a headland, but not very often because of the drainage ditches and canals. There were also drainage ditches and canals that had to be crossed throughout the sugar cane field. There are drainage ditches between each square of sugar cane. A square could be fifty yards wide and 300 yards long. It could be larger or smaller than this depending on roads, houses, canals, etc., in the area.

As we made this right turn onto another headland, two large rabbits ran in complete opposite directions. I shot at the one running to the right toward the high sugar cane first. I expelled the shell on the bolt action sixteen gauge shotgun to get another shell in the chamber and swung the gun to the left. As I was falling off the fender of the truck because Daddy had hit the brakes, I let another shot go. Daddy got out of truck and said "good shot, you got the one on the right." I replied, "yea, I got the other one too." "No way," was the reply from Daddy as he was picking up the dead rabbit several feet in front of a cane row. "Daddy, I think I hit it," I said again. Dad did not think so, but said he would take a look. The old truck was still running and we could see pretty good because both headlights were working fine. On our left was a large drainage ditch and the Johnson grass there was about waist high. This headland had not been cut yet. Dad went to that area still doubtful of my second shot. I went also. We were both looking and neither one of us wanted to get into the ditch. We could not see that well into the ditch. There are some critters in these ditches and canals that we did not want to meet up with anytime of day and surely not at night. We were about to give up when I saw a little blood on some grass. Dad had a flashlight. I showed the blood to him. He said, "I'll be damned!" Before he could finish saying that he did not think we would find anything, we heard some grass rustling near by. Dad walked a few steps further and right where the ditch was starting, some Johnson grass stalks had held the rabbit up from falling into the ditch. Dad reached and retrieved the rabbit.

I had shot his ears off. The noise we heard must have been his last kicks before he died. I felt really good. Not for killing two rabbits, but for being able to shoot two of them on the run going in direct opposite direction. And the second shot made while flying through the air, with a bolt action sixteen gauge shotgun which happen to belong to my Uncle Nolan who lived with us. Daddy just kept shaking his head from side to side. He was in awe of me.

Daddy owned a double barrel twelve gauge shotgun that he lent to Mr. Joe Mabile several years before this which we never got back. When Mr. Joe moved from the plantation in 1960 or 61 he took the shotgun with him. I guess Sonny or Mark Mabile must have my daddy's shotgun if they did not get rid of it.

HEAD LIGHTING WITH THE MABILES

Later that same year we went out into the fields with Mr. Joe and his oldest son, Ronald. Ronald was four days younger than me. I got my usual spot on the right fender. Ronald sat on the left one. We were driving in the field really slow because the driver did not have a full view of the headlands. We were out for about forty minutes. Nothing was happening. There was not much light from the moon this night either. We got to this one headland and up about forty feet in front of us was a full grown skunk. It was in the middle of the pathway. Ronald and I both let out a yell to stop the truck. We stopped when our dads decided that was a skunk alright. Mr. Joe was driving. He turned out the headlight and turned off the engine. We were whispering to not alarm the skunk. After several minutes, Mr. Joe turned the headlight back on to check. Sure enough, Mr. Skunk was still there but a couple yards closer to us. The skunk was content on doing what it was that he was doing in the middle of the pathway. Out went the headlights again. Ronald and I wanted to get off the fenders and into the back bed of the pickup, but our dads told us to not move. If we moved or made noise, the skunk might charge and spray us. That is the way that skunks are. They will attack if they feel threatened. Well I felt threatened and I am sure that Ronald felt the same way. Here we sit afraid to move and cannot even whisper for being scared of getting skunk spray on us. It was very quiet. We could hear the skunk but could not see it. After about fifteen minutes, Mr. Joe said to hell with this. He started up his old truck, turned on the lights and ever so slowly moved forward. The skunk was still there. Ronald and I started talking louder now. "STOP," we yelled. The skunk looked up. We thought that he could not see us because the lights were blinding him. It never occurred to us that he might be able to smell us. Mr. Joe stopped the truck, the skunk was closer now. Our dads started joking about how happy they were to be inside the truck and that Ronald and I would get most of the blast from the skunk. They would be alright, they said. They made the decision to drive ahead slowly thinking that the skunk would run the other way. I made the decision that I was going to shoot the skunk and let it be known to everyone. As I was raising the shotgun, both Mr. Joe and Daddy shouted "NO, we'll back up." Which is what we did. I know Mr. Joe could not see where to back but he kept it in the middle of the headland. After we got a little further from the skunk, Ronald and I jumped off the fenders and followed the truck until Mr. Joe got it to the shell road. We told them that we had enough hunting for one night. We got into the back bed and started home. We had a story to tell.

We hunted several times with the Mabiles but none as memorable as this one.

MY LAST RABBIT HUNTING TRIP WITH MY DADDY

I was sixteen when I made my last rabbit hunting trip with my Daddy. I had been in my position for some time. The rabbits were well hidden this night. They must have gotten the news that I would be head lighting this night. They probably got a rabbit gram, or by tell-a-rabbit or smoke rabbit signals- I don't know. It was not by e-rabbit because the computer was not invented yet. Al Gore was still in diapers. I did say diapers because pampers were not invented yet either. Anyway, nothing was happening.

We turned from one headland onto another. There one goes. Daddy stopped the truck. The rabbit had darted into the cane rows. I decided to go and have a look. It was probably long gone. I walked slowly to where I last saw it. I had a little headlight strapped to my head on this trip. As I looked into the cut, there he was still there. I raised the shotgun and BOOM. Daddy yelled, "Did you get it?" I think so, I responded. I did not move from where I stood. Daddy came over to get the rabbit. This was our deal. When we first started this rabbit hunting business, I would shoot them, but daddy would find them and pick them up. I would not have to touch a dead rabbit. Daddy would skin them, gut them and clean and cut them up for cooking. Momma would cook them. But before she cooked them, she would try and take all the pellets/shots out of them. After all this, I would get involved with the rabbit again. I would help to eat them. My momma made a great rabbit stew. We just did not have it very often. Momma cooked a great everything.

When daddy went into the cut with his hand held flashlight, I followed and we looked on the ground where the rabbit was when I shot. It was a very young and small rabbit. I had gotten excited when I saw it just sitting there and did not think. I just shot. All that was left was a little fur ball about two inches in diameter. I must have blown it to pieces. We could not find any other remains. It had been raining early that morning and the shot may have pushed it into the ground. If so, it was buried. We were not going to dig what would be just pieces-up. I asked daddy to take me home. We went home. Daddy and I never hunted together again. I just did not want to.

SUGAR CANE PLANTING

Harvesters would cut the cane to be planted. Sugar cane loading machines would load it unto cart pulled by field tractors. The tractor driver would transport the cane to the area to be planted. Men would be in the cane carts which was loaded down with the sugar cane. They would throw the cane storks from the carts to the ground trying to place as much as possible into the furrow/row. We would walk behind the planting carts and place the stark straight in the open row. We planted two stalks side by side then would over lap those stocks with two more and so on and so on. When we finished one row we went down another than another until we planted the whole square. A tractor would come after we finished a square and cover the sugar cane with dirt from the sides on each row. At a later time during the planting, we would walk these same rows of freshly planted cane and sow the pea seeds by broadcasting them by hand on the sides of each row. To do this we had to carry the seeds in sacks strapped over our shoulders, reach into the sack for hands full of peas then broadcast them. You tried not to run out of peas in the middle of a row. At the end of each row was a cart with the peas. You refilled you sack when needed there. Several weeks later, after the seeds sprouted and was about eight or ten inches tall and the rows was green with foliage, a tractor would come and turn the peas under into the soil. The peas provided nutrients into the soil for the sugar cane to draw from as it grows. You must have a lot of fertilizer when growing sugar cane. The Overseers usually left a square to make mature peas for folks on the plantation to pick and process for use later in the year. I picked many peas so we could process and put in the freezer.

SUGAR CANE HARVESTING

When the cane planting was finished, and sometimes before it was finished, grinding/harvesting started. It usually started about mid October. This kept the workers working seven days per week.

During harvesting, I worked during weekends and holidays. Cutting cane by hand on the ditch rows, or scraping behind the cane cutter, or scrapping behind the cane loaded which was a really dirty job, or burning the cane after it had been cut for several days to get the shucks or leaves off before loading for the mill. This is why scrapping behind the cane loader is such a dirty job, there is black soot on the cane stalks and everywhere else. My favorite job of all was running the two man cane loader with my Dad. I would drive the loader into the cut/row, piling the cane as I go in a large pile and Daddy would work the loader grab by scooping up the cane and swinging it to the left to place into a cane cart which was pulled by a field tractor which was in the next row over from us.

When cutting the sugar cane, the harvester driver knows where to start to cut the first row. It is important to know this. Sugar cans stands ten to twelve feet tall. The cane harvester have a circular blade at the bottom to cut the cane about two inches above the ground and another circular blade at the top to cut the leafy part of the stark off. There is no sugar in the leaf. The sugar is in the cane stalks or joints that are fully developed. Both blades are adjustable up and down. The driver of the harvester sit on the top part of the machine about fourteen or fifteen feet up from the ground. he control the top cutting blade. The bottom blade is controlled by a man the sat behind the harvester and near the ground where he could really see the bottom blade well. He is close enough to the ground that he does not have to jump off or down from the harvester. He just slide into his seat.

The bottom blade man had the dirty job on the machine.

It was and still is, very important to cut the cane as low to the ground as possible because this is where most of the sugar content is, without cutting below the ground level. When you cut at the ground or below ground level you will disturb the roots and possibly kill next years crop. You also dull or ruin the bottom blade which is thirty six inches in diameter and very costly to buy and very time consuming to replace. Sugar cane is a three or four year crop that will grow back after harvesting. So you must be very careful not to disturb the root system or you will be cutting your own throat.

After the harvester cut the first few rows, the bottom blade man set the throw arm of the harvester to make several heap rows in a square of cane. A heap row is the rows where several rows of cane was cut and laid down on the one heap the length of the rows. To accomplish this, the harvester has what is called a carrier arm/throw arm. It has chains and grabs attached onto the chains. When the harvester cuts the very first row, it throws or leans the cut stalks on the next row that is still standing straight up. When it cut the row that has the cut cane leaning on it, the front end of the harvester has a shield designed to scoop the leaning cane and place it along with the row it is cutting the same way across the two rows. The cutter does this at two or there different spots in the square. When they are ready to cut the third row next to the two rows already cut, the bottom blade man pushed out the extension arm part of the way. This extension is designed to hold the newly cut stalks in its grasp and drop the third row on the heap row. The harvester is designed to place about six to eight rows of cane unto the heap row in a square. A square of sugar cane has from thirty to forty rows in it. A square goes from drainage ditch to drainage ditch.

When harvesting sugar cane, the harvester need to start and stay about three to five days ahead of the loading operation. This give enough time for the leaves/shucks to dry out a little so the cut cane can be burned, thus getting rid of extra weight and what is call trash when the loads arrive at the mill. This also burns the tops that was cut off when the cane was cut. This will help the stubble to grow better for next years crop. Burning leaves the square of cane in better condition for next year cultivation season.

Within a day or two after the stalks/leaves are burned, you need to have this square loaded and at the mill. You do not want burnt cane to stay in the field very long. It can and will go sour and this is very bad. You do not get any money for sour cane. You get paid for sugar content. The more sugar, the more you get paid. The less sugar content, the less the farmer gets paid for his crop.

It take a tremendous amount of planning to pick the variety of sugar cane to cut at the right time. Some varieties have more sugar content early in the harvesting season than other varieties. You have to burn at the right time, haul it come rain, cold, ice, snow (does not happen very often), shine, hurricane and whatever. You work day and night if that is what it takes to get your crop in. You must get the whole crop to the mill before a hard freeze or you can/will lose whatever crop you have left. Luckily, there are not very many hard freezes in South Louisiana.

After the harvesting came the first of the new year. There is not a lot to do during January if harvesting is over, and when we had heavy rain. When the workers were not working, the Store bills started getting more than they could pay. So the cycle started all over again. Before you could be out of debt for a month, you were back in debt.

My daddy would offer work during the slow times to give the men some income. Some of them would not work when it rained. The tractor drivers did not like to work with a shovel or hoe which was all that could be done during the rainy season. Some folks took advantage and worked every day that was offered. If I had to put a number on it, I'd guess about forty per cent of the workforce worked whenever it was offered. The other just laid up. It is very hard to work off debt at the Company Store when you do not work every time it is offered. I guess sixty percent or more of the field hands owed the Store year round. They were just caught up in this cycle and wages was to low to get out of it without working every time it is offered.

In the years to come, many new innovations came to the sugar cane industry. Things like larger tractors that could cultivate three rows at a time instead of just one. One man operated cane loaders and harvesters. Harvesters made much easier to operate and eventually a two row harvester. Sugar cane planters where not much is done by hand. Ditch cleaners or drain cleaners on tractors and not by shovels by hand. Mowing equipment pulled by tractors, not mules, hay bailers by machines instead of the way we used to do it by hand. Even corn harvester was used and you stopped harvesting by hand and many other innovations.

They even planted Milo on the plantation and built several grain storage bins. Whoever would have dreamed a large grain crop besides corn on sugar cane land. And lets not forget Soy Beans by the thousands of acres planted in sugar cane ground. What a deal. The farmers had to buy different equipment to work these crops. They may use some of the same tractors, but needed new type of cultivators and harvesting equipment. This meant another large investment into the hundreds of thousands of dollars.

MEETING MY TO BE BROTHER-IN-LAW

Back in the mid 1950's, my sister sang with a band. Angelo Michelle and his band use to come to our house on the plantation and practice. My sister used to sing Kitty Wells songs. She was pretty good at it too.

One time Angelo brought this guy that sang the French songs for all the French speaking people. His name was Gene Bertrand. Gene is the only other member of Angelo's band that I can recall the name of. He could talk some French and could really sing a French speaking song better than any other member of the band, which is why he done it.

On Sundays, I believe, the band played and sang live on the local radio station. The station was in White Castle and called KEVL. They played country and pop hits, some soul, blues, French, Cajun, and any other songs that you requested. They made it work for several years before they finally shut down. They actually help some new young singers to make it by playing their songs on the radio.

I remember that we used to play bingo for prizes over the air, but it was called KEVLO, not bingo. They called out numbers over the air at a certain time each day. They only called out so many numbers each day, so you played from day to day until there was a winner. This was a ploy to get you to listen to their station each day. It worked for several years. If you KEVLOED, you called in, they verify that you won, then they started another game. You made arrangement to pick up your prize at the station or at the sponsor's location.

Gene started coming around more and more without Angelo and the band. Pretty soon he and my sister were going together. He was working for Conoco Oil then. This was the hottest brand going according to there television advertisements. He drove the crew boat taking the workers into the bayous to work on the platforms. He told me that one day he would take me with him for a ride on the crew boat and to see where he works.

Before long that time came and my cousin Roger Dale Delaune was visiting from New Orleans. Roger Dale was a year younger than me, but I could not leave him home while I went for a weekend with my to-be brother-in-law.

We spent the weekend with Gene and a recap of the events is as follows.

MEETING THE MICHELLES OF PLAQUEMINE

I met Angelo Michelle during my early teenage years when he played in his band. Gene was the first to take me to Angelo's house near Plaquemine where I visited with these folks several time over the years and we ate dinner at their house on this visit with Gene.

Besides Angelo, his Mom and Dad, there was brothers Joe, Johnny, Carlo, Peter and a sister, Stella, still living at home. They had another brother living in New Orleans, and three other sisters. This was one big family. At dinner, Stella and her Mom did all the cooking and serving and the step, run and fetch it for the Dad and all those boys. If this was an indication of what happened at every meal, these boys would run poor Stella ragged. I thought that Stella should hurry and get married and let the guys get up and serve themselves. On this visit, we had a big baseball game at the Mancuso's house next door down the road a bit. They had a big pasture and used it to play baseball on occasion. Between the Mancuso's and the Michelle's and me and Gene and my cousin, Roger Dale, we had enough to play a game. Roger Dale was visiting us for a couple of weeks. He lived in the New Orleans area. He came with Gene and me to visit the Michelles.

Roger Dale was playing first base. I was at third base. On one play, Paula Mancuso hits a ground ball and was running toward first base. The ball made it through the infield. Roger Dale dropped his glove and ran to cover first and open his arms wide as if to really welcome Paula to first base. Just he and I knew he did this. Everybody else was watching the ball. I was watching Paula run and so was Roger Dale. We did not give a damn about the ball or where it was. He and I laughed a long time over his antics. He had dropped his arms by his side by the time Paula made it to first base. I always wondered what she would have done if he kept his arms open to hug her when she got there. I do not remember who won the game, but Paula was the hit of the game for Roger Dale and me.

All through high school and after, my friendship with Johnny, Carlo and Peter continued. These are great guys. Davis Callegan and I used to hang with Carlo and Peter at the Youth Center Dances and sporting events that we used to attend at Plaquemine and St. John High Schools in Plaquemine. We also bumped into them and Johnny at different outings around Plaquemine. Johnny started dating a girl from White Castle; we saw and talked with him on a regular basis.

This visit to the Michelle's house was when my cousin, Roger Dale, and I spent a weekend with Gene Bertrand at his Mom and Dad's house in Plaquemine. Mr. and Mrs. Bertrand were out of town this weekend. The plan was to go to work with Gene on Sunday. The dinner and baseball game with the Michelle's was on Saturday.

This was about mid 1957 when Gene worked for Conoco Oil. He drove the crew boat from the landing at Bayou Plaquemine to the oil/gas platforms in the bayous. He brought guys to and from work and picked up supplies and such for the rigs in the swamp.

We got up really early that Sunday while it was still dark. Got dressed and got in Gene's 1956 Ford and went to the landing. Roger Dale and I sat around while Gene saw to the things that needed to be done before it was time to depart. One or two other guys showed up for the ride to work. We departed for about an hours ride to the platform. We may have gone to two rigs before we tied up at the second one. There was a push boat and a barge taking on product from the platform storage tanks. I did not know it then, but this turned out to be a ten thousand barrel barge. It was going to take a few hours for the barge to load.

We were invited aboard the tug by the pilot. He showed Roger Dale and me around the tug and everything that it was equipped with. Before long it was getting to be time to eat. The pilot invited us to have a meal with them. We said yes. This was my first meal on a push boat. Little did I know that it would not be my last one on a push boat.

I do not remember what we ate, but it was good, I remember that. I also remember feeling like a fool when I spilled a glass of milk. I usually don't even drink milk, but when the cook placed glasses of milk for everyone, I just grabbed mine and took a swallow. I guess I forgot how small our table was and just tipped the glass of milk over. I said that I was sorry about ten times. The cook and pilot said to don't worry about it, shit happens. Everything is a little smaller on a boat. There is not a lot of space. The sleeping area is small, the shower, the head, the eating area- everything. You just learn to live with it when you work on a boat.

I was really impressed by the guys and the jobs they had. I did not realize it then, but ten or so years later I would make my living for over thirty years, hiring and contracting boats and barges to move cargo up the Mississippi River from Baton Rouge, New Orleans, and Houston areas. Push boats and barges worked for me on the Intercoastal Canal from near Brownsville, Texas to Mobile, Alabama. And also on the Illinois, Ohio, Tennessee and Missouri Rivers and the Tombigbee Waterway as well. I even chartered several ships/chemical tankers to move product to international location around the world.

I also contracted for other modes of transportation to move product, but my first love was and still is barges and tugs/push boats. I ate in a number of them, as well as tankers and had parties on them and attended a few christenings for new vessels as well. As long as I live, I will not forget the first tug that I was on with Gene and Roger Dale.

After a number of hours in the bayous, we headed back to the landing. Gene secured the crew boat and locked it up. We went to his house to clean up for church. It was Sunday and Catholics had to go to church or they committed a Mortal sin. This is the big one. You could not afford to die with this sin on you soul. It was hell for sure.

We went to Sunday afternoon service at the big Catholic Church in Plaquemine. This was a much larger church than ours in White Castle. They had a balcony that you could sit and kneel in. I had never gone to church in a balcony before so we went up there. I guess I could say that I went to "high mass." Ha, Ha.

We were settled in our seats when the services began. Roger Dale got up and moved to the very front row in the balcony where there were some empty seats. He was on the rail. After a short time, he kept turning and waving for me to join him there. I ignored him. This is not the movie theater. You don't jump around from seat to seat in church.

When in the front row in the balcony when you knelt down and lean on the rail that was the support for the balcony, you could see over the rail and below it as well. You had a good view of the folks setting down below. I notice Roger Dale kneeling down when we did not have to. He just stayed kneeling most of the time. I knew that he was not that good of a Catholic to be kneeling all that time. After the service was over and we were outside, I asked him what was all that kneeling business about. He pointed to several ladies outside that were walking to their cars. They had rather low-cut dresses on. He said that he could see their tits, so he did not move from that good vantage point. Sometime when the ladies would move, he could even see nipples. He had a great time in church. All I could say was "damn." Gene then took us home to Cedar Grove Plantation.

CHAPTER 9

MAKING POPGUNS AND OTHER TOYS (WEAPONS): AGES EIGHT THROUGH SIXTEEN

I mentioned the playing of games and things we did on the plantation when I was younger. As I became a young teenager, some of the games changed. I (we) could actually make and build things. We had to make do with what we had or could find somewhere nearby since we did not travel much past the River Road, where we lived and the highway, La. #1, which was just past the field hand quarters. This was the shell road which started at the River, ran between our house and the Plantation Store on to La. #1. Along this shell road after passing our house and the store, was the gas pumps behind the store then the gathering area where the field hand wait for work near the small mule lot, than Mr. Tan Miller's house, which was on the same side of the shell road as ours, than the water well that supplied all the water for the river side of the plantation, than a short road to the left that went in between the two mule lots to Mr. Barby Miller's house. On the corner of the shell road and the road to Mr. Barby's house was where Mr. Granier lived than past his house is where the big mule pasture was and it went all the way to La#1 on the left side of the shell road. About one hundred yards from Mr. Granier's house started the field hand quarters/houses. There was a shell road that went to the right than turned left. On this shell road and the main shell road, was the houses that most of the field hands lived in. There must have been about eight houses on each road. These houses was built like our house. They were four to six room houses. Between Mr. Tan Miller's house and the start of the quarters was about one hundred fifty yard and was all pasture for cows. This was an area about one quarter of a mile long.

I made popguns out of elder berry limbs and bamboo reeds. Daddy would take me into the field to find the elder berry bushes. The bamboo was closer and I got those myself. My first choice was to use an elder berry limb. When I found one that had a limb about one and a quarter inches in diameter and straight for a foot or so, I really had something. A fourteen inch long, straight limb could get me two pop gun barrels. The elder berry plant was almost hollow inside. It had a soft spongy type center, almost like that of a corn cob. Either I or Daddy would cut the limb in the field. When we got back to the house, I went to work making a pop gun. I cut the limb about seven inches long. Check it out for roundness. I used a straight wire or a coat hanger wire to push and pull all the insides of the pulp out to make a barrel. I rotated the wire to scrape all remaining spongy substance out. Blow through it, look through it to be sure there were no obstruction and see if the hole was straight. Sometimes the limb would be straight as and arrow but after I got it all cleaned out; the center would not be straight. There may have been a knot in the wood or some other obstruction that rendered this barrel useless. After the barrel was completed, I needed to make a push rod or piston.

For the piston, the part that was used to push the projectile through the barrel, I used a piece of cypress wood. We had a lot of cypress around the plantation. It was the wood of choice to build with because it lasted many, many years. It just would not rot like other woods. All the houses, sheds, barns, and picket fences, were made/built of cypress. It seams like there were miles of cypress picket fences on the plantation and a good supply to replace a picket should it split or otherwise get unusable by a cow or horse going through it. So we always had pieces of cypress lying around the yard.

I would chop a piece of cypress about one and a half inches wide by ten inches or so long. Square off about two or three inches for the handle and whittle the rest of the piece down to about a half inch in diameter round rod to be used as the plunger. I whittled so that the plunger would be as close to the middle of the handle as possible. I used a sharp pocket knife to do this. To smooth out the knife cuts on the plunger rod, I used the blade to scrape the wood while rotating the stick. This action really smooth out the plunger part and made it almost round. If I would have had any course sand paper, I would have been in heaven, but I did not know of such a thing at this time. The plunger had to fit snuggly into the elder berry barrel. It had to be able to slide back and forth without getting hung up.

When the piston fitted into the barrel the way I wanted, I would then add the finishing touches to my pop gun. The piston was usually on inch or two longer than it needed to be. It went all the way through the barrel. I would measure and cut the piston about one quarter of an inch or less before it would protrude out of the barrel. I needed to have a space here to place the item or projectile that I would shoot.

After measuring and cutting the portion off the piston that I did not need, I proceeded to spit on the end of the piston and use the blade of my knife to splinter the wood just a little. Using light taps on the end of the piston and spiting on it to keep it moisten, would make the end of the piston frayed. It looked like fine hairs on the end of the plunger stick/piston rod. I would spit into the barrel a couple of times and run the plunger piston back and forth several times and then be ready to try it out.

I could only make these types of popguns in the spring and early summer. This was when the elder berry brush (barrel) and the chinaberry (ammunition) trees were growing and producing the china balls (berry).

After deciding which end of the barrel was the loading end and which end was the firing end, I was finally ready to test fire my new weapon. I pull a few china balls from a near by tree in our yard. I waited to pick the china balls because they stayed fresh while on the tree. If I picked them off too soon before having my popgun ready to use, they would shrivel up and dry out and would not work in a pop gun. So do not pick the ammunition several days before it was to be fired, or you would have a dud. I place a china ball over the loading part of my barrel, use the handle of my plunger to hit and otherwise smash the berry into the barrel hole. Part of the chinaberry went into the barrel whole and part splattered chinaberry juice all over the barrel and me and whatever/whoever was standing nearby. This was a good thing, because I needed the chinaberry/ball juice to help lubricate the inside of the barrel and make the plunger/piston rod slide easier into the barrel. I use the plunger to push the china ball all the way to the projectile end of the barrel. The quarter inch space between the end of the plunger piston and the barrel is where the china ball stayed when I withdrew my plunger. I am now ready to test fire. I repeated the action of placing a chinaberry over the loading end of my barrel, smashed it into the barrel with the handle of my plunger and used the plunger piston to push the berry about and inch or two into the barrel. My popgun was now cocked and ready to fire. There was always some anxiety at this point because I would not know if It would work right or if the compression created by the juices and tight fit of the plunger piston would split or otherwise blow apart the barrel which did happen on occasion. It happen more often than any of us wanted it to happen. It is for this reason that I (we) preferred to use elder berry limbs instead of bamboo joints. The bamboo split about fifty percent of the time. It was not nearly as strong as elder berry. I would even rap electrical tape around the loading and firing ends of a bamboo barrel and it would still split. We only used bamboo if we could not find and elder berry plant large enough to get a good limb off of it.

It got so, we would stake out and make claim to a young elder berry bush. We watched it grow until it was large enough to get a limb or two from it. We get the word out that this was our elder berry bush and nobody better mess with it or we will tell our dads who was the bosses and could fire the field hand because his kid bush whacked our elder berry bush.

I am right handed, so while holding the barrel with my left hand, I push the plunger piston with my right hand and POW, the projectile would shoot out thirty feet or more. Every pop gun I ever made worked for a while. They lasted a month or so. After the elder berry barrels really dried out on the outside, they would eventually split open after firing a shot.

We would often have pop gun fights trying to shoot each other. Sometime it was great fun to sneak up on some poor unsuspecting sole who did not know that you made a popgun and shoot them in the butt. Even when you missed, the sound the gun made would scare the heck out of them. We did not think that these things could put an eye out. We were just trying to have fun. When you did surprise someone with a shot in the butt, you would be the talk of the Plantation, until the dreaded day that somebody got you. And you would be got. Nobody was left un-shot during popgun playing time. I have to say this again. What made this so much fun was the noise that the popgun made and noise that the person made that got popped. Almost simultaneously, before you finish reacting to the noise, you felt the sting, and there was nothing that you could do about it. I had this feeling on the receiving end several times although I like to believe that I was on the giving end and laughing end more often.

SLING SHOTS OR NEGRO (POLITE) SHOOTERS

I (we) made sling shots too. Although I did not know them as sling shots at the time I made them. I was about seventeen years old before I knew the nigger shooters were actually sling shots. The derogatory name was all we knew to call them because we just did not know any better. It was a normal thing for us to refer to them as nigger shooters because this is the only way that this item was referred to. I actually do not know what the black folks on the plantation called them. Honky shooter sound like it could be a good name for them to refer to this item as.

We needed strong wood for these. They were U shape with a tale in the middle of the bottom of the U. We had to find a fork on a tree limb to make the sling shot. We could/would not use the elder berry bush because the limbs were hollow and we need something with solid limbs. There were plenty of these type trees around.

We could only make sling shots when someone found or was given and old tire inner tube. We did not come by these very often. Our dads did not make much money, so the only inner tubes we came by was when one of the cars or trucks tubes had so many patches in it, it just could not take another patch and they had to buy a new inner tube. Our next problem was to try and find a part of the tube that we could cut out two strips that was three quarters of an inch wide and ten to twelve inches long.

We usually could get material for several sling shots from one inner tube that would go into a fourteen inch wheel and tire.

To make a sling shot, get the fork of a strong limb about an inch or a little smaller in diameter. Cut it out of the tree. Each prong should be about five or six inches long. Cut a little grove or notch in the two parts of the limb that goes up. The other part of the limb that goes down is the handle. Lap one strip of rubber over the top of one of the upward prongs and over the notched or grooved area. With string or small gauge wire, tie the rubber to the prong at the notched or grooved area. Do the same with the other upward prong. Now there are two rubber strips attached to the top of the fork and just hanging down. A pouch is now needed. The pouch is the leather piece that the rock or marble goes into and become the ammunition or projectile to be projected. We used the tongues from old leather shoes for the pouch. We would cut the tongues about two inches square or smaller, depending upon the size of the shoe that we got the tongue from; punched two really small holes with an ice pick into two sides of the pouch. Past good twine through one hole and out through the other hole on the same side and tied the ends of the twine to one of the rubber strips. Did the same thing on the other side of the pouch and tied it to the other rubber and WAL LA - we had a sling shot that was good for a long, long time or until the rubber dry rotted or just broke. We would just replace the rubber or twine with fresher material when we had the occasion to come up with some fresher rubber.

I made a sling shot one time with a clothes pin (not the kind with the wire spring). It has the pouch attached to one rubber strip which was tied to the head of the clothes pen. It looked pretty good to me. I had seen other guys shoot these type sling shots with very good accuracy. When I tried to shoot mine, I nail the thumb on my left hand that was holding the pen with a marble. I hollowed and screamed loudly as it was very painful. I never tried to shoot that damn sling shot again because when I stopped crying, I threw the bastard away. It may not have been the workmanship as much as the lack of knowledge to operate this type of projectile instrument. Anyway, I never tried to make or shoot another one rubber strip sling shot again.

MAKING A CORN COB PIPE

Not long after the Nou Nou corn crib ordeal, I started making corn cob pipes. I would cut the large end of a corn cob off and leave it about an inch and a half long. I gouged out the center of the cob about an inch down, leaving a half inch in what would become the bottom of the cob. I would drill a small hole (about a quarter inch in diameter) into the side of the cob just above the solid bottom part. I got some bamboo which grew behind the levee in front of hour house and other places on the Plantation. I would cut one bamboo stock and then cut the smallest joint off the top of it. I would hollow out the stuff inside the bamboo joint with a stiff wire and cut the joint about eight inches long. Then taper the end if I had to, to fit in the hole I made in the bottom part of the cob. It was now a corn cob pipe.

Some time later, after I had rounded up some more tobacco, I tried my new pipe out. After sucking on the bamboo stem to hard and getting some very hot ash or something in my mouth, I learned to draw on it just right not to get hot stuff in my mouth. I made several puffs. By the way, I do not remember ever sharing my pipe with anybody else. What I found out during this experiment was, before I could get half way through smoking a home made corn cob pipe, the cob part burned clean through, burned my fingers and thumb, then fell apart when it hit the ground. Why did it hit the ground? Because it get to hot to hold in ones hand, I did not know how to treat the cob and bamboo to prevent it from burning up. So I did not bother making any more corn cob pipes. I thought about soaking it in water for a day or two but it still would have dried out and burnt up the first time it was smoked. The main thing is that I know how to make one if I ever decide to make one again. Later I remember seeing corn cob pipes being sold commercially. They must have figures some way to keep the cob and bamboo from burning up. I out grew this smoking business until I was nineteen or so and would smoke a cigar that I could afford to buy already rolled and everything.

RUBBER BAND (STRIP) SHOOTERS

A very simple weapon that again was made of cypress wood whittled into the shape of a sort of gun. We made it about twelve to fourteen inches long. It looked like a long wooden gun. It was one piece with a stock or handle and a sort of square barrel about ten inches long. Nothing fancy at all. We put a pincher clothes pen (one with the spring in it) on top on the gun near the stock or handle. We would tie it on with twine because trying to nail it on would split the clothes pen. We would cut rubber strips about one half inch wide and eight inches long for a twelve inch gun. With a thumb on the top of the pincher clothes pen, we opened the mouth of the pen, placed both ends of the rubber strip in the mouth than removed the thumb. The spring loaded pincher pen held the rubber strip in place while it was stretched and looped around the nose end of the gun. The top of the pincher pen was the trigger. You could shoot it left or right handed, just as you could the sling shot and popgun or any of the other toys we made. Hold the gun as you would any gun, aim at the target, with the thumb of the hand holding the gun, press down on the pincher clothes pen and WALL LA again. The rubber strip would shoot out like a projectile toward the target. It depended upon how much you stretch the rubber strip as to the distance it would go forward; sometimes fifteen feet, sometimes thirty feet. We would use these for close in fighting.

BOW AND ARROWS AND WILLOW REEDS

We made bows from willow reeds and certain limbs from the chinaberry/ball tree. Both has some flexibility in them and could be bent a great deal before breaking. My bow would be five to six feet long. The hardest part of making a bow was having strong enough string or twine to make the thing work.

We would just find a limb or reed long enough and about three quarters to an inch in diameter. Notch it about one half inch from both ends, tie the twine at one end, in the notch, put the tied end down by your foot and bend the reed down and loop the twine over this end and tie it in the notch also. This would leave about a ten to twelve inch gap between the reed and the twine at the center of the bow. The twine would be good an taunt. This was very good for projecting arrows.

I made my arrows from good old cypress wood. Again striping and carving them out of old used to be picket fence wood.

We only use these to shoot at targets. This was a serious play toy and could have really hurt somebody if we tried to play cowboys and Indians. I would have harmed a lot of cowboys, because I made a good Bow and Arrow set and I would have always been the Indian and put my bow and arrow against all the rubber guns and popguns they could make. Of course the sling shot would have been against the rules. We all made better than average sling shots. The only thing that kept us from mass production was the lack of rubber strips.

MUD-SLINGING WILLOW REEDS

Sometimes we would pay behind the levee. This mean the River side of the levee. We did not do this very often as we would catch a whipping if we got caught by daddy or any other adult who told on us. They considered this a safety issue and they would tell your parents if they saw you even act like you are going behind the levee.

The few times we did, we enjoyed it. There is several kind of ground makeup behind the levee just as there is on the plantation. Close to the River is the sandy type land, then there is a gray color sort of sticky kind of dirt then the gumbo or black jack dirt as we referred to it as. The black jack/gumbo was really good for mud ball fights. You could roll it up into a ball and it stayed in that shape. It stayed in that shape when it was thrown at somebody. When you got hit in any area that was not covered by clothes, it would really sting. It was heavy and solid.

When we really wanted to get some distance on our throw, we would cut a young willow limb. They grew by the tens of thousands behind the levee. Get one about one inch thick at the base and tapered to a quarter inch at the top. I would cut a six foot long limb and cut it back to about four feet or so. I reach to the ground and get a hand full of black jack and squeeze it into a ball and stick the smallest end of my willow reed into the ball. The clump of mud stuck to the willow reed very well. You would use a motion like you was using a bull wipe and fling the willow reed forward toward your target area. At the top of you swinging forward movement, the mud ball would let go from the reed and go for as a hundred yards. The whipping motion you make and the speed with which you are going forward, supplied the impetus to make the mud ball go. This was not something just anybody could do. You had to practice it. Greenhorns could not get the mud to stick on the willow reed. If it had been dry weather for some time, we had to wed the mud a little to get the right consistency to make it stick. Most greenhorns lost their mud on the back swing. The mud would fall off before the forward motion was made. I even lost some mud balls at the top of the arch and they would just be lobbed up in the air and come down far short of the target. We very seldom hit each other playing this game and I thank God for that. I got hit by a willow reed thrown mud ball only one time. I never got hit again after that one time because I quit that game and have never ever played it since. I got hit on my right cheek. Besides hurting for two days, my cheek was red for two weeks. I could have lost my right eye if I would have been hit there.

Some of the games we just had to try at least until we got hurt. Most of the things we did and learned how to do was by watching the older kids on the plantation do. These were mostly games handed down by older brothers and sisters who played them before us.

Some of the older kids would have gun fights with bee-bee guns. I never did this. That would have been really stupid of me to do.

CHAPTER 10

OUR HOUSE IN WHITE CASTLE
AGES FOURTEEN AND FIFTEEN

Another photo from Catholic School (1956 - '57)

THE TASTE OF FRESH BREAD

    Sometimes during these years, Daddy purchased a lot in Adams Addition in White Castle. He decided to have a house built on it. In 1957, he got Mr. Meaka Burnstine (a black Carpenter) to frame the house and build the cabinets and do most of the work that us and relatives and friends could not do. That same year, we left the plantation for the city life of White Castle. This house had a fan in the attic and a furnace in the floor in the hall.

During the Winter months, I would sleep with just a sheet covering me. I could not believe it. It was great. I did not know this was possible. The Summer nights were cooler with the attic fan on. This house was smaller than the plantation house and had eight foot ceiling instead of those fourteen footers in the plantation house. This had to help with the cooling and heating of it. I just did not know that city folks had it so good.

Another thing I leaned while living in town in 1957 was, Daddy would come home for Dinner (served at twelve noon) and one day Momma asked him to get a loaf of bread for supper when he came in from work that day. Daddy forgot to go by the Plantation Store to get the bread before he left the plantation, but remembered it when he got to White Castle. He stopped at Dominick Sciortino's Grocery Store in town which was on the way to our house and purchase a loaf of Sunbeam bread, our usual brand. At supper time (the evening meal), I could not get over how soft the bread was. It was so good. I had never had bread this soft before. We purchased all our bread in town from that day forward- even after we moved back to the plantation two years later.

What I came to learn sometime later, was that Mr. Joluette, the Office Manager for the Plantation, and a man who cheated many people over this lifetime, would buy old stale bread to be sold at the plantation store and charge prices for it that was even higher than the stores in town. When Mr. Charlie Guercio (the Sunbeam bread man) would pick up all the stale bread at the grocery stores in town, he would deliver them to Cedar Grove Store and sell it to Mr. Joluette for almost nothing. Mr. Joluette had Mr. Braus and Milton sold it to everyone on the Plantation for a very high profit. What a bastard Joluette was.

The bread I ate for my first fourteen years on this earth was stale. It was like toast bread but it was still white. What a crook Joluette was. There were other things that we paid full price for that was used or old. I do not blame Mr. Burton for this because he lived in Lake Charles, Louisiana. I blame Mr. Joluette. He cheated many people in his day. He cheated many area farmers out of money and just lined his pockets. I know, because of Joluette's efforts, W.T. Burton made some money too. But I do not believe that Mr. Burton knew of the dealings of Joluette.

FRIENDSHIPS IN WHITE CASTLE

It was during the years that I was fourteen and fifteen year old that I began to bond with good friends like Alvin (Slim) Barbier, Bobby Pearce, who lived a couple of houses over from us on Adam's Drive in town, Davis Callegan, Nickie (Crowbar) Guercio and others. Donald (Duck) Aucoin was like my cousin. Since I was a very little fellow, we visited with his Mom and Dad on a regular basis. Mr. George (Duck's Daddy) and my Dad had worked in the cane field for my Grandpa when they were young. My Daddy started working full time the cane field for his Daddy when he was seven years old. My grandpa took him out of school to work in the fields. I believe Mr. George trained Daddy on field work. Mrs. Maude (Duck's Mom) had really helped and supported my Momma when she was young and living with Nan Noon and Paran Charlie Pansono. They were really strict people and Mrs. Maude made it possible for Momma to go out with them sometimes and have some fun or just to get away from the house and the old folks for a while. The Aucoin's looked after my mom and dad when they were young. The Aucoin's were a little older than mom and dad. Our families were very close. Some years later, Duck and I would go into the Army together.

When we were teenagers, Duck worked for the Chat and Chew with was a barroom, pool hall, and hamburger/poor boy sandwich place. Mr. George Ourso and Pechun (LeRoy) Aucoin (Duck's brother) owned the place. When ever we were out of school, Duck worked there. He worked like seven days a week. He was the "step and fetch it boy," he also clean up, wash glasses/dishes, did a lot of work with a broom and other chores that needed to be done there. The Chat and Chew was a large place and took a lot of sweeping with a broom to keep the floors clean. Duck just could not run around with us because he worked all the time. As an older teenager, he did take time off of work here and there to do some things with us, but it was far and in-between. All those Aucoins knew how to work. They was not afraid of work. Mr. George and Momma Maude would not have it any other way. This was one hard working family.

NICKY (CROWBAR) GUERCIO

Me and Nicky 1961

As best I can recall, I first met Nicky in the fourth grade at Sister School (Our Lady of Prompt Succor Catholic School) in White Castle. It was a school with grades from first through eight. Many kids attended through the eighth grade then went to White Castle High or Catholic High in Donaldsonville, Louisiana for the ninth through twelfth grades. Donaldsonville was ten miles south of White Castle on La. Highway #1.

Our school was referred to as "Sister School" because most of our teachers were Nuns. The Principal was a Nun. The top person in charge was the head catholic priest of the local church.

We were required to ware uniforms to school. The boys wore khaki pants and white tee shirts or white short or long sleeve button down dress shirts. The well to do boys wore the button down shirts. The rest of us wore the tee shirts. The girls wore white blouses and navy blue pleated skirts.

Nicky was always the tallest kid in class. During our pre teen years he was considered tall for his age. By the time he got to the eighth or ninth grade, he was lanky and skinny. He kind of leaned forward when he walked. Thus the nickname Crowbar came into play. He was known as Crowbar throughout his high school years.

At Sister School during recess we used to play tag, marbles, softball, with yo yos, spend our tops and other games. When we were in the fifth grade, we were all playing outside at recess. Nicky had on a long sleeve button down dress shirt. It was a really nice shirt. I do not remember the circumstances, but some how I tore his shirt at the chess pocket. It was not a large tare but I was afraid of getting into trouble with the Nuns or even worse - Nicky's parents may want me (my parents) to pay to replace the shirt. I was really scared. Nicky did not seam to care about the tare. I became more and more preoccupied about it so much so that I do not remember or know what Bully Daigle did to make Nicky so mad. He was trying to catch Bully. Nicky was red in the face and just had a mean disposition about him. He had a little tussle with Bully but could not grab him like he wanted to and this scuffle made the tare in his pocket a little larger. I yelled at Nicky that he was tarring his shirt more and to calm down. But he was really mad now. Madder than I ever saw him before or during our later years. I kept telling him that his nice shirt was tarring more and this seam to make him madder. Thank God that he was wearing a tee shirt under his nice dress shirt, because he tore his long sleeve shirt all to pieces. He just ripped it off his body to the shock and awe of the several of us around him. We all backed further away from him at this time. He was cursing and stomping around looking for somebody to hit. He was what you call "pissed off." His actions, as bad as they were, made me feel better because I now knew that I will not have to buy him another shirt. About this time the bell rang- thank goodness. We all went back to class where things settled down. At the next recess nothing was said or done to start this wanting to fight business again. Everything was forgotten and over. I never did learn of any problem that Nicky had when he went home without his nice white long sleeve button down dress shirt. If he was punished, he never let on to anyone about it.

    Nicky and I had a lot of good times together during our pre teen and early teenage years. I used to spend nights at his house on Saturday sometimes. It was a big joke in their house that I would baby sit with Nicky when Mrs. Virginia and Mr. Dominick went to a function. We had good times just watching the television or listening to Nicky's short wave radio. One time we listened in on guys talking back and forth for about an hour. Their conversation was about supplies and how cold it was where they were. I do not remember all that was said but I do remember one guy telling the other fellow that nobody in his group could walk on the floor because it was to damn cold. They were in a hut with their feet off the floor. It was colder than forty below zero Fahrenheit. They were somewhere in Alaska. I cannot remember their location. When I heard where they were, I thought about how costly that short wave radio must be to pick up conversations from Alaska to somewhere else. I was in awe because of this and listening to pilots of airlines talking and police and ambulance drivers, etc. I had heard about radios like this but this was the first one that I ever seen. It was just amazing.

    Over the years, Nicky and I hung around the gas station his dad and mom owned and ran. As a young teenager, Nicky was put in charge on many occasions. This gave him some business training along with handling workers and giving out orders. Watching the cash register was his number one priority. Number two was not pissing off customers. Some of the black guys that worked there did not like a youngster ordering them to do things. They took orders well from adults but had a problem with a kid ordering them to do what they know was their job to do. I can relate to this. I would have the same problem. Sometimes they mopped around, pouting until Nicky said he will tell his dad or here comes daddy now. They would get in high gear and get back to washing, greasing and changing oil on cars being serviced, and whatever other jobs they were suppose to be doing. Nicky just had to give them that motivation - here come daddy.

When there were no customers for gas or oil change or the grease rack, they would sweep and or wash the whole area around the station with a water hose. It was all cement.

In the early years, the Guercio's ran the gas station on the corner of La. Highway #1 and Bowie (main) Street. Some years later, they moved about one hundred fifty feet north to a bigger station across the highway on the corner of La. #1 and East Street which is the street that they lived on. Their walking distance to work was shortened by about one hundred fifty feet.

After all these years, I do not remember which brand of gas the Gurecio's sold at either gas station.

There was this time at the old station when I was about sixteen years old and Nicky was fifteen and left in charge. His dad went home for dinner at twelve noon. We call this lunch nowadays. Sometimes Mr. Dominick would stay home for two or three hours to have a nap after eating. We knew when he had Nicky watching the station; he would stay at home longer than normal. After all, he got up before daylight everyday, seven days a week to open the station for business. He had to be ready for the early morning folks before they went to work in case they needed gas.

He would work until ten o'clock at night or later. When Nicky was deemed old enough to help out, he spent a lot of time running the station. For many years before Nicky was old enough to help, Mrs. Virginia would be there alone running it while Mr. Dominick had dinner, or needed a break or had business or a doctor's appointment, etc. It was a family run business. Nicky was the only child so it came down to him to put in many hours at the station. This really helped his mom and day to spend more time together. As they got into their mid forties, they finally got a chance to spend more time with each other - thanks to Nicky.

Getting back to this time that Nicky was in charge and I was with him. There were a couple of black guys who was just two years older than us working there at the time. It was winter time. It was cold enough to have the gas heater on in the station but not freezing cold. The conversation somehow got to rubbers (condoms) and how much water one could hold. Nicky got the cigarette machine key from the desk drawer. The rubbers were locked inside of the cigarette machine to keep them out of sight and to keep them from disappearing. The black guys begged Nicky to give them each just one rubber but he said NO. They did not want to pay for them. Nicky said that his dad may have counted them and he could not take a chance on taking more than one. Nicky got just one rubber out and relocked the machine. The station had a water can with a spout on it. Nicky got the can and went outside to the water facet and got some water. Upon his return, I fitted the rubber opening over the spout and Nicky poured the water into the rubber. We were surprise to see how much it stretched. Nicky made another trip outside for water. The black guys just could not believe that we were abusing a perfectly could condom in this manner. All the while this was going on, we kept an eye out for Mr. Dominick. We could see out the window to the other gas station near the side street where he would be walking from. It never occurred to us that he may come back by car. Anyway. If we would have seen him coming, we would have had the time to empty the rubber into the hand washing basin inside the station where we were and stick the rubber into one of our pockets out of sight. Although the hand washing basin was near, we could not use it to get water for the rubber because it restricted us in the way we wanted to do this scientific research.

During this whole time only one customer showed up for gas. Nicky sent one of the black guys to pump it. We were hoping and praying that the customer was not a lady and would not come into the station as many customers did. We were scared shitless with no place or time to hide a three foot plus rubber with water in it. I do not remember if the customer was a man or woman but they never got out of the car. Thank God it was cold and damp outside. After the customer left we got back to our experiment. I was very happy the customer did not come into the station. After all, I was the guy holding the bag, er I mean rubber partly full of water.

Nicky started pouring the second container of water into the rubber. It really stretched now. It was almost four feet long. We got a chair for me to stand on so the rubber would not touch the cement floor. It was getting heavy and I had to have a very good grip on it to keep it from slipping out of my hands. Nicky got more water. The rubber was over four feet long when I bent down a little to look out of the window for Mr. Dominick because we had not done so in several minutes. This was a mistake. This is when all hell or should I say all rubber broke lose. The rubber touched the floor and burst. Nicky was outside getting more water. When he returned and saw the mess he shouted "OH SHIT what happened?" It popped, it touched the damn floor and popped, I retorted. We quickly got the mop and a broom. We asked the black guys to help us. They said NO. They did not want any part of it and was not going to get involved

We started mopping and sweeping water toward the door. I never worked so fast in my life. This was harder than working in the damn sugar cane field. We kept looking out of the window for any sign of Nicky's dad. We got up all the free water. Now we needed the whole area to dry. I started using the broom to fan the floor. Nicky turned the heater up higher thinking that more heat will dry the floor quicker. For fifteen minutes we worked and worried. All the while the black guys were laughing at us and lamenting on how we ruined a perfectly good rubber. They kept shaking their heads from side to side and showing their white teeth while laughing. This kind of pissed us off.

"OH NO! Here he come, Nicky." The floor was still damp in a place or two. Mr. Dominick was a short man and took small steps and walked slow. Nicky got his height from his mom who was a head taller than his dad. I thought if someone was to talk with Mr. Dominick that would slow him down even more. He would stop to talk. The black guys would not do it. I could not think of anything to say that would not cause suspicion in his mind if I ran from the station to him just to talk. He would be there soon enough if I just wanted to talk. We were scraping our tennis shoes on the floor thinking that it may help to dry the damp spots.

Mr. Dominick came in and looked around. I do not know what kind of expressions we had on our faces. The two black guys went outside to look busy before he crossed La.#1. They were still smiling. He asked how it was going. We said fine. Nicky told him we had a couple customers and it had been quite. No problems. Mr. Dominick walked over to the heater to get some warmth. With his back to the heater, he looked down and saw the dampness and asked what happened here. One of us said that a cup of drinking water was spilled and was mopped up. That was all there was to it. We were safe. He told us to go on about our business. We walked to Nicky's house. On the way we laughed about the whole thing. To this day, we still don't know how much water a regular condom can hold. I am sure we had close to a gallon in that one before I let it touch the floor. There is one thing

I learned that is still with me today. These damn rubbers are waaaaaaaaaaaaay to big for my apparatus.

As far as I know, the black guys never told Mr. Dominick what happened. Mr. Dominick is long gone and so are my parents. Mrs. Virginia is in her eighties and still going strong at the time of this writing in October 2003.

During our late teenage years, Nicky and I did not spend as much time together. He spent many hours at the gas station. For that time spent there, he was allowed to use the family car a lot. He also always seemed to have a girlfriend. He had many girlfriends from the tenth grade on. He went steady with several of them, at different times, of course. When not going steady, he dated on a regular basis. He also played sports for several White Castle High teams. These activities took up much of his time. He was always on a date, or otherwise doing something on week days and week ends when not working. He was always on the go.

Dating was a relaxing time for him between working and sports. Much of my time was spent with my other friend- Davis Callegan. We did not date that much during high school so went everywhere together.

Nicky had this saying that we like to quote. We talked about using it when talking with girls but none of us had the gonads to do it. It went like this, "if you make it hard on me, I will hold it against you." Well, one thing I do know is, he dated a lot of pretty girls, and ended up marring the prettiest one of the lot. Other stories about Nicky and me will be saved for another book.

HALLOWEEN IN THE CITY

I was fourteen when we moved to White Castle. I will have more to say about my friend Slim Barbier later. Slim's dad would drop him off in town and he, Bobby Pierce, me and others would just roam about town playing and getting into things. One Halloween night we watched the older boys (about seventeen/eighteen) give Clayton (hop along) Hebert, our Chief Deputy (and only deputy in my early life) headaches all around town. They did this not only on Halloween but on other holiday night also.

They would light off cherry bombs and drop them into the fifty-five gallon drums that was used for trash cans at the high school and other locations around town. When they went off, a very loud boom could be heard in most of the town proper. If any trash was in the drums, it would be blown all over the place.

We would sit on the bench in front of Mr. Clarence Martinez's store which was across the street from the high school gym. The older boys would place lit cherry booms into the trash drum that was near the high school gym. We had a good view of the goings on but could not make out who the boys were that was doing this mischief because it was just a little to dark. We would not have wanted to rat on them but would have to save ourselves from the likes of Clayton Hebert.

Shortly after a bomb went off, here come Clayton with the sirens blasting just letting everybody know that he was on the way. The older boys would have it set up that as soon as the cherry bomb at the gym went off and Clayton was on his way there, another one was lit and dropped into a drum at the baseball field near the Catholic Church and than another one behind the high school property and several other locations throughout the town.

Us younger teenager, in training, would watch Clayton coming in the police car with his lights blinking and the sirens on after the first blast. Just after getting out of the car and putting his flashlight on to start looking about the place, the next cherry bomb would go off. He would jump back into the patrol car; make a u-turn in the middle of the street an head toward the boom. Within a minute he would be heading back to get to the street behind the school as the next cherry bomb went off. As he arrived there, jump out of the car to look around, another one would go off. They would keep this up for a half hour or so. Skip a half hour and go to the center of town where all the bars are and hold up parking meters and listen to Clayton tell them and the adults there what he was going to do when he catch this gang of delinquents. Then they would tell everybody that they were going home and start the cherry bombing all over again.

It occurred to me that Clayton never walked where he went. It might be because he had this bad leg which caused him to limp or he just may have been lazy. I do not know which. But using the patrol car, he was not ever going to catch anybody and maybe that was the way it was suppose to be. Perhaps the Chief, Mr. Eddie Boudreaux did not want him to really jack up a kid. He just wanted to see to it that they did not do any harm to property or persons. And by Clayton keeping them on the run and them keeping Clayton on the run, no one was ever hurt that I am aware of.

My first Halloween while living in White Castle, I teamed up for part of the night with Robert Dimm. He was one of Ronnie Dimm's (of Quinn Falcon's knife fight fame while we were in Sister School) brothers. Robert was really tall for his age, which was odd because Ronnie was really short for his age. All the Dimms had blond hair and really white and looked alike.

Robert and I trick or treated on the north side of town near the River. We was kind of old to be trick or treating, but I was making a good haul. Robert did not have much. Even through he was younger then me, He was almost a head taller and folks refused to give to him because they thought he was to old or to big or just knew that he was a Dimm or something.

I was ready to quit, but Robert did not have much stuff so he went on the porch where we both knew a really old women lived. He called upon me to join him, which I did. We knocked on the door and call out "trick or treat" several times. We knocked louder. We got no answer. We made noise on the porch, still no answer. We then looked through the blinds on the front door. We saw the old women in a rocking chair in the front room just sitting there staring. She was not rocking or nothing. Just staring and not moving. It got spooky. Robert, the bastard, who just before we peeked through the blinds, was ready to do a trick on her porch, shouted "she's dead." He took off and ran down the steps and when I turn around, he was running in the street. He just left me there on the porch all by myself, the shit. I turned and started to run off the porch and missed the steps and fell to the ground dropping my number twenty-five paper bag with all my goodies. I yelled for Robert to wait for me but the bastard was going up the street. I reached in the dark and felt my bag and tried quickly to reach in the dark for some of my stuff but was not very successful. I took off after Robert.

The next block over we stopped to catch our breath. I was really breathing hard. I had to run extra to catch up with Robert. I thought that I would catch a heart attack. My bag was three quarters empty of what I had. Since Robert did not want to go back with me, we decided to let the old women have all my goodies that was in her yard in the morning if she was still alive then. If she was dead, then someone in her family could have them when they came and found her body. Anyway, I was not going back by myself. I will just do without the stuff that I worked so hard for. We made it to downtown, Robert and I split up. I teamed up with some other guys and we ambled over to the south side of town to be near home when I decided to call it a night. Which I did shortly thereafter.

When I was a year older, on Halloween, Slim was hanging with me. He was brave enough to light the cherry bombs if I would let him use my bike for a get away. I did not think that he had the guts to do it, so I said that he could use my bike to run. I believe Bobby Pearce, Nicky (Crowbar) Guercio, and maybe Elmer Boudreaux (who was a year younger than his good looking sister Bobbie Boudreaux who was in our grade at school) and I went to the school yard. We then went to Mr. Clarence Martinez store. Slim stayed in the school yard near the gym, lit the cherry bomb threw it into the fifty- five gallon drum and started hauling ass towards us. He grabbed my new bike (this was a new, new bike I had gotten several months before Halloween for my birthday or something) and started running with it than jumped upon the seat like Gene Autrey and Roy Rogers did on their horses in all their movies when they were in a hurry. As I felt sorry for my bike taking the punishment from Slim's wide ass the cherry bomb went off. I was sorry I had made the deal. But a deal is a deal. I did not think he would go through with it. He was over two hundred and fifty pounds for God's sake, and the slowest one of all of us. And this load was on my bike getting smaller in the distance as he was now hauling ass (a really big ass) on my bike. He made a good getaway.

After the boom, Clayton came by, knew we did not do it because we was still there in front of Mr. Martinez's store. Someone pointed in a direction that Slim did not go and off went Clayton with the lights blinking and the siren screaming.

We teamed back up with Slim a little later. We felt like the eighteen year olds now. My bike was never the same after Slim hopped skipped and jumped on my seat making his getaway. The next week, I had to replace a broken back axle on it. Another time I let him ride it, the next week after that, I had to replace another back axle. I did not have a heavy duty bike. It was never the same after that. The frame must have gotten twisted or something. I could not keep the chain on the sprocket and the rear wheel axles would screw up. It got so my bike was not ride-able any more. I know that this was due to the punishment it went through when my buddy Slim rode it. This was O K. Slim was one of the good guys, and I needed to walk more anyway. This was the last bike that I remember having until after I married and purchased one for myself.

Mr. and Mrs. Martinez live next door to their store. In fact their house was attached to the store. They had a couple of sons who were several years younger than we were. They did not let them out to much back then. Somebody had it in for Mr. Martinez, as they would not give treats or anything on Halloween. It seemed like each Halloween (unless it is just my memory) someone would place a burning paper bag with shit in it on their porch. Light it, yell trick or treat, bang very loud on the door and run. I saw Mr. Martinez stomping to put out the fire and spreading shit all over himself and his porch. The movie Hollywood Knight did not have anything on the teenagers of White Castle in the late 1950s.

MY BROTHER GOT MARRIED

My brother and Liz Giroir got married on September 29, 1957 in Bell Rose, Louisiana. They went together for several years before they married. The reception was at a hall in Bell Rose and everybody past a real good time. I remember Liz's brother Russell and brother-in-law, Pete Sanchez, working as bartenders or as beertenders as was the case. All the folks there love to drink beer.

Liz have four sisters and two brothers. Three of her sisters married guys from Cedar Grove Plantation just as she did. Ruby married Irvin Ponsano. Bell married Pete Sanchez, who was not raised on Cedar Grove as all the other guys were, but worked for Cedar Grove Plantation for many years. Vivian married Quinn (the Knife Fighter) Falcon. This is amazing to me. Four of the five sisters married fellows from Cedar Grove/White Castle. The youngest sister, Lois Ann, married Big Moose. He was not from Cedar Grove. All of these marriages lasted. Irvin and Quinn has past on. Pete and my brother, Put, are still going strong. Big Moose died about seven years ago.

Liz and her sisters are in fairly good health. Liz's brother, Nelson has some medical problems and her younger brother, Russell is in good health. They must all have their Momma's genes. Mrs. Giroir is nearing her mid nineties and still going strong. Liz's Dad got killed while working in the sugar cane field in a tractor accident many years ago.

Some time after they got married, my brother built a house in the woods between White Castle and Plaquemine called Random Oaks. But my sister-in-law was afraid to live there because my brother worked all over the state and was gone all during the week. So she would live with us during the week and live in Random Oaks during the weekend when my brother was home. She worked her buns off cooking and cleaning and doing all other household chores in that big house we lived in on the plantation. This went on for several years until my brother got on the I-10 project and worked out of a more local yard. He stopped traveling the whole state and was home every night during the I-10 project and all the years he worked for the state after that project was over. They had two or three kids when they moved into their house to stay. I believe Brian Paul was born after they were living at Random Oaks. And they been there ever since.

CROP DUSTING ON THE PLANTATION

When farming for a living, there is certain kinds of work that must be preformed at a particular time of the year. Such as cane planting, cane harvesting, fertilizing the crop, plowing or chopping the land to reduce the grass growth, running the drain cleaners, (did this by hand with a shovel during my early teenage years), spraying by tractor for bugs and grass and Crop Dusting by airplane.

Two times a year, the plantation hired Mr. Bob Gunn of Yazoo, Mississippi to come down and spray and/or dust the sugar cane crop. This happened after lay by time when the crop was to high to drive the tractors through it.

At a predetermined time of year, Mr. Gunn would fly in from Mississippi, and land at the Cedar Grove landing strip on the back part of White Castle Plantation. This is the same landing strip where Daddy's bosses would land and the very same one that I went on my first airplane ride. You may remember. This was the airplane with four seats that we landed in the Mississippi River with. Anyway. The plantation would have all the supply needed for the spraying or dusting operation.

When it was spraying time, Mr. Gunn would fly down with his airplane rigged for spraying. It had a large tank in it that would contain the liquid.

When I started working for pay at fourteen years of age, I was on of the Overseers sons that usually worked specific jobs during the spraying/dusting operations. Most of the time, I was a flagman. This meant that I had to carry this fifteen foot long pole with a three foot square on the top with red cloth stapled onto it that covered the three foot square area. The "flag" was just red cloth. The pole was two inch by two inch wood, about fifteen feet long with a three foot square wood frame attached to one end of it. As mentioned, a red cloth was cut out to fit the square and stapled onto the wood frame. It was a fairly sturdy instrument. I carried it on my shoulder with the flag end up in the air and most of the pole part in front of me to counter balance this long object.

Since the plantation was so large and at certain spots over a mile long where sugar cane was planted, three to four flagmen were used. The Overseers would take us in their pickup trucks to a designated starting spot. Usually this was the border of White Castle on the east side of the plantation. We would cover all sugar cane to the boundary on the West Side of the plantation, which was Catherine Plantation which we called Supple's Plantation because the Supple family owned it.

Cedar Grove Plantation was much wider at the back of it than on the River front part of it. So the flagman would not start in a straight line. This is hard to explain. From the air looking down the flagman would look to be in a diagonal line. The line was straight but not as a straight edge of a carpenter's level and a board would be. We were in a straight diagonal line.

From the River front of the Plantation, if I could have seen the next flagman up from me, he would have been in a line to my left and not straight ahead of me. I hope that this make sense. Here is that word again, ANYWAY

When the airplane got in the air, we were all at out post. We walked to the city of White Castle property line, than make about thirty or forty paces/large steps, away from the boundary. Then stand our flag straight up with the red cloth in the air so the pilot could see it above the sugar cane. At this time of year, the sugar cane was eight or nine feet tall or taller. It was much taller than we were which is why a tractor could not do this job. We usually had to lift the flag up higher to be sure that the pilot could see it.

After the first pass of the airplane, we would pace off twenty one steps and set the flag straight up for the airplane pilot to line up on it after he turned around. Each time he flew over us, we would continue this twenty one paces throughout the plantation until we got to the Supple's boundary.

This would sometimes take several weeks to accomplish. It all depended upon what liquid chemical or dusting powder that was being used, and the weather. Whether it was raining or not, fog, too windy, any number of things could delay the spraying/dusting.

If we were spraying for tie vines, we would work from day break to maybe ten or eleven o'clock. We usually would not spray in the afternoon because when the sun was out for this many hours it would be very hot and the spray would evaporate too soon and not do any good. These chemical were just to expensive to not utilize them properly and when they would do the most good. We could not spray in windy weather because the chemical would blow all over the place and not get the application needed to do what it was suppose to do.

When we started from the White Castle property line, I mentioned that we paced off thirty or forty steps. This was done because the chemicals could drift on the garden and flowers of residence and kill them which made all the folks that lived on the boundary very upset. Se we would try and start twice as far from the boundary line than the Supple's boundary line.

Supples grew sugar cane across the ditch/canal property line, and would love for Cedar Grove to spray there crop. They sprayed/dusted just as we had to do. Sometime, the pilot that worked for Supples used our landing strip to load from. Supples used there own supplies and personal to work their flags.

There were time that the chemical still drifted to the border residence and the Plantation paid to replant shrubs and flowers, etc.

When we use the airplane to dust/powder, it usually was to kill the sugar cane bore. This was a small worm that bored tiny holes into the cane stalks and eventually killed it or otherwise made it sour. It took us several weeks to spread dust/powder over the plantation also. We would start at daylight and quit about ten in the morning each day until we passed the whole plantation. We only applied the dust when the cane still had dew on it. We needed the moisture to make the dust stick to the leaves and stalks so it would do the most good. Again if it was windy, we could not dust, because the application would not be spread evenly or stay in the area where we were trying to dust.

When spraying or dusting, we usually got started flagging between six and six thirty in the morning. When I was one of the flagmen, Daddy would show up about eight with my breakfast each day. Momma fried two eggs for me and made two fried egg sandwiches. She would break the yellow and fry it hard. Daddy would take my flag and work while I sat on the running board of the old truck and ate my fried egg sandwiches and drank coffee to wash it down. I did not like milk, still don't, but I liked coffee with milk in it.

As the airplane sprayed and/or dusted overhead, I ate my sandwiches. The spray and or dust would get all over me (and anyone that was flagging) and my food. I just ate it anyway. We did not know any better. I ate many fried egg sandwiches with the chemical 2-4-D sprayed all over me and them and my coffee milk. This was the chemical of choice to kill tie vines and other broad leaf grasses and vines that got into the sugar cane crop. The powder/dust used was poisonous also. I am just lucky to still be on this earth and not under it. In the 1970s, 2-4-D was band from being used in food crops by the Federal Government. It is a highly poison product. I can still remember, after spraying this chemical in the fields, when it rained, a lot of it got washed from the fields with the rain water and eventually drained to what is known as the White Castle Canal. This was a location about four or five miles from town and away from the Mississippi River. Fisherman and fun seekers launched their boats in the White Castle Canal and went to Shell Beach, Lake Verette, and many other places that was even forty miles away. You could get to the coast if you knew the waterways well enough. That word again, anyway. After the rain, water from miles around made it to the canal, where there would be a large fish kill. The 2-4-D from the fields even diluted with all that water was still enough for major fish kills at the White Castle Canal and other bodies of water in the area. It was a very poisonous product. This stuff is really bad.

I want you to know that every farmer in the United States was using 2-4-D to control certain weeds and grassed that hurt their farm crops whatever it was. South Louisiana just happen to grow more sugar can than any other crop.

I mentioned earlier that we usually used three or four flagmen and the plantation was wider in the back then the front near the River. When I worked the flag at the front end of the Plantation, an Overseer would arrive just before I got to the Supple's property line. After the airplane made his last pass over me, I jump into the back of the pickup with my flag placed across the top of the truck. The driver would deliver me further away from the River. We would go to a predetermined spot where I would pick up the airplane pathway, walk off twenty one paces and hold my flag up to make the pilot's return path.

I guess now would be a good time to tell you that the twenty one paces was the distance of the spraying or dusting pattern. It was the length of the wing span on the crop sprayers. From the cockpit, the pilot could see the four red flags above the cane crop. He would line up on the first one on either end of the plantation and fly where the engine came directly over the flag. It was really scary most of the time. All the flagmen could hear the airplane coming but could not see it until it was passing over hour heads. We could hear the engine getting louder and louder and closer and closer until the roar was upon us. I trusted all the pilot over the years, but that did not stop me from being afraid sometimes.

On one occasion, the wheel of the crop duster hit my flag and broke my pole about seven feet high. Mr. Bob Gunn was not doing this job for us. I was really afraid when I saw the airplane. I thought that I was a goner for sure. They always flew low but this was lower than normal. I heard it. I saw it. Bam, the top part of my flag flew twenty feet behind me and landed on the other side of a large ditch. I was working up front again. I was the last flagman that the pilot passed which meant I had to march off the twenty one paces in a hurry, get set up before he made his turn to come back. Well, after he broke my flag, I immediately ran toward it, jumped over part of the ditch, climbed out of the rest, picked up the top part of my flag, ran back, got across the damn ditch, and almost made the twenty one paces before he was back over me again. I had recovered both pieces on my way to the spot where I needed to be. He passed me by and I kept going for forty two paces. Then stopped, took a deep breath, maybe two, and started sweating profusely. Now it hit me. I was so afraid that I was shaking. I had time now to be scared because it would be several minutes before the airplane would make it to the other end of the plantation and back to me again.

I calmed down in a couple of minutes. I looked over the two pieces of my pole and flag. I could not put it back together without some tape or a lot of string neither of which was on me at the time. As the airplane approached, I lifted the flag as high as I could but the pilot could not see it because he past about forty feet in front of me. He could see me when he made the turn and lined up in the right spot on the way back.

All flagmen got a break each time the airplane went to reload. This gave us a well deserved rest for about ten or fifteen minutes. Daddy was at the load area when the pilot went back to reload and learned from him that the knocked the flag out of my hands. I could hear Daddy coming down the road. He looked to see if I was alright or hurt. I was not either. He looked at the broken flag pole while I was telling him what this cowboy pilot had done. He had some twine and we tied the lower part of the pole to the upper part of it that had the flag still attached. I finished the day with this patched up flag. But with a little more fear each time the airplane flew over my head.

After a couple of years of being a flagman, I became a loader. When we sprayed the liquid, we would have thirty five gallon barrels of liquid poison. We also had a large flat bed truck with a five hundred or more gallon water tank on it. We had a formula that we used for each application. It was so many gallon of water for so many gallons of poison. We would mix the poison and water in another tank and hand pump it into the airplane tank. While the pilot was spraying, we were getting the next batch ready. Our water tank was not that large, so during the spraying operation, we would have to drive the truck back to the shop area and refill our tank with fresh water. All of the loading operation took place at the landing strip on the Plantation.

When we dusted with powder, it came in fifty and eighty pound bags. We had to walk with a bag from the flat bed truck, throw the bag on the side of the airplane over the hopper opening, cut the bay open and pour it into the hopper. It would take twenty or thirty bags to fill the hopper. After the pilot took off, we would line up another twenty to thirty bags to be ready for his return then took a few minutes well deserved rest.

I had all this fun while earning forty three cents an hour. There was never any overtime pay. If I worked sixty hours a week, it was straight pay for the sixty hours. There was never any overtime pay for farm labor. That is just the way it was, maybe still is.

One time we was waiting for the pilot to come back and land. We all was watching. There was about six or seven of us out there. Me and two other workers and two Overseers (one was my dad), Mr. Luban Colliet, the Chief Engineer in the sugar mill, and Mr. Lu Lu Henry, the Shop Manager. I was on the ground, behind the flat bed truck watching the airplane come in. After being a flagman for a couple of years, I always watch the airplane approach from a safe vantage point. The other two workers were on the flat bed truck. Mr. Luban shouted "look out, he is dragging something behind him."

The fellows on the flat bed, jumped to the ground on my side of the truck. Mr. Luban starting running and dove to the ground. My Daddy turned around and also dove to the ground.

The airplane landed with a wire trailing behind him. We could hear it whistling as the airplane came in for landing. The pilot would always come in to land over us. This gave him room to stop going away from us than he turned around and taxied back to the loading spot. He would then take off from the loading spot.

After he passed over us, we went to the spot where the trailing wire cut the ground. It was nearest to my Daddy. If he had not jump out of the way and hit the ground, we all believe that he would have been cut in half by that wire. I thanked God and Mr. Luban for seeing the wire dangling from the wheel set under the airplane.

After landing, the pilot knew that had hit some telephone or electric wires, but did not know he had about fifty feet of it following him in. He cut the wire from his landing apparatus while we were reloading the cargo compartment. After he took off for another run, we then had time to sweat and wonder what could have happened if.

MY UNCLE'S 1954 DESOTO

I remember one time when I was fifteen and still living in town, my Uncle Nolan let me use his 1954 four door Desoto to knock around town. His car was loaded; it even had power steering which none of our autos had. My uncle showed me how to drive it one day. I was not used to the steering being so easy. We were heading towards town from our house on Adam's drive. We came to the intersection and I had the stop sign. I stopped to show my uncle how good a driver it was. When the path was clear, I started turning right. Well, this got my uncle all excited and he had to reach out of his window and grab the stop sign and twist it around at the same time as shouting for me to stop. I got my first lesson in the power of power steering. I would have scrapped the passenger side of the car if Uncle Nolan would not have grabbed the sign. He was hot for a little while but realized this was my first time driving his car. We rode around town for a little bit and went back home. I learned how to drive his car. It was a smooth riding and large car but I got used to the power steering and power brakes and the power windows, etc. etc. I liked everything about this car.

This one time my uncle let me use his car by myself it surprised everyone in our family. I went to down town. There was no way that I was going to leave town because the gas needle was near empty. I saw Duck holding up a parking meter in front of the Chat and Chew and asked if he wanted to go for a short spend. He said "wait here," which I did while he went inside to talk with his brother. He was out in less than a minute. We were off. I picked up Bobby Pearce and Wayne Sandifer somewhere, I do not remember where, but we now had a foursome and no gas. The only one with money was Duck. He always had money. He was always working. He was also very tight with his money. I lamented that I had to get home before we run out of gas and Duck said to pull into the gas station that we was near. This is what I was hoping to hear. All the stations had attendants in these days so we could not put gas into our own car, the attendant did. We sat in the car while Duck told the attendant how much gas he wanted to buy. All of a sudden we heard this loud cursing and hollering. We all got out of the car. It seemed that the black attendant had went over the amount that Duck was willing to pay for. A number of folks from inside the station and gathered with us around the gas pump now. Duck was still cursing and reaching into his pocket for some money. The black attendants was saying how sorry he was but he thought Duck wanted a dollar worth of gas. Nobody ever came into the station and wanted fifty cents of gas. Especially not in a Desoto, maybe for a lawn mower.

After Duck paid the seventy cents or so for the gas, we took off. Duck was still upset with the attendant and could not understand how the man mistook a gallon of gas for a dollar of gas. He was really pissed off. This upset his whole day.

White Castle is a small town and this gas station altercation got all over town. We had to listen to the story being recounted at school, and home, down town, back of town and everywhere else we went. You know, stories like- did you heard about the boys that drove into the gas station with the biggest car and gas gussler in the parish and ordered one gallon of gas. It took several months to die down. The important part was that my uncle laughed with all the other folks in town when the story broke so a month or so later I got to use his car again. But this time it was at night.

BURNING UNC'S CAR UP

About a month or so after the one gallon of gas stories had died down, I was again driving about town in my uncle's Desoto. I picked up Duck, Bobby Pearce and Wayne Sandifer and we were just cruising the streets listening to the fine radio and minding our own business. We had more gas in the car this time, thank God. Or is should say, thank Uncle Nolan. I had checked the gas gauge as soon as I got in the car. If it would have been low, I would not have accepted the offer to use it because I was not about to get the gossip going around the parish about the gas thing again. I wondered when my uncle said that I could go to town in his car, if there was any gas in it. I did not know if he was trying to set me up again or not. Anyway there was almost half a tank, so we were not being set up.

We had been cruising about twenty minutes or so when while driving North on the street behind the Catholic Church, I hit a pot hole. The head lights blinked off and on again. This was night time so I had the headlights on but this blinking on and off was unusual. I stopped at the corner and made a left turn heading the less than one block to get to Bowie Street, which was the main street in town. As we got to Bowie, the headlights went out all together. I pulled over a little and stopped the engine. We were all wondering what was going on. The Catholic Church was on our left and Bowie Street was fifteen feet in front of us and residences was on our right. Just before I cut the engine off, we started to smell something like burnt rubber. I popped the release button for the hood. We all jumped out and when I lifted the hood, the engine compartment was on fire. Now we had some excitement. I did not know what to do. It had rained earlier in the day and there was a little puddle of water near by. Wayne and Bobby cupped their hand and got some and tried to throw on the fire but that did not work. On the side of the church was as water faucet but we did not have a container to put water into. I believe Duck went to call for help. Wayne took off his shirt and dipped it into the water puddle and got it soaked with dirty water and threw it over the burning area to smother the flames. I thought about using my shirt but I really liked the one I was wearing. I did unbutton a button or two but started helping Wayne stuff his shirt over the flames. Why ruin my shirt too if Wayne's would do the trick. Which it did. Wayne got the flames out and now he was standing bare chess for everyone to see. Until this day, I do not remember if I properly thank Wayne Sandifer for the sacrifice of his shirt and burnt hands and skinned up arms. Thanks Wayne.

By this time a number of folks had arrive to see what all the commotion was about. Then the Chief Deputy, Clayton (hop along) Hebert arrived and shouted "what's going on here?" to which Donald "Duck" Aucoin retorted "read the Morning Advocate and find out." Which a number of the growing crowd thought was amusing and had a good laugh about. But not I. The "Read the Morning Advocate" was a big promotion that was going on for one of the leading newspapers in the state at the time. Duck jumped on the fraise at Clayton's expense. I told Clayton that the car had a fire but I thought it was under control. He came to take a look. He had a very nice flashlight and we could now see much better into the engine compartment. The fire did seem out but some smoke was still there.

Shortly after Clayton's arrival, came the White Castle Fire Truck and the fire brigade led by Mr. John Marque who was the Fire Chief. They strung out the hose and had the nozzle aimed at the engine compartment of Unc's car which was still smoking a bit. NO, NO, don't open the nozzle I pleaded. The fire is out; it is just smoking a little bit. I knew that if the opened the nozzle and hit the engine with that stream of water, they would blow a lot of the engine parts from here to kingdom come. Where ever that is. I had seen what a fire hose at close range could do. Mr.

Marque told them don't open it up yet. He looked at the engine compartment and surveyed the situation for himself and was satisfied that the fire was out. I was happy for a short while. Now I had to call my uncle and tell him that I burnt up his car. I made the call, from where I do not remember. He cussed and said "you burnt up my damn car." He borrowed Daddy's 1953 Chevy and came to the scene. He arrived shortly and looked over his car. I was concerned that the hoods paint job would be ruined by the heat, but we just could not see good enough to tell at this time of night. Uncle Nolan reached under the hood and pulled out a hand full of wires and threw them on the ground while mumbling and cursing. He said we would leave the car there and get the wrecker at Dixie Sales and Service, where he was the head mechanic, and get it in the morning. Which he did. All my buddies walked home because I was not about to ask my Uncle to drive them. Anyway, White Castle was such a small town they would not have to walk far. Bobby lived only two doors down from us, but I still would not see if we could give him a ride. I believe that there were so many folks there that the guys all got rides home or had and good time doing something else while I was on my way home and had to listen to an ear full. In fact, two ears full.

The next day, after school, I went to Dixie Sales to look at the Desoto in the daylight. I got some compound polish and worked on the hood area where the fire was and it come out great. The car did not need to be painted. The electrical wiring was bad and my uncle told me that is what caused the fire. The wires had a short in them and it was not my fault. This could have happened at any time and he could have been driving the car. But he wasn't, I was and it did happen with me at the wheel. I felt really bad about all this. I offered to pay my uncle for all the cost. But I would have to pay a little at a time since I did not have any money on hand. He said no, do not worry about it, it was not your fault. He replaced all the electrical wiring under the hood and the spark plug wires also. His car was as good as new. It was a very long time before I drive the car again. It must have been, because I do not have a recollection that I ever drove it again.

This was the best car, most fancy car that we ever had in our family up to this time. Even though it was over four years old when Unc purchased it, it was newer than all the cars Daddy could afford to buy. I believe Mr. Johnny Latino purchased this car brand new from Dixie Sales and Service in 1954 and traded it in on a new Chrysler that he purchased in 1958. His son, Johnny Jr. and I ran together for a while in 1964 after he got out of the service. Then Johnny Jr. moved to Baton Rouge for a job.

CHAPTER 11

HANGING WITH ALVIN (SLIM) BARBIER: AGES FIFTEEN AND SIXTEEN

Alvin's Dad would pick me up at my house in White Castle when they would go to Plaquemine to visit relatives. Alvin (I named him Slim when we were in the sixth grade or so because he was so fat; the name stuck all through high school until he moved away) and I would be dropped off at the movie theater there. Mr. Pete Goutier had closed his theater in White Castle because of lack of business. All the teenagers in our town did not want to go to the local movies with dates that there Moms and Dads might be at, so they went to Plaquemine or Donaldsonville. Both towns were ten miles from White Castle. One north of us and the other south of us. So we had no choice but to go the movie in the town that our parents would visit.

I remember one double feature that Slim and I watched one night. Showing was "I was a Teenage Werewolf," which stared Michael Landum (later to become Little Joe Cartwright on Bonanza) and the other was "The Thing from Outer Space," staring I do not know who. The Thing was not as spooky as the Werewolf movie. That night, Mr. Barbier dropped me off at my Grandpa's house on the main drag coming out of White Castle. Our house was on another street behind Grandpas. Grandpa owned this empty lot which had waist high and higher weeds between his house and ours. Daddy later purchased the lot from Grandpa. The moon was very full and I wanted Mr. Barbier to drop me off at my house especially tonight. This route saved him time because our street was a one way street and he would have to back track to get back to the main street out of town. It was now after ten p. m. but well lit with the full moon out. Did I mention that I did/do not like spooky movies? Never did and still don't. There was an old fence and gate between Grandpa's yard and the property line for his back lot then the weeds started for about eighty feet or so then you get to our back yard, which had low grass because I CUT IT EVERY DAMN WEEK. I made it to the gate from the Main drag where I was dropped off in pretty good shape. I was whistling softly and trying to be cool and not to think of the full moon and damn werewolves and stuff like that. It must have been about two hundred feet between our house and Grandpa Adam's. That night, I thought it was a mile. I made it to the gate then heard a rustling sound in the bushes and weeds. And that's all brother, I took off. I bet that I would have beaten Jessie Owens in a hundred yard dash. I must have done a nine flat one hundred. I hit our back cement covered patio and slid to the steps of the back door. I just could not get in the house fast enough. I was out of breath and it was hard to breathe. Somebody took the oxygen out of the house. I stood in the utility room a while with the light on trying to catch my breath. When my pulse rate came down a little and I was not making a lot of noise trying to breathe, I made it to my bedroom, changed clothes and slept with one eye open.

The next morning, Momma asked me what all the commotion was about last night. I said "nothing." She asked "did you see a scary movie?" I said "yes." She just smiled and said nothing more about it.

Slim and I saw quite a few movies that summer. The best one was Dr. No. The first James Bond movie. We really enjoyed it and knew that they had something special here. I believe that I saw all of the James Bond movies with Sean Connery in them. I did not care at all for the other actors that took his place after he decided not to do those movies anymore. It just wasn't the same without the original 007.

MEETING DAVIS CALLEGAN AGAIN

Davis and I was in the same grade for a couple of years at Sister School. Then he went to school at Samstown and we did to see each other for several years.

It was a year or so later that Davis Callegan and I teamed up for all of our high school years. I used to visit his house at Lone Star and spend all day on Saturdays there. We would ride their horse- when we could catch him to put the saddle on. Mrs. Mandy (Davis' Mom), had to cook for a large bunch of kids. Davis was the youngest of six boys and three girls. Mr. Alex (Davis Dad) said that I was eating grobeck at a meal one time. A grobeck is a large skinny black bird that lived in the swamp. It may have been gorbeck stew. I don't know. What I do know is it sure was good eating.

One time Davis, Calvin (Davis cousin) and I went riding in the back of Mr. Dewey Callegan's (Calvin's Dad) pickup truck. Mr. Dewey, his wife and her mother rode inside the truck. We rode in the fields and along the canal looking for cattle I think. Well, Mr. Dewey was a tobacco chewer and Davis was sitting on the driver's side in the pickup bed. He picked his spot first and argued to keep it. I was on the opposite side and Calvin was behind the passenger side close to the cab. Mr. Dewey was doing about thirty-five or forty miles an hour and had to spit. He did and most of it his Davis right in the chest. He had a white tee shirt on. It was really nasty. Davis hollowed and started cursing his uncle who could not hear him inside the cab. His aunt and her mother was looking out of the back window of the pickup because they could tell there was something going on and started laughing so loud that I could hear them. Calvin and I was laughing too. We were also very happy that we did not pick that side of the truck bed to ride in. I believe Davis may have thrown that tee shirt away. It had tobacco juice all over it.

THE GUITAR

When I was about fourteen, I ordered a guitar from Santa Clause instead of a 410 shotgun. It came at Christmas time. It was a large Spanish style guitar. When we moved to town, I took it with me. It was either in 1958 or 1959 that I traded my guitar with Bobby Pearce for his guitar. Neither one of us could play them. Bobby's guitar was smaller than mine; it was white and had a caring case, which mine did not. During the late 1950s and early 1960s, I wrote several songs. I still have them put away in my guitar case with my guitar. I was afraid to send them off to some publishing company for fear that they steel my songs. I wrote them for me, or Elvis or Jerry Lee or Little Richard or Larry Williams to sing and record. Since I did not trust any of the guys to be fair and record my songs and give me my half of the revenues they would bring in, I never sent them off. Over the years, a few songs had the same subject matter as mind did. This had to be by coincidence as the only person to see my songs was Nicky (Crowbar) Guercio in 1964 when we went to Spencer Business College in Baton Rouge, together. We retyped the songs then. This was the last time they were retyped. Maybe I ought to put them in this book. Hummmmm. Maybe not. I still have not gotten them copyrighted- yet and I still do not trust folks to do right by me. And after all, they were written for the Rock and Roll era. I just have to wait until the new Rock and Role era come or change them to the Blues, which is my first love.

It is now the year 2001 and I still have Bobby's guitar. I still cannot play it, but I enjoy taking it out of its case every now and again, cleaning it and making like I can play it. My brother-in-law came to my house in August this year. He used to play a guitar when he had one. I showed him my old guitar and he started playing some Blues, which we both love and turning the knobs trying to tune it. After a while a string broke. He was upset that he broke a string and I told him to not worry about it. The strings on this guitar are over forty-five years old. It is time for something to give. When I get a little more time on my hands, I will get new strings put on it and have my guitar tuned and learn to play the Blues. This is a goal of mine to play the guitar and sing the Blues.

I saw Bobby at our friend, Donald (Duck) Auction's funeral earlier this year. I asked about my old guitar. He does not remember what happened to my old guitar that I swapped with him many years ago. I told him that I still have his and he is not getting it back. Bobby said "no problem, I never learned to play it anyway." And that was that.

MR. ALEX'S 1954 CHEVY

In the early part of 1959, Davis Callegan would drive up to White Castle from his home at Lone Star near the White Castle Canal. His dad (Mr. Alex) would let him borrow his car. The car was a 1954 Chevy four door Belliare, I believe. It looked pretty good from the outside but most of Davis's brothers had used this car and Mr. Alex thought that it might have transmission or rear end problems. Mr. Alex would tell Davis not to cross the railroad tracks in down town White Castle because the car may fall apart.

Davis would come by my house on Adams Drive in White Castle (this was before we moved back to the Plantation), and pick me up. We would putt-putt around South White Castle. We go by the high school. Park at the tennis courts which was between the baseball field and the school gym and just hang around. If someone was there, we would stay and just mess around. If no one was there, there was nothing to do. All the action was in down town at Mr. Eskine's pool hall, where teenagers hung around, and the Chat & Chew, where Duck worked, and several gas stations where some of our friend's worked and hung around their Daddy's station. We was restricted to the dead part of town, if a baseball game or tennis game was not going on we were in the right place. Sometimes there was roller skating at the gym.

We parked near the railroad tracks several times and walked to see where the action was. These spots were close to the tracks. In fact, all of North White Castle was close to the tracks. There were only about three blocks from the tracks to the River. But this is where most of the business places was.

One time we met up with Bobbie Bourgeois and Dot Irwin at the tennis courts. They wanted to go riding so we all jumped in the old Chevy and rode around a little. Before long, they wanted to know why each time we got the tracks, we turned around and traveled the same street back to the tennis court. I do not remember if we told them the rules or not. They wanted to go across the railroad tracks. This was something we had never done before in this car. But the girls wanted to go. So off we went. It took us about two minutes to cross those damn tracks. I was happy that there was not any traffic that night. We could have crawled both sets of tracks four times in the time it took us to cross. But we made it and we listened with the radio off for something big to fall off. But it never did. We were happy now. This paved the way for later trips across the tracks. We could not afford for anything to go wrong on this side of the tracks.

My thoughts was that Davis had a lot of older brothers. He was the baby of the family, and I always hoped we would not get caught by on of them. I am sure that they knew of Mr. Alex's rule to not cross the track in this car. We had made it. We headed to River Road at the end of Bowie Street which was the main street in town. This was the same River Road that past in front of the house on the Plantation where I used to live and would live again with the next year or so. But this part of River Road was

Southeast of White Castle. The part of River Road that I used to live on was one mile Northwest of White Castle. Or something like that. Let's just say that it was a different part of River Road.

Bowie Street went from the River all the way to SamsTown, I believe. All the bars and pool halls, the bank, clothing and furniture stores, city hall, the fire station, both hospitals, the Western Auto, appliances stores, food stores, Ford Dealership, jewelry store, all the drug stores, picture show (before it closed down), the baseball field, tennis courts, high school, and a gas station or two were all on Bowie Street. Bowie Street was White Castle.

We headed toward the White Castle Ferry, although I do not remember it being installed there yet. Davis got in the back seat with Dot and Bobbie moved to the front seat with me. I was driving now. While Davis and Dot was wrestling about some disagreement they had, Bobbie was steering the car while I had my foot on the gas to control the slow speed we were going. I did not want to go fast, hit a pot hole and lose a transmission or rear end this far across the railroad tracks that we were not suppose to cross.

I never would give up my driver's position. It just looked like two persons was driving the car. We were close together and this made me feel really good. I suppose I should have told her that. But I was a bashful boy. Davis was not

As I was finally about to put my right arm around Bobbie who was really leaning on me, Dot finished kicking Davis's ass in the back seat and words were said and the party was over. I never did put my arm around Bobbie Bourgeois. My loss.

Davis came back to the front seat to drive. Bobbie got back in the back seat with Dot and we made the trip back to the tennis courts where we found them, again taking two minutes to cross the railroad tracks.

Later during the year, Mr. Alex purchased a brand new 1959 Ford Galaxy. Four of his sons bought new 1959 Fords also. Floyd, Joe, Curtice and J. D. all purchased new cars if I am not mistaken. Davis and I rode in all of them at one time or another. His bothers used to take turns dropping us off at the Youth Center dances in Plaquemine and picking us up when it was over.

When Davis came over with his brother J. D. driving, my momma always like to talk with and see J.D. He had the rugged prize fighter's face. Momma would call him Crook, because she thought he looked like a gangster from the movies. She would ask, "is the Crook going to pick you up tonight?" J. D. was a good guy. All of Davis's brothers and sisters were good guys. Two of Davis's sisters used to take us out also.

J. D. had this girlfriend in Plaquemine named Jackie. She was a very pretty girl and so was her little sister, Dickey Lee, who was several years younger than Davis and I. We would sometimes go with J.D. to pick up Jackie before he dropped us off at the Youth Center when we were early. We did this often enough for them to get to know me.

Several years later, J. D. and Jackie got married. A number of years after that, Dickey Lee married Eddie Boy Boudeaux Jr. who was also from White Castle. Eddie Boy was the son of Mr. Eddie Boudeaux who was our Chief of Police. He was a year younger than Davis and I, but a grade higher in school. Yea, I think he was smart.

LEON MILLER BASEBALL STORY AS DADDY TOLD IT

As I mentioned before, Leon loved baseball. Occasionally a group of white guys would play hardball with a group of black guys all from the plantation. They played in the mule pasture.

There was a very large area where the home plate was about four hundred fifty to five hundred feet from the fence of the pasture. Pass the fence was a large drainage ditch than the shoulders for La.1 then La.1, than the shoulder on the other side of La.1, than some ground than a ditch then the gravel for the Texas and Pacific Railroad tracks. All this was just to give you the lay of the land. The field/pasture was really wide also, so foul line were decided before the game would start.

I should have mentioned long before now the Leon was a little clumsy. He was also tongue tied. When he got excited, nobody could understand what he said until he calmed down. When he talked with you, he kind of looked up and sideways. He did not always look straight at you all the time. His eyes would roll upwards. NOW back to the GAME.

As Daddy called this game.

Leon is a bat in the bottom of the ninth. The black pitcher reared back and threw a fast ball. Leon reared back an swung at it, this time with his eyes opened. He hit it. Boy did he hit it. It was well hit. A very long fly ball to deep center and over the center fielder's head. Leon threw the bat down and started for first base. He fell down. He got up fairly quickly and again started for first, made eight steps and fell down again. He got up and took off again. He rounded first base and fell down. He jumped back up and headed for second. At the same time that Leon was rounding the bases, the center fielder, when the ball flew way over his head, threw down his glove and started running in the direction that the ball was going. He had to stop and get through the barbed wire fence, which he got snagged on, got himself loose and had to wait for several cars to pass by on La.1. In the main time Leon had made it to second base and tripped on it and fell down. He got up made six more steps and tripped and fell down again. He is back up and heading for third. At this time the center fielder had crossed La.1 and was by the railroad tracks looking for the ball in the weeds and tall grass. He found it and ran back to La.1 where he had to wait for a dump truck and several sedans to pass, ran back across the highway, jumped the ditch got his britches caught again in the barbed wire. At this time, Leon was approaching third which he fell head first into. Everyone, both the black and white fans were cheering and hollowing and jumping up and down. Some were so excited that they were hitting each other with the hats. Leon rounded third base- and - yes he fell down again. He pulled himself up and started for home. Now the center fielder got unstuck and fell through the fence back onto the playing field. He ran twenty or thirty feet and threw the ball to the short stop which was his cut off man and who had ran toward center to be in position for the throw. He turned just after catching the ball and fired it to the catcher. Leon had fallen two more times but was up again and steaming toward home plate. The catcher, without any catching gear whatsoever, not even a mitt, and in tennis shows, was trying to block the plate. Here came the ball, here came Leon. There was a big cloud of dust and mule turds flying everywhere. Even the spectators had to duck for cover. When the dust and turds had settled, the catcher had the ball and Leon was two feet from home plate. He was OUT at the plate. The black folks rejoiced and sang praises to the LORD. The white folks hung there heads in sorrow about the game that got way from them. Leon wanted to know what happened. The game was over. As everyone was leaving, Leon shouted, "YALL WANNA PLAY TOMORROW?"

MY SISTER'S WEDDING

My sister was graduated from high school the end of May in 1958. She married Gene Bertrand on June 7, 1958 at the Our Lady of Prompt Succor Catholic Church in White Castle. The after wedding reception was held at a hall on the River Road in White Castle.

There was a band to play music and alcoholic beverages and food and cake served to the invited guest.

I was fifteen years old at the time and very much in my shy shell. This is the shell that made one not outgoing, the bashful shell which stayed with me until my mid thirties. At least I think I outgrew that shell in my mid thirties- I don't know. It may have been my mid forties during my separation and ultimate divorce from my first wife that I came out of my shell.

At my sister's wedding, I remember that Cousin Fallon and Jabbie Trabeau and their four daughters was there. Or maybe three of their four daughters was there. The girls names are, Gloria, Jackie, Sharon and Delta, who was the youngest. Sharon is my age and Delta is a year or two younger. All the girls were very pretty. I remember thinking what a shame it was that they are my cousins. Being raised a Catholic meant that you should not get serious about your cousin. It was a sin. I was afraid to get serious with a girl who would by my sixth cousin. Where does the cousin business stop with the Catholics? I had some pretty girl cousins but would not ask them out on a date because I was afraid it might lead to a Mortal Sin. That is the big one -you know. When I was around the Trabeau girls or any Quatreuingts, or Tulliers, and some other cousins, I was especially careful because we were double cousins. Explain that you ask! Alright, I will.

My mamma's daddy and his sister was Correls. They married a brother and sister who was Quatrevingts. So a brother and sister married a brother and sister. All the children from these unions became double first cousins. They are first cousins on their daddy's side and first cousins on the momma's side. Hence, double first cousins.

The Trabeau girls were my mamma's double second cousins and my double third cousins- I believe. Anyway, being Catholic and having this cousin thing over your head, can you imagine if you had a relationship with any of your double cousins what will happen to you. I can. You would double burn in Hell. I just could not afford to do/chance that. Anyway, I was bashful. So I kept my distance from all my girl cousins no matter how far down the line they were. This also applied to the Breauxs, Sanchezs, Richards, Bertrands (who I thought was my cousins because my sister married one) and the Giroirs (whose family my brother married into).

Many cousins and friends attended my sister's wedding. The Boudreauxs from New Orleans was there. Uncle Henry and Aunt Bertha and much of their family attended. My cousin, Paul Boudreax, was the youngest of this family. He was about two or three years older than me. Paul was a bookworm and a scientist to be. He was into designing rockets and shooting them into the air. He made/mix fuels to make that happen. He was a very smart guy.

My sister's wedding became a coming out party for my cousin, Paul. Several of the Trabeau girls taught him how to dance at the wedding. I watched as he changed before my eyes. He became outgoing, developed a personality and danced every dance. Paul was having so much fun and I wanted to dance also but was just to bashful to try.

Aunt Bertha said that Paul had never took the time to even look at girls before this day. She and Uncle Henry and his two older sisters and their husbands was happy to see Paul having such a great time. Aunt Bertha called momma two weeks after the wedding and told her that Paul had a girlfriend, his first ever. As soon as they got back home to New Orleans, he started looking for a girl that he could go steady with.

A year or two later, Paul attended Tulane University, got his degree and for a while taught at LSU. He was one of the youngest Professors there, if not the youngest. This is where he was the last time I talked with him. This was in the late 1960s or very early 1970s. When he left LSU, he went to Washington, D.C. to work for the Federal Government, I believe. The last I heard about him was that he had FBI and/or CIA clearance. For what, I do not know. It was during the 1970s that I heard this from mamma who talked with Aunt Bertha.

I used to see my cousins Sharon and Delta Traubeau at the Youth Center dances in Plaquemine on a regular basis. I cannot remember if we ever danced. You know- this Catholic and cousin thing that I had in my head.

I just recently found out that my cousin, Delta, published a book of poems that she wrote in 1993 which was inspired by our Lord, Jesus Christ. My friends, Davis and Cathy Callegan gave two of her books to me on a trip I made back to White Castle area in November 2001. I gave one to my sister, who already had one but it was not autographed by Delta like the one that I gave to her. I enjoyed reading the poems very much. Yes, I believe Delta had inspiration from our Lord to complete these works of art. She even noted the date and time of day that she received the inspiration. I am very proud of my cousin. And I now want to publicly apologize to Delta for calling her "Delta Tank," which was the name of a company in Plaquemine that manufactured storage tanks. It just seemed like a natural thing to do at that time. I am sorry for it. I must be getting old. I am trying to make piece with family, cousins, friends and God.

NINTH AND TENTH GRADE SHENANIGANS

I took Agriculture for five years in school. I started in the eighth grade. All this time, I was a member of The Future Farmers of America Club or the FFA as it was referred to. Jervis (Pee Wee) Campesi was our chapter president in high school senior class.

The Agriculture classes were in a building away from the school proper. It was off by itself behind the gym. To the right of the Ag classroom was the school shop where I learned to weld and cut steel with a cutting torch and do very little carpenter work. This was tied into the Ag learning. To the left of the shop started Mr. Bill (Easy) Brown's yard that was fenced in. Mr. Brown and his family lived upstairs above the school cafeteria. Easy Bill Brown was the school's maintenance and handy man. He was nicknamed Easy because of his great disposition and slow movements when he move around. Easy never seemed to get in a rush or hurry whatever the situation was. He was constant and kept a cool head. I never saw anything that Easy Bill Brown could not handle in my thirteen years at this school. He was respected by all the kids, even though they put the Easy Bill moniker on him. To the right of the cafeteria was an open play ground area. This open area was about forty yards behind the three story main class building. All these building, the Ag classroom, the shop, the yard, Mr. Brown's Quarters and the cafeteria, faced a public street that cut through the school property. The baseball field was on the back playground across this street. Later a football and track field would be located there also.

From the shop to the open field past the cafeteria was about fifty-five yards.

Mr. Leo C. Carmouche was our Ag teacher. He also taught shop. I liked Mr. Carmouche very much. He was truly a good guy and would try and help you if he could. He gave me a lot of help and advice. But other kids did not like him so much. Mr. Carmouche was different than the other teachers, but I cannot explain how or why.

He liked to smoke a pipe which he did in class many times. He would leave has pipe on the black board eraser shelf when not in use. On several occasions, some guys, I honestly do not know who, or I would tell all here and now, would take his pipe behind his back and put some horse shit in it and replace a little tobacco on top. I remember word getting around to us before our group went to Ag class that Carmoushe's pipe had been set up.

I guess he would forget that his usually habit was to place his pipe on the eraser shelf empty, because we saw him pick it up as he was talking to us and get ready to put some tobacco in it, but notice that it already had tobacco in it. He put his tobacco pouch away and grab his box of wood matches. We were all sitting there in disbelief. He lit her up. I do not think any one of us could remember what he was teaching at that time because we all had our attention on the match and his pipe.

He sucked in several times as you normally do when lighting a pipe. The tobacco got lit. He made several more puffs and had that baby smoking. It was all any of us could do to not fall to the floor laughing. We were holding back as best we could. Some guys had their heads down so Mr. Carmouche could not see them. Some put their note pads over their faces and some used their hand over their mouths to keep from laughing. I had both hands over my face just rubbing up and down and rocking in my chair.

In this class we usually sat four to a table. This class did not have desks. We had about fourteen students in the class.

Mr. Carmouche smoked his pipe for about ten minutes. We all had settled down by this time and figured that the other class before ours had lied to us or Carmouche was just too stupid to notice, or maybe horse shit was the same as tobacco. We did not know what to think, so we were getting back into the class subject matter when all of a sudden, Mr. Carmouche made a funny face. He puffed again, shook his head like gesturing no and took another puff. We all knew that something was up. He usually stood near the front side door nearest the cut through street when he taught. We normally entered the classroom through the back door which was facing the back of the gym. There was a cut through from the main three story building between the girls' bathroom and the gym on one side and the cafeteria, Easy Brown's yard, and the shop on the other side to get to the back door.

Mr. Carmouche walked out of the front side door and started spitting and cleaning out his pipe. Some of us did laugh out loud but muffled it as best we could. He did not hear the commotion we were making or even if he did, he had his mind set on emptying that pipe. After a minute or two he came back into the classroom, placed his now empty pipe on the eraser shelf, started to walk to his desk which was across the room from the front side door, than stopped suddenly. He retraced his steps back to the eraser shelf, picked up his pipe, walked over to his desk, opened a draw and placed the pipe in it. He had a look of disgust on his face but did not say anything about his recent experience to our class. Of course we had one hell of a story to tell; which we all did, over and over and over. I felt sort of sorry for Mr. Carmouche. But not too sorry to not tell anyone what I saw.

Mr. Carmouche had this other habit. After lighting his pipe he would blow out the match and place it back into the match box. He did not throw it on the ground as most folks did. He was not going to litter. Several times during my high school career, I saw him with several fingers on his right hand bandaged. He would not blow the match out completely and place it in the match box and the whole thing lit up in his hand. You would think after you did this one time, you would not do it again. I did mention that Mr. Carmouche was sort of different.

Some boys also stuffed Irish potatoes in the exhaust tailpipe of his car. This was done to his car several times and to other teachers as well. The compression that would build up when trying to start the engine was so high that it would blow a hole in the muffler and/or blow the potato about forty feet and make a very loud bang. You did not want to stand behind a car with a potato in the tailpipe. When we heard this noise, we knew what it meant. This was not a good thing to do nor was it funny. I often thought that if I know who did this, I would like to do it to their car or truck. I do not think that they would have like it one bit.

OTHER WILD TIMES IN AG CLASS

Lester (Beaver) Hebert, Calvin (Poochie) Colliet, Davis (DAC) Callegan, Jervis (Pee Wee) Campesi, Jean (Lil Jean) Austin, Barry (Butch) Raffray- that's me, and others whose names escape me, went to Ag class in the afternoon each day.

Beaver usually sat up front near the front side door by the cut through street. Poochie sat at the table near the wall at the back of the classroom closer to the back door facing the gym. Davis and I always sat the table closest the back door. Poochie and another guy sat at the next table over from our. So he was not really close to the back door.

Poochie had larger than normal size ears and was very self-conscience about it. He did not like to be teased about it at all. He was a big guy and was ready to fight in a hurry when he got teased. At all other time he was a really easy going guy.

When Poochie and I were little kids and he was still living on Cedar Grove Plantation, his nickname was Rabbit because of his ears. Even very young, he kicked enough butt and Rabbit was dropped many years before we got into high school. When we were in high school, the only person I ever heard call him Rabbit was my Daddy because he could not remember Poochie or Calvin, which was his real name. Momma used to get on Daddy about calling him Rabbit.

Anyway, some days Beaver would tease Poochie in Ag class or either make fun of Mr. Carmouche when his back was turned. It was about fifty-fifty which one he would try and agitate each day.

Sometimes, Mr. Carmouche like to stand in the middle of the room when he taught. He usually paced in an area in the middle of the classroom. From this location, he could talk and turn and ask questions and point to student that he wanted the answers from.

When Beaver was mocking Mr. Carmouche, he would make gesture about his bald head. Like the glare from the lights bouncing off Mr. Carmouche's head was blinding him. Of course this made us laugh. Beaver also made like he was flogging his log and when it popped off, the juice went into the air and hit Carmoushe on his bald head. He acted out all these things and he was really good at it. It almost seemed real. With Carmouche pacing back and forth with his attention on my side of the class most of the time, and his back to Beaver, the beaver got really animated. We would use our handkerchief and stuff it in our mouth, hide behind out text or composition books. We grunted, coughed, turned away from Carmouche's view, and did what ever we could to not laugh out loud. Beaver would stick pencils in his ears, his nose, his anywhere and just kept the class in stitches. Poochie would laugh at these antics along with the rest of us.

When Beaver wasn't making fun of Carmouche, it was usually Poochie that got the treatment. He would hold a composition book/pad on each side of his head, as ears and point to Poochie.

Or he hold one composition book/pad to one ear and with his free arm make like it was an elephant's trunk and raise it up and down. This was calling Poochie "elephant ears."

Beaver did all this when Carmouche's back was turned to him. We just could not always control ourselves and there would be a burst of sudden laughter. Carmouche would ask us what's up. We always said nothing. He would ask if we like to share with the class and we would answer "no Sir." He never did press any of us to fess up or rat fink on The Beaver. But he knew something was going on behind his back. He would whorl around really fast to try and catch Beaver but The Beav was very fast and never got caught by Carmouche much to our amazement.

Poochie on the other hand would get so mad that his face would turn blood red. Boy he really lit up. His neck and arms, everything would turn red. We could see all this and Poochie would grit his teeth and when Carmouche would spend around to try and catch Beaver, Poochie would point at him and mouth "I am going to kill you," which we all believed he would do it he got a hold of Beaver at that time. We would all be on alert because if Poochie ever jumped on anybody to do bodily harm, it was going to take all of us to get him off.

Every time Beaver teased Poochie, as the class was near it end, Beaver would start edging his chair closer to his door at the front side exit. Poochie would start edging his chair closer to my table to be near the rear exit.

We all had to go toward the main three story building to get to our next class. Beaver went into the building, Poochie and the rest of us went near it to go to the side entrance of the gym for PE. The bell would ring and they were off. We would not get in front of Poochie because he would just run over us. Beaver was out the front door like he was shot out of a canon. We would all and I mean all, everyone in the class would run to the path that

Poochie went because it was a shorter distance to get to our next class and also to see it Poochie was going to catch Beaver this time.

Beaver had to run around the shop, Easy Bill Brown's yard, the length and the width of the cafeteria, than the open space of about forty yards to get to the entrance door of the main building.

Poochie, by bar had the shortest run. Thank God that Beaver was much faster. Beaver was a short stocky kid about five foot, maybe. Pochie was stocky but about five feet ten inches tall. We all run to see it today would be the day we had to gang up on Poochie to keep him from killing Beaver. I can still see this race for life (Beaver's life), in my minds eye. Beaver making it all the way around those building, his short legs just a pumping, and Poochie cutting across between the buildings. Poochie reaching his arm out to grab Beaver but just could not catch him before he ran out of gas. This allowed Beaver to get to the large door, open it and be gone down the hall before Poochie could get there.

I believe Poochie even tried to lose weight one time to make him a little faster, but it still did not work. There were many times that Poochie was just an arms length away, than faded badly only to live and run another day.

This happened two or three times a week. Poochie was such a good natured fellow that he got over the teasing quickly after it stopped. He did not hold a grudge and would just forget it ever happened until the next day when Beaver would start it all over again and the race was on. We actually made bets some days. It was days the Beaver looked pooped out or Poochie was really pumped up and feeling good. We would make the bets in class when Carmouche was not looking at us.

Poochie never did catch Beaver that year. Mr. Carmouche never caught him in the act either but knew the little bastard was up to something all year long. But Carmouche got even. He failed The

Beaver that year and so did some of the other teachers. Beaver finished high school the year after we all did. We all took it hard at year end when we found out that Beaver failed. But if he stayed with us, we may have all failed eventually. He just entertained another gang of kids.

Mr. Carmouche had a saying that he used each time he saw one of the students in his classroom looking at the clock. He used this saying on me several times during my five years in his classroom. The saying was "time is passing, are you?"

CHAPTER 12

SNEAKING INTO CLASSROOMS DURING RECESS: AGES SIXTEEN AND UP

As far as I remember, it started in the eighth grade. Some of the guys would sneak back into a classroom during recess to change answers/add answers to a test paper or just replace the paper outright.

The doors to each classroom was about nine feet tall. Over the door was a glass window on a swivel. It could be pushed opened. The top section would come into the hall and the bottom of the one piece window would go into the classroom. This made it easy for two guys to get into the room. One would have to lift the other up high enough so he could push on the bottom of the window frame, get a hold on the window sill, lift himself up, climb through the window, drop down into the classroom and unlock the door for his accomplice.

Apparently this had been done on a routine basis when I found out about it. I do not know who started it but I eventually participated in a couple of the intrusions as lookout.

I remember a time that we entered Mr. Clarence Elliott's classroom on the third floor by the means I mentioned earlier. I do not remember all the players but beside me, Alvin (Slim) Barbier, Bobby Pearce, Gerald (Termite) Hebert, and one or two others were in attendance. A couple of the guys were changing test answers on their paperwork. I never changed any of my papers.

While up there, Slim had to pee. He was nervous and had to pee bad. We used to write in ink with fountain pens. I don't think that there were many ball point pens around back then. I found an ink jar and told Slim to pie in this jar. He grabbed it and started his pee operation. He soon realized that it would not be large enough and said so. Someone found a used paper coffee cup in Mr. Elliott's trash can that held the balance of Slim's pee. He closed the lid on the now very full ink jar and put it back on the desk that I took it from. We made our escape back to the playground just before the bell rang to go to our next class.

Several days later, we are all sitting in class. We had about thirty kids in the classroom. Eleven boys and the rest girls. They outnumbered us almost two for one all through high school and I was too bashful or stupid to take advantage of it. We had a nice girl crop. Woe is me. While in class, Doris Ruth (Dot) Irvin blurted out, "Mr. Elliott, this ink taste like, hee, hee, hee, well it taste like pee." Mr. Elliott did not believe Dot. She insisted. Five or six of us in the class knew that it was in fact pee and started to worry a little and wished she would shut up. I looked at Slim; he had a real worried and scared look on his face. I motioned with my palms down to stay clam.

Dot had this thing about putting pencils and fountain pen tips on her lips. It was just a habit of hers. She did not even know that she did this. She wanted Mr. Elliott to taste the ink. He would not. We all laughed at her preposterous statement. She challenged the whole class to taste her ink. Nobody did. She stated that she was not going to use that ink anymore. The class said good, don't use it. And she quit saying anything about it, but let out that big hardy laugh of hers every now and then. Of course, when she laughed, the whole class laughed also. Slim now had a look of relief on his face. This is another one of the things that happened that I never told anyone before. Keeping a secret for forty four years is long enough. Anyway, poor old Slim pass on a number of years ago. I think Dot is still with us though. If she ever read this passage, she will be vindicated and I am sure will tell all her friends that she was right when she made those statements well over forty years ago.

A year or two later, I was lookout on the bottom floor for a sneak in into Miss. Gilmore's Science classroom. Some of the same guys as in the past was involved.

The school started enforcing the rule of no students in the building during recess unless you had a pass. They also had a teacher do hall monitoring during recess. Miss. Gilmore was actually the hall monitor the day of the sneak in into her classroom.

I caught a glimpse of her shadow on the other side of the building on the bottom/first floor. I gave the warning signal, which I do not remember what is was, than to buy time for my friends made a noise that she heard to come and investigate. She waddled herself over to the side of the building where I was. I could here her coming all the way. She was trying to walk fast. I had to get her into this side hall so the guys could get out of her classroom into the big hall and take another side exit. She rounded the corner, I was now making like I was drinking water from the fountain. She said, "Barry, fellow, what are you doing in here?" I said, "getting a drink of water, Miss. Gilmore." Which she retorted, "don't you know you should not be in here?" Why are you not drinking water outside?" I made up the story that the water inside the building was cooler than the water at the outside fountains. She order me to get out.

At this time, she had one hand on my shoulder. Miss. Gilmore used to like to touch the boys and hit them too. I don't think she or Mrs. Goutreaux liked boys very much. As I turned to head for the exit door, I notice her right arm being raised. This old woman could hit hard, I already knew that. She had her left hand on my left shoulder now that I had my back to her. Her right arm was cocked and ready to come down on my behind with a lot of force as I walked away. Well, surprise! surprise! I started to run and broke away from her grasp, which did not happen very often-I really surprised her. I look back after taking several running steps and saw her arm with the large hand attached, follow through so hard that she fell off balance into the other side of the hall wall. She would have lifted me off the floor if she made contact. I hit the door a running and met up with my buddies outside. They all wanted to know what she did to me. I told them what happened and my only pain was in my left shoulder that she had a hold onto when I broke away. We all had a good laugh, but my shoulder hurt for most of the rest of the day. This was a very powerful and strong old woman.

A PROBLEM WITH TEST PAPERS

Here we go again. One time the guys snuck into Miss Gilmore's classroom to make changes on their test papers. They improved on their old method of just writing correct answers on the original papers to making a completely new paper and exchanging it for the old test paper. I do not really know how they did this, but they did. It was quicker to get in and out this way. So the risk factor for getting caught was less.

What happened was Bobby Pierce and Termite Hebert was called to the Principal's office. It seemed that on one of our tests, there was two test papers for one of these guys and no test paper for the other. It took Miss Gilmore a while to figure on this before getting the Principal involved. She first ended up with the two test pages with the same name than she had to figure or go to the roll call for class that day to see how many of us was there to take the test, than find out whose test papers she did not have. The two boys said that they did not know what happened. I never did find out how this mess was resolved. I believe the teacher could tell by the hand writing on the two papers that they were from the same person. I am inclined to believe that both boys received a zero for that test. I do not ever remember sneaking back into a classroom at recess after this. I got out of the "lookout business." The teachers may have also tightened up security also. They definitely knew that something was up.

One time in Miss Gilmore's Biology class, we each had a section in the book to read. David Callegan had started teasing Poochie about his ears before we went into the classroom. We all sat in individual desks. These were the curved type desk with a high back. It was a two piece desk with the top part bolted to the seat and storage part. This was a very sturdy desk. Davis was sitting in the middle of a row. Poochie about two rows over and further back. It was Davis's turn to read a paragraph. His section happened to have the work "years" written about eight times in it. Each person had to stand to read. When he got to this word, he used "ears" instead of years. After the second time he used it, several of us looked back at Poochie, and sure enough, his neck and face was getting red. Davis kept reading and said "ears" again as he was trying very hard not to laugh. So were the rest of us who knew what was going on. Davis read on. Several of us was trying to smother out laughter. Davis said the word again and Poochie just could not stand it anymore. He jumped out up out of his seat. We all jumped when he did this. My thought was, boy the shit is going to hit the fan now and it will be Callegan shit. Poochie shouted, "Miss Gilmore, I'm going to kill that boy." Miss Gilmore jumped up from behind her desk and said "Poochie, fellow, what's wrong with you"? She waddled over to where Poochie was standing and got between him and Davis in no time at all. We were all laughing so much, I do not remember if Poochie told her what Davis was doing or not but she told Poochie to calm down and sent Davis to the Principle's office. Which was a place that Davis was very familiar with.

Davis was used to going to the Principle's office. Miss Gilmore sent him there every day whether he deserved it or not.

There was this rule of not talking between classes. We had to come down to the bottom floor for Miss Gilmore's class from the third floor. She would be waiting at the foot of the stairs where the entrance to her classroom was. Davis and I would walk down together every day. We did this for four years. Miss Gilmore taught ninth grade Science, tenth grade Biology, eleventh grade Biology II and Lab and another subject we had to pass in the twelfth grade as well. She taught all the Science courses.

One day before we started down from the top floor, Davis told me not to talk to him because he was not going to the office today. He did not talk. He did not say one word. We got to the bottom and there was Miss Gilmore pointing to Davis and told him to go to the Principal's office, he ask why? I did not say a word. Did you hear me talk, he said. No, she remarked, I did not hear you today but you must have done something so go get a slip to come into my class. This is when I really knew that she was picking on him.

Other students had problems with two female teachers. They did not like girls who wore makeup in class. It is a shame what those two women did to several girls because they wore some makeup or did not like the way the girls dressed. They would physically grab and hold them while rubbing the makeup all over their face. This was done on numerous occasions. I witnessed it several times. In the 1980s, teachers would have been sued for doing what these two did during the fifties and sixties.

Several times a week, a female teacher would grab a hold of Davis and shake him in his desk. She would push him down in his seat with his head on the backrest of the desk. With one hand she would hold his hair to keep his head on the backrest and with the palm of the other hand; she would smash it into his forehead four or five times. She would leave a read palm print on his forehead. The back of his head was taking a beating as well. One time she remarked as she was pounding him, "I try and try and try to teach you and all I ever get out of you is a hand full of grease." Davis did use a lot of Vaseline hair tonic in his hair to help keep it in place, and perhaps so our teacher would have to wash her hands after women handling him. I think there was a man inside of her, because she grabbed a hold of me one time in the tenth grade. I must have made a smart ass remark or something. I usually got away with such things, but not this day. As I was in my desk, she grabbed both my arms near my shoulders and starting jerking me up and down. I was a bigger than average guy and was holding on to my desk as hard as I could. She was lifting me and my desk off the floor. I got the message and never acted cute in her class again. At least I never got caught again, because I chewed gum in her class every day and every other class I ever had. Chewing gum was against the rules.

I did have the personally that allowed me to get away with a lot of remarks and gestures that if anyone else tried, especially Davis, would have been punished for or had to get a slip form the Principal after being thrown out of the class.

I am proud to state that in thirteen years of school, I never was sent to the Principal's office.

MORE TENTH GRADE WOES

In the Tenth grade I failed Biology and Algebra I. I still cannot see how I failed either. I had a B average in Algebra. Mrs. Goutreaux taught all the math in high school. As mentioned earlier, Miss Gilmore taught all the sciences.

I went to summer school in Plaquemine to make up these classes along with many others from White Castle High. The same teachers who failed us wanted to have summer school in White Castle. Us kids would not have any of that shit, so we went to Plaquemine. I saw several of the White Castle teachers there trying to get a summer teaching job. They did not hire any- thank God.

I made some new friends while in summer school that lasted until I left Louisiana for Texas in 1979. I made friends with kids from Donaldsonville, Plaquemine, Brusly, and guys from down Bayou Plaquemine.

I made an A in both subjects during summer school. Both teachers and the Principal there did not know why I was there. The Plaquemine High Principal wrote a letter to the White Castle Principal about it. My first day back to regular school in White Castle, the new Principal, Mr. Lyle J. Docoute came to find me. He showed me the letter that the Plaquemine Principal wrote and said that it was part of my file. I told him that I thought that I got screwed, and I did not deserve to fail. I don't know if it had anything to do with the letters from the Plaquemine folks or not, but the next year Mrs. Goutreaux was gone. And two years later, Miss Gilmore retired also. Of course these old women were old enough to retire and that is what most likely happen. They just retired.

I got hurt two ways going to summer school that year. I could have driven a dump truck on the Plantation for most of that summer at eighty-five cents and hour. The other thing was that I had to pay for the two classes with my own money. I had worked all the summer before in the sugar cane field for forty three cent an hour. I started a saving account at the White Castle Bank of Commerce owned by Mr. Cleve Joseph and had saved a total of fifty five dollars that year. It cost me fifty dollars for the two classes. I know that I would have made over two hundred dollars driving dump truck that summer. I never got that opportunity again because that was the year that all the big ditches and canals were re-dug out for better drainage. Mr. Reed Ardoin would dig out the canals with a drag line and put the dirt/mud directly into a dump truck and it was taken to a place on the plantation that had a low spot and dumped. Ronald Mabile and Wayne Henry were two of the kid drivers. I did drive a little on Saturdays when Mr. Reed worked. None of us had driver's licenses to drive dump trucks. But we stayed on private property, most of the time.

After paying for summer school with the hard earned money I made the summer before, I promised myself that I will never fail again. And I didn't. In the end, I am happy that my Daddy made me pay for my summer school; it taught me a big lesson on the value of a dollar. I should have done this same thing when two of my sons failed in college. I should have let them come home, get a job, earn their own money, than go back to school. Instead I kept pouring my hard earned money down the drain. I would have another eighty or so thousand dollars in the bank by now. I am counting the interest I would have made also if I did not pay for them to retake classes that I had already paid for. I did not know at the time that both would eventually quit college and not go back. I feel that I lost this amount of money because my two sons does not have a college degree. If they would have degrees, it would have been money well spent, as the money I spent on their brother who has two degrees. I paid for one of his degrees; he paid for the other and is thinking of paying for still a third degree. Well, more power to him. Carry on, Lane.

SHRIMPING IN THE BIG MUDDY

The Big Muddy is the Mississippi River of course. The plantation owned over a mile of river frontage. Whoever owns the property along the river's edge owns the right to use the levee and all the way to the river itself. Some places on the Mississippi River the distance from the levee to the water was a quarter of a mile or so. This section could be fenced in from the edge of the public road on the dry side of the levee to the water at the river's edge. It could be fenced as long as a gate was available for the Levee Board, the Corp of Engineers, and other government officials and workers to have passage onto the levee. There also had to be opening on the top of the levee. Cattle guards were placed at both ends of the property line by the folks who fenced in the levee for cattle or horses or to make hay or all three. The top of the levee holding the Mississippi River within it banks in Iberville Parish was wide enough for two vehicles to pass each other going in opposite directions. During the spring thaw, much water flows down the river on its way to the Gulf of Mexico. We referred to this as the May/June rise. These were the two months when the water level in the river was usually the highest. It took several months for the snow and ice up north and the northeast to melt and finally make its way past our house on the plantation. We lived on River Road about a mile west of White Castle. The gravel road was at the base of the levee. Our yard was where the gravel road ended and the river was on the other side of the levee. During the regular months, we would have to walk over one hundred yards from the bottom of the levee on the river side to get to the water/river. During the May/June rise, the water was hitting the sides of the levee itself. At times it was less than five yards from the top of the levee. All traffic on top of the levee was stopped during these very high water times. The water level was usually higher then the tallest part of the roof on our house. If that levee ever broke at high water, we were gone pecans. Never to be found again.

During the "high water," we and other folks in the area took advantage of it by putting out catfish lines better known as trout lines in the ponds between the river and the levee. Although we could hardly know where the ponds ended and the river began because it was all water. The willow trees marked where the ponds were for us. The trout lines were tied into the tops of the willow trees. Many sixty, seventy, eighty, and even one hundred pound catfishes were caught on these type lines. To do this, one had to have a boat, very strong wire and large strong hooks. The wire/line was tied to the top of the trees and baited. The boat had to be used as transportation to and from the top of the levee to the trout line.

I also caught crawfish in the river during high water. These crawfish were different in color then the canal or spillway variety. These were tan in color or a river sand color. Generally crawfish are reddish in color everywhere else in Louisiana.

Shrimping in the Mississippi River was by far the most exciting and dangerous of anything else we ever tried to do in/on the river. It was hard work and more dangerous than all of the other activities I was involved in.

The times Daddy and I did it, I was not to happy doing it. I do not remember if daddy and my older brother did this or not. Since he was eight years older than me, he was gone from home when I had my experiences shrimping in the Big Muddy with daddy.

Since the river frontage in front of our house did not have a good place or foundation to work from, we went to White Castle for river frontage more suitable. The Corp of Engineers had laid down mats to help stop erosion some years earlier. They do this sort of work when the river is at its lowest level. The mats ran from the bank of the river for about forty feet or so into the water. During the May/June rise, the water would rise higher than the mats. But for about eight or nine months during any year the water level would flow against the mats. Willow trees grew through the mats just as they grow on the banks of the river. The river banks are loaded with willows.

We use to put our shrimp trap out in late June after the river started receding but well before it got completely within normal banks. The trap was made of wood and wire. It was about eighteen to twenty-four inches square. The sides were made of mostly wood. The wire was on the top and bottom. A close mesh type wire was used so the shrimp could not get out. All four sides had six inch holes with the small wire shaped as a funnel inserted and nailed fast to the wood opening at the middle of each side. The funnel shaped wire had the large opening facing the flowing water on the outside part of the trap and the small end -a little over one inch in diameter was on the inside of the trap. It was made this way so the shrimp outside the trap had a large opening to crawl in through. After in the trap, it was harder for them to find their way out through so small an opening.

So we had four funnels leading into the trap. There was one on each side. The trap was large enough that the ends of the funnels did not touch inside. We had a string nailed down with a staple in the middle of the trap to keep the bait secured there. We used throw away chicken parts or beef or fish cut up tied to the string as bait. We also used pumpkins or squash sliced in half and placed in the middle of the trap. Occasionally daddy purchased cotton seed meal which attracted shrimp really well as bait. We also use a small cylinder shaped container made of small mesh wire with a wire trap door to place in the bait into and place it in the middle of the trap. The cylinder had each end made of wire also. This cylinder made the bait last much longer. The shrimp could smell and see the bait but could not get to it easily because of the wire cylinder.

The four entrances made it easier to catch shrimp. The current of the river would move the trap back and forth and sideways. No matter how good or tightly anchored/tied it was to secure it, the current would move it. You wanted one opening always facing the current because the river was moving the shrimp downstream.

To place the box into position was kind of scary. We wanted it to be forty or fifty feet from the water edge. I would tie a rope around my waist. I would pick up the trap and walk up river as far as the rope would let me. We had to pick a spot to place the trap before hand. We had to see that there were no large debris or trees in the path that I needed to take before getting into the water. After getting to the end of my rope, so to speak, I would start into the water. The trap was heavy but I could handle it. I would try to fight the current while keeping the rope between me and daddy taut. At about thigh deep in the river it was really hard going. Trying to hold onto the trap and trying not to step in a crevices of the mat and trying to navigate around young willows was hard. After the first couple of times, it became easier. One thing I learned was not to fight the current. I could not win that battle. Make a good path plan and letting the current take you there was the key to success. The spot we were looking for was always directly in front of daddy. With the life line taut between us, I would tie each corner of the trap to a young willow. We had attached loops on the trap at each corner with length of small ropes tied to each loop. After securing the trap, I would move slightly down stream a few feet and daddy would start pulling me in.

I usually tied off the trap when the river water reached my chess. I always wore long blue jeans and a tee shirt and above the ankle tennis shoes. Even working this close to the bank, one had to be aware of the immediate surroundings and always be on the lookout for driftwood and other floating objects as well as larger than normal snakes. The river takes huge tree trunks and just pulverizes them into splinters along the mats and rocks along the shoreline. This was one of my fears. The large floating trees could come along the bank and just run over the willow trees and anything else in its path. I've seen world pools in the river that large trees would drift into, circle around and around, sink down and I never saw them come up again. This did happen more toward the middle of the river- thank God.

After being pulled out of the river, we untied our rope from each other and watched to see if the trap was staying put, picked up our buckets and gear and went home. We also looked around to see if anybody was watching us. We tried to do this at times when there were no other folks fishing or just milling about. We did not like the thought of anyone raiding/poaching our trap when we were gone. Everybody in White Castle had a taste for large Mississippi River shrimp.

We would check the trap daily, sometimes twice daily. If we put the trap out in the morning, we would check it that evening while still daylight. With the river dropping a couple feet a day, we had to not only retrieve the shrimp, but re-bait, and tie the trap lower each day. The last thing a river shrimper needed was a shrimp trap tied up several feet above the water. There are no flying shrimp that I know of, so the trap needed to be repositioned at least once daily.

Each time we went to check the shrimp trap, I had to follow the same procedure as when we place it. Tying the rope around us, walking up stream, making way to the trap, untying the trap and having daddy pull me in with the trap. Once upon shore we flipped the latch and open the wire framed top and grab the shrimp by hand and place them into our bucket. We would place fresh bait in the trap, latch it up and back to the usual routine of replacing the trap. When the river receded several feet, we kept our same depth for the trap by placing it further out. We had more bank each time we came back to check the trap. After checking the trap several times, if we did not catch many shrimp, we would give up with the idea of trying again the next year.

I mentioned earlier about fear. Another fear I had was getting a foot caught in the cracks of the mats and not being able to get it out. The only good thought was that the river was usually going down at this time of year. So in a couple of days I would be out of the water and help would come. If this ever happened, I would be pointed at and laughed at for years to come.

We would not have tried to catch shrimp if the river was coming up two feet a day. This was way too dangerous to try. Why did Daddy stay on the bank and I go into the murky water you ask? Well, it was because he was Daddy and I was the kid. He was also over 200 pounds and I was about 140 pounds. I do not know if I would have been able to pull him in out of the current. Probably not.

Another detail of the trap placement was. I would place it just below the water level. We did this for three reasons. Number one is that we wanted it lower in the water so we would not have to change its position more than once a day because of the receding water. Number two is that the shrimp schools and feed near the top of the water. When they are feeding, the water is just bubbling with activity. If they did this near a pier and you had a net, you could scoop all the shrimp you want without a trap or bait. This is as much as I remember about shrimping in the Big Muddy.

Oh, what about the third reason you ask. Weeeeeeell, I do not know what the third reason was.

CHAPTER 13

MOVE TO THE BIG HOUSE NEXT TO OURS ON THE PLANTATION: AGES SEVENTEEN AND UP

Sometime in 1960 or 1961, Daddy had replaced Mr. Joe Mabile as Plantation Manager. Mr. Grady Roper offered the job to him. Daddy did not want to take the job of his friend and coworker for many, many years. We all watch him get sick. He was sick with worry and physically sick. He lost plenty weight and was throwing up daily. Since Mr. Roper lived in Lake Charles Louisiana, he was not there to force Daddy to make this decision quickly. Daddy tried his best to see that Mr. Joe kept his job or at least was offered something else. Finally after several weeks, Mr. Roper told Daddy that Mr. Joe was gone from Cedar Grove and if Daddy did not take the job, he would hire someone that was not from Cedar Grove to run the show and Daddy would answer to that person. He also said that there would be just two overseers from then on and Mr. Jules (Gayle and James' dad) would lose his job also. Reluctantly, Daddy took the job. The Mabiles had lived next door to us (except for our short time in White Castle) for all my life as I knew it. They lived in a ten room, fourteen foot ceiling, two to three feet off the ground, rain drop splitter, tin roof house. They had to move from The Plantation when Mr. Joe lost his job. They eventually moved to a rent house in White Castle. It was another old wood frame type house just as the ones we live in on the plantation.

Everyone who worked for the Plantation was furnished a house to live in. This also applied to the black field hands. This meant all the folks who worked in the fields, all the folks who worked in the sugar mill year round, the shop personnel, the blacksmith, the horseler and some tenant farmers like the Falcons and later the Trosclairs and the Medines, lived in plantation owned houses.

VALUABLE RECORDS LOST FOREVER

Just before the Mabiles moved, one day I noticed Sonny Mabile on the levee sailing large seventy eight records into the woods on the river side of the levee. I went to talk with him. He said that they were moving soon and his Momma did not want the records anymore as he pitched the last one. The really sad part of this for my Momma and my family was that many of those records was ours that the Mabiles had borrowed and never returned. We lost some great music by Jimmy Rogers and Hank Williams and Hank Snow and Earnest Stubb and his Texas Trupperdoors, and many others. I remember the names because I went down the levee to where they landed to see if I could find any that had not broken. The records in those days were made of a material that if you dropped it, it would break in many pieces. All of then was broken. I knew that this was wrong for anyone to do. I was pissed, but I never mentioned anything to Sonny about this. After all, it was not him who borrowed our records years earlier and just forgot who owned them.

There is another item that our family never did get back from the Mabiles. Mr. Joe had borrowed my Daddy's double barrel sixteen gauge shotgun many years before he left the Plantation and just kept it. After they moved, we wanted Daddy to ask Mr. Joe for it back. Daddy would not. All he would say was "Joe knows who the gun belong to." I believe that Mr. Joe had come over and borrowed the shotgun and Daddy was a man that if you came and borrowed, you have the responsibility of bringing it back. Mr. Joe may have remembered who the gun belong to but apparently never told Mrs. Violet or Ronald, Sonny, Sister or

Mark. Because he died some years later and to this day, The Mabiles still have my Daddy's shotgun. Maybe they got rid of it years ago, I don't know. One of these days, I will ask Sonny if he know what happened to my Daddy's shotgun. Ronald left for New York City after spending some time in College and I have not seen him in many years. Ronald and I are only four days apart in age. I am four days older than him. Kenneth Blanchard is two days older or younger than me. I do not remember his exact birth date. I see Sonny occasionally when I go back to the White Castle area to visit the graves of all the Raffrays at the Catholic cemetery there. There are four generations of Raffrays buried in the White Castle Cemetery. Several older generations are buried in the Brusly graveyard. Brusly is about seventeen miles North of White Castle on La. 1.

After the Mabiles moved out of the Big house, we moved into it. I believe we had some furniture in each room. Where the furniture came from, I do not know. We now had at lease four bedrooms, but only used two, unless someone came to visit. My brother and sister was already gone. My uncle Nolan and I shared the same bedroom and it stayed this way until I got married about seven years later.

My brother built a house in the woods between White Castle and Plaquemine called Random Oaks but my sister-in-law was afraid to live there because my brother worked all over the state and was gone during the week. So she would live with us during the week and live in Random Oaks during the weekend when my brother was home. This went on for several years until my brother got on the I-10 project and worked out of a more local yard. He stopped traveling the state after that.

LATE TEENAGE YEARS: AGES SEVENTEEN AND EIGHTEEN - ELEVENTH AND TWELFTH GRADES

Me around 17

With the modern cane equipment and chemical plants buy up farm land in our area, many folks left the Plantation. Older folks retired and was not replaced. I saw the plantation come from fifty to sixty families down to about twelve or so families. During cane planting/harvesting time, they still needed to hire a few extra folks to help out, but not near a many as in the past.

Better chemicals, fertilizers, pesticides and herbicides, helped to improve the yield of the crops such that hand labor was almost extinct. Improvements in harvesting and planting equipment also help to reduce the labor force. With all the petrochemical industry coming into the area now, the farmers are lucky to keep the labor they had. They had to pay them better than in the past and also treat them better than they used to also.

My brother, who is eight years older than me, and my sister, who is four years older, got married soon after getting out of high school. My sister's wedding was really soon. She got married about three weeks after she graduated. She married Gene Bertrand who was living in Plaquemine with his Mom and Dad at the time. My brother took a couple of years after graduating before he married Liz Giroir from Belle Rose, Louisiana. This left me to do their chores that needed to be done after they left home.

There was a period of time that I milked three cows a day before and after school and on week ends. We did not take vacations like other folks would. We just could not be gone that long. We would occasionally spend one night in New Orleans at Daddy's sister's house. But as soon as we got home, I had to get the cows into the pens and start milking. The cows were ready to be milked. They would just be mooing all over the place. They did this when they needed milking. Their utters would really swell up and it hurt them. They needed to be milked for relief from the pain.

I had a number of dates with girls, not many during these years. Davis Callegan and I were very good buddies and he would drive over and pick me up almost every Friday and/or Saturday to go knock around White Castle or Plaquemine. When we were several years younger, one of his older brothers, (he had five of them) would drive Davis and I to the Youth Center dance in Plaquemine each Saturday on their way to where they were going. They also took us to the movies and a fair and would always come back and pick us up when it was time to go home before midnight. Several times, one of Davis' older sisters would do the same. He had three older sisters. Davis was the baby of his family as I was in my family. Come to think of it Donald (Duck) was the baby of his family also.

TED HYMEL AND I

Ted Hymel, (the baby in his family), Bobby Pearce, or Steve Landry (I doubt you), would pick me up for ball games, movies, going to dances, or just getting out of the house. Ted Hymel and I became very good friends. He was a year behind me in high school. We went many places together. I really enjoyed the trips we made to Baton Rouge to hang out with his older cousins. I cannot remember their names, but we would park at his cousins house and ride all around Baton Rouge with them in this candy apple red two door hard top Chevy. A very special car. It was beautiful and these guys accepted us like we was one of their gang. They did a lot of crazy things when they were in high school. They use to talk about the things they got into. It was just mischief and some very funny stunts. They worked for a living at the time we ran with them. I learned a lot from these guys; some good things to know and also found out things not to do. Like jokes that could lead to problems. They taught us these things by us just listening to some of the things they did.

I dated one of Ted's sister-in-law's cousins for a while. She was from New Iberia, Louisiana; a very nice girl that I met through Ted's brother Rodney and his wife. They got us together. Lou Ella Landry was petite and well built and cute as a bug. She was raised by her Grandmother. Her mother died at her birth because she was a very small person also. Lou Ella never did marry because of her size. I think that she was afraid of getting pregnant and not being able to have the baby in the normal way. It is a shame because she was a lovely person and would have made some man a good wife.

Ted and I built up a trust between us so much so that when he was in the Army and stationed at Fort Polk in Pineville, Louisiana (North Louisiana), he asked me to drive with him and his girl friend back to the Base on a Sunday because I was the only guy he trusted to drive the car back to White Castle with his best girl alone. This was a two hour trip one way. Nothing happened between me and his girl on the trips back. In situations like this, I was the best friend any guy could have to not mess with their girl friends; even the ones that might want to mess with me. I just did not play that game. I have no regrets.

Me and the guys would mostly hang around town at the Chat & Chew (Duck worked there) or Bullyepp Shaheen's place. We would shoot pool or watch the older guys play the slot machines which was in every bar in Iberville Parish. The adults would play high stakes poker in the bars in town. At any time in one of the bars was a big game going on. Sometimes we teenagers would play low stakes poker; very low stakes. I lost with three kings to Steve Landry's full house one time. I bet everything that I had on me and lost. I never told my Daddy or Momma about that. I never gambled for money again— playing poker.

I can still remember our town gambler, Mr. Rodney Erwin. He never worked that I know of. He fished during the day to help feed his family and I guess took a nap in the afternoon because I know he gambled all night, every night. He was a card playing fool. He would win big one night and need a body guard to watch over him. One time he won several rent houses, a car, over ten thousand dollars cash and I do not remember what else. He was loaded. The next week, late one night when I was going home, I saw him and his whole family being put out of his house after eleven o'clock at night. He had lost everything he won and had gambled his house away also. It is a bad life. I went to school with three of his kids. The others were much younger than me and I do not remember them. He had five or six kids. Did I say that I do not play cards for money anymore? I do not want to lose my hard earned money or anything else I worked so damn hard for. Don't get me wrong, I am not against all gambling. I believe if you do it, do it under control. Set a goal or and amount that you are willing to lose. If/when you reach that amount, be a man, walk away. Or you will lose. The odds are that you will lose. There are very few folks that ever come out ahead while gambling.

Davis Callegan and I did just about everything together. We was a team like Mutt and Jeff, Abbett and Costallo, Lewis and Martin, Seemore and Doless. You got it. We hung around together all through high school.

UNCLE NOLAN'S PASSION

Uncle Nolan loved to go fishing. He always owned a boat, motor and trailer and used to have two vehicles also. His older one, he use to go to work and pull his fishing boat. The newer one was for honky-tonking with his pals.

His fishing buddies were Mr. Shorty LeBlanc, Mr. Harry Kimber, and Mr. Edmond Rodrigue. Usually just two and sometimes three of these guys would team up every Sunday and go fishing. Unc worked on Saturdays as he did all through the week as head mechanic at Dixie Sales and Service in White Castle, so there was no fishing on Saturdays. Although he fished every week end, we very seldom saw any fish. He liked to catch them and eat them, but he did not like to clean them. So ninety nine point nine percent of the time, he gave them to whomever went fishing with him.

Unc used to like to go out honkytonking on Friday and Saturday nights. He went out every night, but during the week, he only went to town and held the parking meters up. A lot of guys, including me when I was a teenager, when I did not have anything going on, went to town and just stood around leaning on the parking meters, talking to others who were also leaning on parking meters and watching the traffic pass by.

When Unc went honkytonking, he took Mr. Edmond Rodrigue and or Mr. Harry Kimber with him. These guys and Mr. Shorty LeBlanc (who did not go honkytonking) was about twenty years older than him. He just liked hanging with the older guys. Unc was in his forties and fifties during these times when I was a teenager.

One Saturday after going out in Baton Rouge, on their way home, they (Mr. Harry and Mr. Edmond and Unc), stopped at Dup's Cafe in Plaquemine, which stayed opened until about three a. m. to catch the honkytonking crowd before they went home, for a hamburger. This was a weekly event for this trio, so every body knew them. They go out and on the way home stop and get something to eat. They ordered their usual three hamburgers. Dup's used to serve their hamburgers on a small cardboard throw away plate not much bigger in diameter than the hamburgers. We called them paper plates. As Unc related the story, Mr. Edmond kept saying that his hamburger was tough and hard to chew. Mr. Harry and Unc did not pay him no mind. They all used to drink pretty good, but I believe Mr. Edmond could out drink both of those fellows. I might add here that I never, in my life, remember seeing my Uncle Nolan drinking alcohol. I know he did but I saw him often in town when I was a teenager and holding up the parking meters but I never saw him drinking anything but soda. I believe he drank when he went out of White Castle. Maybe it was something about the way people gossip in town that he did not drink locally.

Back to Dup's Cafe. When they finished their hamburgers, the waitress came with more coffee and to get their little plates. She got Mr. Harry's and Uncs and ask Mr. Edmond where his plate was. He said, "you did not give me one." She replied, "I most certainly did." They looked under the table, on the floor around the table- no plate. It all became clear in a minute that Mr. Edmond had eaten the hamburger and the plate at the same time, and was to drunk to tell. It became apparent to the guys that Mr. Edmond's hamburger was not any tougher than theirs was, but he was eating the cardboard plate at the same time. I don't believe Mr. Edmond ever lived this one down.

One more story about Uncle Nolan and I'll save the rest for another time. When I was eighteen, which was the legal age for drinking alcohol in Louisiana, my buddy, Davis Callegan and I went out on the town in Plaquemine. Plaquemine was five times larger than White Castle, had more barrooms and had a number of dance halls. So we spent a lot of our time there. It was also the largest town in Iberville Parish, about ten thousand people. It was also the Parish Seat. You know, like County Seat, except Louisiana does not have Counties, they have Parishes.

Anyway, Davis and I had stopped at the Rendezvous Lounge to have a beer. The next morning, Uncle Nolan, me and Momma was in the kitchen drinking coffee. Momma asked what Davis and I did the night before. I recap our stops and then said on the way home we stopped at this new place, The Rendezvous Lounge for a beer. After hearing this, my Uncle propped up and said, "the Rendezvous Lounge, you should not go there, Josie, he should not go there." I ask him "why." "Because only no-good people go there, I know, I go," said my Uncle. After hearing this, I laughed and said, "Only no good people go there, you know because you go there." "Yea," he said without thinking. I could not stop from laughing and Momma started laughing also. It was just so funny not only what he said but how he said it; with conviction. Unc mumbles something and got up and left the house, pissed off. Momma and I laughed for fifteen minutes. When the laughter stopped, she said, "baby, you should not go to that place."

THE FEE FEE EXPERIENCE (BOY WHAT A RIDE)

Several times, Fee Fee Suarez and I teamed up to go places. One place was a dance hall near Parieville on the west side of the River. Parieville was about fifteen miles east of Baton Rouge on highway 190 that went to New Orleans. A lot of LSU football players and other athletes went there. He heard that the chicks were hot and very good looking. We also heard that they had fist fights there on a regular basis. We certainly did not go there for the fist fights. On this trip, Fee Fee, Frank Messina, Wayne Henry and I were in attendance. We paid our buck or two to get in. Van Broussard with Bobby Loveless on the saxophone was playing that night. Van had a very good band and had recorded several hit records and was very popular during the late fifties and all the sixties and into the seventies. Van's sister Grace (who I met and talked with a number of times) used to sing also and later teams up with Dale Houston to make the duo of Dale and Grace a very popular singing team that made it nationally for a number of years.

Fee Fee was well over six foot tall and well over two hundred pounds. But he looked small when standing side by side with many of the guys in the place. We started walking among the crowded hall and made our way to the band just watching the crowd dance and the goings on. We said a few hellos to band members that we knew and just kept on moseying along. After about ten or twelve minute, we had circled the hole dance hall and made it to back where we started from. Fee Fee was standing by a guy about three inches taller than him who was talking to another guy about the same size. All of a sudden there was pushing and shoving and the four of us got moved/shoved over a bit and these two guys were rolling on the floor fighting. The floor bouncers got there in a hurry. These two guys made the other two look small. We sort of forgot about all the good looking chicks and just looked at each other. I do not remember if any one of us said "lets go." We just all started walking toward the exit. The bouncers had no sooner threw these two guys out when another fist fight broke out as we were heading for the door. We did not hang around to see how it came out. We got out of there.

Another time, Fee Fee and I went to Donaldsonville to the Town and Country Club that was very popular at the time. It was a great dance hall and brought in all the good bands on Friday and Saturday nights. I believe we went there on a Thursday night and just sat in the bar and had a couple of beers. Couples went there and danced to the juke box when a band was not there during the week. We did not stay very long.

On the way back to White Castle, Fee Fee opened it up. He buried the speedometer needle past the one hundred twenty miles per hour mark. Using his tachometer, he said we were doing about one hundred thirty or so. He was driving with one hand and laughing. I think he was trying to get a reaction out of me. I stayed calm and did not say anything. I was thinking that if we hit a pot hole or had a blow out, we were goners for sure and inside, I was cutting buttons holes. Which meant that my ass hole was so tight that it could cut a steel bar so you know it would not be any problem to cut button holes.

This may have been the fastest that I ever went in an automobile.

THE BOBBY SQUIRREL STORY

This was not during Halloween, but one night several years later than the tale above, things was slow around White Castle. A number of us was just handing around listening to the grown ups bull shit. We decided to pay a trick on someone. We were not sure who it would be on at the time the idea festered. We got the idea from conversation that the grown ups were having.

There was Phillip (Fee Fee) Suarez, Wayne Henry, Frank Messina, Steve Landry and me. There may have been someone else. I just do not remember.

We heard that Mr. Bobby Ourso (Bobby Squirrel-I do not know how he became Bobby Squirrel) was getting ready to head home for the night. He usually started leaving about fifteen minutes before he actually left. He was a single man in his upper forties or older and lived at Richland with his Momma. We knew he always took La.1 to Hw. 992 and went to Richland Road. Hw. 992 was now black topped. If you remember, it was a graveled road where I rode my new used bike home many years before. You know, the bike that Wayne Henry put a scratch on my new re-paint job. Anyway, we got into the cars and hurried to Hw. 992. Turned left from La.1 crossed the Railroad tracks and pulled into a headland on Cedar Grove Plantation where sugar cane was growing on both sides of Hw. 992. The headland (a dirt road that leads into the cane field) was very grassy with tall Johnson grass and it was after ten o'clock at night. From Hw. 992, you could not see very much of anything on either side of the road.

Earlier that night Fee Fee had shown us a stop sign in his car that he stole, errrr, I mean came by some kind of way. At least, I think it was in Fee Fee's car. It could have been Steve's, Frank's or Wayne's car. I know it was not in my car. At the site, we propped up the stop sign in the middle of the road. We pulled up big clumps of Johnson grass from each side of the road near the sugar cane. The clumps came up with dirt attached. Johnson grass has a shallow root system and pulls out of the ground easily. The grass was four to five feet tall. We lined both sides of the stop sign in just a few minutes. Since each car was parked on each side of Hw. 992, well onto the head land, they were well hidden and could not be seen from the road without a spot light. We waited. It did not take long. In less than five minutes, here came a car. We could see the head lights. There was the left turn from La 1 onto Hw. 992. We could see and even hear the car as it was coming over the Texas and Pacific railroad tracks. We heard the sound of the engine as it was being gunned to pick up speed for the straight away as soon as the tracks were crossed. And just as soon, the brakes and the slight squealing of the rear tires as the car came to a stop. We could tell it was indeed Bobby Squirrel. The car hesitated about twenty seconds than in reverse it went. It backed then turned forward and backed again than made the rest of the turn and headed back over the tracks, took a right and headed back to White Castle. He laid down some rubber heading back to town.

As Bobby Squirrel started to turn around in the road, we got back into our cars and by the time he turned right onto La. 1, we were backing onto Hw. 992. We got to White Castle about thirty seconds after he did. We listened as he told the story of a big road block on Brickla Lane. He was really excited and stated that he was not drunk. It was all we could do not to laugh. The adults thought that we were there all the time and never had a suspicion that we were involved in this deal. In fact I believe this may be the first time that the details of that night got out. I do not know how many folks will even remember it.

Well, Bobby Squirrel stirred up a lot of curiosity and the Chief of Police for White Castle and a whole lot of other folks started out to the site of this highway blockade to rob Bobby Squirrel because everyone knew that he always carried money on his person.

There was a caravan of vehicles heading out to the scene of the great Johnson grass capper. We all parked where we could find places, and walked up to where the blockade was. It's a stop sign all right said the Chief. And look at all this Johnson grass.

Someone went to a lot of trouble to do this. Yea- about two minutes of trouble thought I. They shined a few flashlights around the area, saw nothing as they picked up the stop sign and grab each clump of grass and threw them into the ditch on the side of the road. The road was opened for traffic again. Hooray for the law, for they made an un-passable road passable again.

I often wished that we would have thought this out and picked up everything before we went to town. We could have done it in less than a minute. Then we could have watch the face of Bobby Squirrel and the others looking at him when they all got to the non-scene that he could not prove was the scene. If we would have done it this way, Fee Fee would still have his stop sign and would have been able to pull this stunt for the next thirty or forty years.

RIDING WITH STEVE (I DOUBT YOU) LANDRY

The second fastest I ever went in a car was with Steve Landry heading to Plaquemine on the same La. 1 that Fee Fee and I was coming from Donaldsonville on. The exception is, Donaldsonville is ten miles below White Castle on La. 1 and Plaquemine is ten miles above White Castle on La 1. Steve and I and someone else were riding around in Steve's daddy's car. It was a big Dodge. I do not remember the year make, it may have been a 1960 year model, but it had a four hundred plus cubic inch engine, and nearly four hundred horsepower, I guess.

We were racing with Eddie Supple Jr. who had a 1956 Ford with a supped up engine. We were trying to pass Lil Eddie at over one hundred twenty miles per hour. (By the way, Lil Eddie was not called Lil Eddie because of his size, but because he was a Junior and his dad was Big Eddie Supple who was one of the owners of the Supple plantation). I knew that we were going over one hundred twenty miles per hour because, just as it was in Fee Fee's car, I was in the front seat watching the speedometer and the needle was past the maximum which was one hundred twenty. This Dodge did not have a tachometer that I can recall. We just did not have enough power to get around Little Eddie. We would run nose to nose and would have to back off for on coming traffic in our lane. One time I thought we bought the dust. We could see the other car headlights coming towards us. (Yes both of these high speed experiences were at night). We were in the passing lane again, as the other car got closer, Steve knew that Lil Eddie would back off and let us in. Well time was running out, so Steve hit the brakes, it so happened the Lil Eddie hit his brakes also. Steve hit the gas and the same time Lil Eddie hit the gas. I thought Oh Oh, this is it. Steve hit the brakes again and Lit Eddie pulled away. As we cut in behind him the on-coming car zipped on by us. It was close but we made it by a good three or four seconds. No problem. We stopped in Plaquemine and discussed our experience. I believe we all had to go for a pee pee. I am amazed that we all did not pee-pee during the ride. Maybe we forgot we each had a weenie is why we did not pee-pee in our pants. We sure had the opportunity too.

   My Momma gave Steve the name "I Doubt You" from a card game that we used to play. I do not remember how the game was played, but if you doubted the hand that the player said they had, any player in the game could make the statement "I doubt you" and make them show the hand to everybody playing the game. If the player had the hand stated the person who said "I doubt you" had to draw extra cars or something like that. Steve never did believe my Momma when she stated her hand. From this one game, from this day forward, my Momma referred to Steve Landry as I Doubt You.

PLAYING CARDS FOR MONEY

Gambling was a big business in all of the barrooms in White Castle when I was a kid. All young teenagers were allowed in the bars even without our parents or another adult. It was just something that was done. Each bar had a food specialty that was well known. It may have been hamburgers, ham poor boys, fried shrimp poor boy, or other foods. Also several bars had pool tables. We were allowed to eat, play pool, and play the juke box. The bars all had slot machines also. If we were under eighteen, we were not allowed to play the slots. If we looked eighteen, nobody bothered us if we played the slots.

Each bar had a back or side room where adults did their card gambling. Draw or stud poker, booray, or down the river was played for high stakes. Us teenagers were on-lookers with the rest of the adult onlookers when big games were going on. The adults got the better position and pushed us out of the way for that position on occasion. We even saw cars, truck, boats and even a house (one time) change hands because of someone losing in a card game.

Occasionally we would get a small game going away from the adults. I remember well the last time I played for money in the room behind the Chat and Chew Bar. There were five of us playing. I was holding my own for a half hour or so. I did not make much money working in the sugar cane field on week ends and holidays and during school vacation. I did not like to spent money to freely. In fact my not wanting to spend money was the primary reason for my not dating very much during all my teenage years. I just did not want to spend the money. But I did play cards every now and then. I always came out even so no harm was done.

This particular night, we had gotten the pot up to twenty five dollars or more. It got down to Steve (I Doubt You) Landry and me. I raised, he saw my raise and raised me back. The other three players had folded by this time. I saw his raise and raised him again. By this time we had several onlookers. We were going back and forth with the raises. I had three kings. I was not going to let Steve bluff me and fold. Even if I wanted to I could not because the onlookers had seen what I have. One guy kept going back and forth between me and Steve, looking at our hands. I looked in his face when he was behind Steve at one point but could not get any help from his expression. I had bet all the money I had and decided to finally call Steve's hand. I thought sure I had won. I laid down my three kings. Steve looked at them. It was then that I saw the relief in his face just before he laid down his full house and rake in all the money. He won fair and square. This finished me for the night and forever. I promised myself that I would never do this again. I worked to damn hard for my money to throw it away like this. I had seen how it affected the adults who had lost everything. I did not want to get hooked on a life of gambling like them. Thanks to Steve Landry I never did.

MR. PERCLE- JUNIOR/SENIOR YEARS

Davis Callegan and I became pretty good friends with Mr. Percle who taught at White Castle High our last two years of school. He was from Plaquemine, and a single fellow. Although there may have been rumors that he was queer, we did not see any evidence of it. We spent quite a bit of time with Mr. Percle. We liked him. He was one of the good guys. Davis and I met his younger brother and worked with him a day or two cutting trees from a lot. We also met up with him several times in Plaquemine and did some bar hopping.

Mr. Percle had this lot in Plaquemine that needed several trees cut down. One day it came up at school that he needed to remove several trees. Davis said that he was handy with a chain saw and his Dad had several at his house. So a deal was struck. I am not sure what the deal was, but we volunteered to help remove the trees. This would take us just one Saturday and maybe Sunday to get the job done- not a big thing.

I knew very little about operating a chain saw. Davis had a large saw. It was a two man chain saw. One man operated the trigger that made the chain run and the other worked the end of the chain bar. It had a handle on the end of the chain bar to help guide the chain blades through a standing tree or a lying down tree for that matter.

We got the saw all fueled and oiled up and ready to go. These were standing trees we were to cut down, then cut them up in small pieces to load into a pickup for transit to the dump. We looked the job over and decided on the area that we wanted the tree to fall. We thought about notching the tree with an axe on the side that we wanted it to fall but Percle's brother was impatient and wanted to get started. We said O K, we do not need to notch this tree. Not us. We were there to cut the trees down and make a better grade in class than we earned, although nothing about grades was ever mentioned. But I thought that this made since to me. We help Percle get the trees down at no cost to him; he owed us better grades as a payback. I cannot find any fault with my way of thinking. This was the deal that I wanted, but still did not mention it to anybody.

We had an axe and a couple of wedges and a mall (large hammer) to be used when needed. But we did not use the axe before the chain saw. We will do this the easy way. The way that Mr. Percle's brother wanted to do it, with only the saw.

It was Davis's Dad saw, so Davis was the one to run it. I would work the guide handle on the chain bar. Davis started it up. The bar/blade was about seven feet long. Percle's brother took over for Davis. He wanted to run the saw. He did not seam to want to be there, and he wanted to hurry up and get this job done so he could go about his business of looking for a job or get back to sleeping or something. He had just got out of the service and needed a job. He did not like having to cut down trees. This just took up his time. He had never cut a standing tree either. I was afraid of his gun ho attitude and wanting to rush into this without thinking about it. This was a formula for disaster and I did not like the position I was in- holding the chain blade bar guide handle.

I asked Davis "don't we have to do something to the tree first?" Percle's brother answered "no, let's go." I placed the bar blade as close to the ground as I could get it. We were going to cut it as close to the ground and just run the blade clean through this standing tree. I did not think that was ever done before. But what the hell did I know. I was not a worldly fellow like Percle's brother was. He had served his time in the Army already. He has to know more than Davis and me.

I believe there are many ways to cut a standing tree down. We picked a way that it could not be done. We started cutting into the tree. Right away I had a problem. If the chain blade broke for any reason, it would have cut me in half. The direction the chain drive was moving the blade led me to this conclusion right away. I yelled a Percle to stop. We had only cut about two inches into the tree. Something is just not right I told him. We looked it over again and he decided to continue. I was really afraid of the chain blade but was trying real hard not to let Davis see it. I did not want him to see how afraid I was. He would have it all over school. He may not have said anything, but this was another of my fears.

At about half way through the tree, the chain blade bar got stuck. We could not go forward or pull the chain saw out of the tree. I was happy that it was stuck. The tree had shifted just a little and squeezed down onto what was going to be the tree stump. Davis told Percle to kill the saw engine. The whole saw was not going anywhere. What the hell were we going to do now?

After surveying the situation, one of the guys got the axe and chopped above the cut in the direction we wanted the tree to fall. This is what we should have done before even starting the damn saw.

We had to cut with the axe over half way into the tree to get it leaning in the direction we wanted. It was leaning in our direction with the saw blade still in it before we started chopping. When it started to lean, this released the chain saw. We checked the saw blade out. Had to adjust the chain on the bar and started it up again. We started cutting the tree again from the back of where the notched area was. We kept an eye on the tree the whole time. Sometimes a tree will roll before it goes down, so you need to be on the lookout at all times. Besides the roll, I was more concerned with the tree kicking up and out before it fell. Any number of these things could get you killed dead.

Finally we heard the cracking that a tree makes before it falls down. It started to go. We all scattered. Davis ran in one direction, Percle in another direction and me in still another direction. No, no one ran in the direction that the tree was falling. I do not remember where Percle, our teacher was or even if he was there at this time. He may have gone to get us something to eat and drink.

After trimming all the branches and cutting this tree down to size, we were much more knowledgeable to attack the second tree. We had much better success in getting it down.

I do not remember if Mr. Percle assisted us with our grades or not. I know that neither Davis nor I failed his class. Neither did any one else in our grade.

Mr. Percle would take us or chaperone us on after school outings. We got away with stuff when he was watching us.

One night after working on decorations for the junior/senior prom, we decided to drive to Donaldsonville for a beer or two. Some of us were already eighteen years old and old enough to drink alcoholic beverages in the state of Louisiana. We had several car loads of folks. Mr. Percle had about five girls in his car. Davis had me and about four more boys in his car. It is ten miles from White Castle to Donaldsonville. On the way over, we would pass Percle than slow down. He would pass us and we would pass again and slow down. We did this a number of times until Percle picked up speed a little. We finally got on the side of him but did not pass. We were just driving side by side. Percle turned out his lights. I reached over and turned out our lights. Percle put his lights on so fast after ours went out that he must have had his hand on the pull knob on the dash board. During these times we did not have headlight on/off switches on the blinkers or automatic shift control handles. The dimmer switch was on the floorboard on the left side, high up and was activated with the left foot.

We tried to play tennis against Mr. Percle but could not beat him. Percle was the one teacher through all of high school that we could relate to. Although he was a number of years older than us, we looked at him as being in our generation. He as not against good, clean fun as the older teachers seemed to be.

Mr. Elliott, our teacher in the eight grade, was the closest to Percle. He quit teaching the year after I had him to support his family better. He went to work for Shell Oil Company at the Shell Field behind White Castle. This was a big loss to all the upcoming students who did not get the chance to meet and be taught by Mr. Clarence Elliott.

CHAPTER 14

ME AROUND THE HOUSE: AGES EIGHTEEN AND UP

During the times that I was not running the street with Davis or Ted Hymel, I pretty much stayed at home. I did not own a car and could not use Daddy's car to "just run the streets." I could use it to go to work or go to the Post Office or run errands for him or Momma, but that was about it. I could not burn his gas for nothing. I would stay home and watch TV with Momma. She loved to watch those scary old movies. Like the Vampire, staring Bella Lagosse, that made me not able to sleep that night, or the Werewolf staring Lon Chaney Jr., that made me not able to sleep that night either, and Frankenstine and the Mummy, staring Raymond Massey, that either made me not able to sleep that night. She watched other spooky movies also. I still do not like to watch spooky movies. They just do not interest me in the least.

On Friday nights, when I was younger, I used to love to watch the Gillette Friday Night Fights on TV. Of course everything was in black and white. The blood looked black and the socks looked white. During this time in my life, I enjoyed the Fights of the Century. I still love the old fights and new fights too, for that matter. These old films was of very old prize fighters in their day. Fights from the early 1900s and 1920s and 30s and 40s. The 1950s, was not old then because I was living them.

Nolan Charles Correl (Unc)

TRYING TO GET MY UNCLE TO TALK

On Sundays we would watch Twentieth Century with Walter Cronkite. It was about World War I and World War II. I mostly wanted to watch the World War II films. My Uncle Nolan, who was in the Army during that time would usually be home during this time and would sometimes watch with us. He had always told us that he was in Canada helping to build a road called the Alcan Run during the war. This was a route from Canada into Alaska for the Allies to get war supplies to areas in Alaska to be reshipped to where they were needed. He told us this for years.

During the time of my upper teenage years, my Uncle would make a comment or remark that led us to believe that he was not in Canada and Alaska during the whole war. One time when watching Twentieth Century and a certain part of the war was in a jungle or very wooded area, he stated that his company was in those woods and the enemy was flying over and dropping bombs in the area. Although it was cold there, they could not light a fire for fear it would be noticed from the planes that flew over them. This particular night, it was very dark and they could hear the enemy airplanes above. They were in black-out mode and some how a black soldier that was there put his flash light on. Many of the men was shouting and hollowing at the guy to put it out. Some of them shouted out to shoot and kill the son of a bitch. The black guy got so afraid that he was trying to blow out the flashlight with his mouth. When my Uncle noticed that we all were looking at and listening to him with our mouths open, he shut up. We could not get anything else out of him. We begged. He left the room. We only know that my uncle made it through the war to come home.

Another time, he and I was watching this program on the Normandy Beach Invasion in France. He mentioned that his unit was on the second wave to hit the beach; that there were ninety percent casualties on the first wave. I just wasn't thinking and I said "I thought that you were in Canada building the Alcan Run." He clammed up and did not mentioned anything else about what he saw while there. If I would have kept my mouth shut, I may have learned more about his experiences during the war. We could never get him to talk about it and had stopped asking him direct question years before. He would just let something slip out every now and again. He had all sorts of medals and I regret to say that I do not know what for. His Medals seam to have disappeared over time. I do not know what happened to them.

I will get a little ahead of myself here…

My Uncle (Momma's brother) never did get married. He lived with Momma and Daddy after they got married. He left for four or five year while he served in the Army during World War II and again lived with us after the war and all the while that I was growing up and until Daddy Died in 1984. My brother moved one of Daddy's house trailers into his back yard and my uncle lived there until he died in 1988.

Momma died in 1980. She had been sick for many years. Daddy remarried in 1982 and my uncle still lived there during those two years before Daddy died. There was two house trailers placed together and a large front screened in porch connecting them. Daddy and his new wife lived in one trailer and Uncle Nolan lived in the other. He was like a brother to my Dad. They had been together for so many years. Daddy was still working for the plantation when he died. The trailers was on plantation land. After Daddy died, my brother moved one trailer to Plaquemine so Daddy's widow could have a place to live and the other older trailer that my uncle lived in, to his back yard as I mention earlier.

My uncle was an auto mechanic. He did this for almost forty five years for Dixie Sales and Service, the Chrysler/Plymouth dealership in White Castle until he retired. Our cousins, Fred and Steve Doiron owned this business. This is where we all purchased our auto from for many years. The third generation Doirons lost this business. Uncle Nolan worked on all our cars during the time when he was off work for nothing. He paid Momma ten dollars a week rent for as long as she was alive. This is the amount that I paid her after I came home from the Army in 1962 and the age of nineteen. I paid this amount until I moved away after getting married when I was twenty-four years old.

MY SENIOR YEAR...

There was nothing exceptional about my senior year in high school. I already covered most of the things I was doing with my high school friends. I turned nineteen two weeks before we graduated. Our graduation was on the football field. We was the first group to do that. I believed that we had thirty two kids in our graduating class. We did not have the football field very long. We were in our second or third year of football. We had a six man team. We had a small school. I believe Class C. There were only nine teams this size in the state. They all played each other. We had an eight game schedule then the playoffs, if your team made it, then you played for the six man team State Championship.

Several years later the team grew to an eight man team with about nine teams in the state. After integration allowed the black kids to go to the same school as the white kids, in about 1968 or so, the team grew to an eleven man football team. Then White Castle High School had the talent to win some state championships in several sports.

One time while just driving about White Castle with Davis, we were making a turn-a-round in front of the high school where the buses parked to pick up the kids. It was a half circle driveway. For some reason, the passenger side door (my door), was not all the way closed. I had been hearing wind whistling through it for some time and it was bugging me. I do not know why I picked this time to open the door, but I did. I was just not thinking. As we were about half way through the half circle, I pulled the handle to open the door just as Davis was gunning the engine to pick up speed to get onto Bowie Street. Sometime we would burn a little rubber here to just show off, if no adults were around. The door flung wide open. I held on to the door and was leaning half way out of the car. It was all that I could do to not tumble out onto the pavement. It all happened so fast that Davis did not notice it because he was looking the other way for possible on coming traffic. Of course there wasn't any on coming traffic which is why he gunned it. When he swung around on Bowie Street and straighten the car out, I was able to pull myself back upright and into the seat. I pulled the door closed. Davis yelled at me and said, "What the hell were you trying to do, you could have fell out?" I answered, "I do not know what I was thinking about." There were no seat belts in those days.

My fingers, arm and shoulder on the right side of my body really ached. I had hurt muscles that I did not know I had. I hurt for several days later, and never tried a stupid stunt like that again.

ATTENDING PROMS

In 1960, I attended a St John High School Junior/Senior Prom in Plaquemine. My date was Judy Bertrand the sister of my brother-in-law. I borrowed my brother-in-law's white sport coat and I wore black dress slacks. I looked good. Yes, I had a pink carnation in the lapel buttonhole. I was the hit of the prom, or something like that. Marty Robbins would know it better, he had the hit record.

In 1961, as a Junior, I went to the junior/senior prom at White Castle High School. As a junior, I along with all the other juniors, worked on the prom program. The junior class sponsored this event for the seniors. A band was hired and a big dance was held in the gym at the school.

When it became time to get a date for the prom, our telephone was out of service. Gwen Allemon wanted me to ask Dianne LeBlanc, her best friend at the time, to go with me. Dianne had quit school that same year. I knew Dianne for a very long time. Our parents were friends and used to play cards one night during the week and go dancing almost every Saturday night when it was not sugar cane harvesting time. Mr. Etienne and Mrs. Mable LeBlanc were sugar cane farmers and hard work folks just like my folks.

I went to Gwen's house, which was on La.1 in White Castle next to Mr. Emile Shaheen's bar. Gwen's momma, May, worked hard all her life to raise Gwen and her older brother Buck, and did a very good job of it.

I called Dianne; she said yes, she would go out with me. I told her we will get all the details to her later. All I knew was the date of the prom and we would be double dating with Gwen and her date Bobby Loveless. Gwen was sitting on the swing on their porch while I called Dianne from the room just off the porch. After hanging up the telephone, before I could get from the room to the porch, which was ten feet, Gwen's telephone started ringing. Gwen ran to answer it while I went to sit in the swing. Gwen was back in less than a minute. It was Dianne telling her the news that she already knew.

Gwen was dating Bobby Loveless from Ascension Parish at the time. The night of the dance, Gwen, Bobby, Dianne, me and another couple, tripled dated in Bobby's car.

After the prom dance was over, we drove to the "Gold Coast" in West Baton Rouge Parish. This was a section on Highway 190 just past the city of Port Allen, where a number of night clubs were located. It was about twenty-five miles north of White Castle. The clubs were located near the Mississippi River Bridge that connected Baton Rouge with the West side of the River. When all the honkytonks in Baton Rouge closed down for the night, the folks that still wanted to party would head for the Gold

Coast in West Baton Rouge Parish. They did not close to six or seven a. m.

We attended a live show where the singer Jay Chervier was performing. Jay was popular locally at the time. He had made a record about the famous Billy Cannon's Halloween Night run for a touchdown when LSU was playing Ole Miss. LSU won the game because of Cannon's run and made it into the Sugar Bowl. The record sold really well in the Baton Rouge area. Jay was still playing music in all the area clubs.

After several Songs, Jay noticed Bobby Loveless, who played the saxophone in Van Brousard's band. Van was very popular and had several major regional hit records out. Bobby was also very well known as an outstanding sax player.

From the stage, Jay started to throw some barbs at Bobby. Bobby, being the kind of guy he is, would throw his own back. This went on for several songs, until a subject matter about family came up and Bobby answered one of Jay's barbs with "yes and my Grandma would be my Grandpa, if she had nuts." Bobby got a bigger laugh than Jay with this one so Jay stopped the barb throwing for the rest of the night, and we all passed a good time.

I met Bobby Loveless about a year or two earlier in Donaldsonville at a night club. He chased Gwen for a couple of years and would come to our school and visit her (and us) during recess. We would not let him be with her alone for two reasons. One of which was, we knew Bobby played with Van, so we wanted to get to know Van better. This way we would meet Van and his sister Grace who also made records with Dale Houston. They made the national scene for several years with several hit records as "Dale and Grace." We did get to know Van, Dale and Grace and talked with them enough that they recognized us as fans and friends.

Bobby later started his own band and made the big time for several years. Two of the songs he recorded were played nationally but he did not/could not follow up with something that caught on to keep the big ball rolling. His record "Night Owl" was played around the country. I heard it on a radio station in Jacksonville, Florida on a trip I made there. This was about 1966. He released "Return of the Night Owl," but did not get the play time on Dick Clark or Wolfman Jack's shows. Either of these guys could have taken Bobby national. I really do not know if Bobby wanted that or not.

In 1967, I went to work for Foster Grant Chemical Company in Baton Rouge and again met up with Bobby Loveless. He was working there full time and playing music on the weekends. Bobby worked at that plant location for over twenty years.

I wonder if he still plays the saxophone!

I do not remember what the second reason was that we did not want Bobby to be alone with Gwen.

Another prom I attended was a Plaquemine High prom. I do not remember if this was in 1961 or 1962 but I had a date with a friend of Barry Landry's girlfriend. Barry, Clay Sonnier, George Alonzo, Wayne Landry and another guy, started a band named "The Checkers." They were a very good local band and paid these guys way through college.

We all got together after the prom was over and went out dancing and had a great time. I am sorry to say that I cannot remember the name of the girl that I had the date with. I knew her before the date but do not recall if we dated after the prom or not. She was a very nice girl, of this I am sure.

I attended another prom at St. John High School in Plaquemine with another girl that I cannot remember her name. It was her senior prom. We had become friends a short time before she graduated high school. I do not remember seeing/dating her after the prom. We went our separate ways.

There were several other invites for me to attend proms that I did not because I had a steady girlfriend at the time. A steady girlfriend just would not understand or stand for her guy taking another girl to a prom. I just do not understand why girls are like that. It must be something in their genes.

I have long since forgotten the reason why I did not attend my own senior prom in 1962. Maybe I should say that I do not remember attending that prom. I may have gone without a date which is why I do not remember anything about it.

Unless this was the one that Rod Bennard played for. He was a local (New Orleans) disc jockey that cut a few records and made it big in the area. During the break, I sat with Rod and talked about the music business. It was something that I wanted to get into for years but was too bashful and very nervous when getting up in front of a lot of people. I just could not do it. I could write and sing songs but performing in the bathroom was one thing, getting up and performing in front of a couple hundred kids was frightening.

If I would have learned to play the guitar, I would have become a member of The Checkers band. Barry Landry wanted another guitar player in the band. He also knew that I could sing a bit.

At one practice in Prompt Succor Hall behind the Catholic Church, we had a live session. All instruments and mikes and amplifiers were set up. I was going to sing "I will be a Wheel Someday," a Fats Dommino song. We were talking back and forth and I said "shit" and it was amplified throughout the hall. Barry got upset because of our location.

This guy from Plaquemine, who was in a good band had come down to help with the practice and give pointers. He grabbed the mike and started singing the song. The band caught on and got going. They had a very good sound. I think that I could have done the song better, but this guy had a good voice too. This got the band going. They played a good number of songs with this guy doing all the singing. They had been practicing a couple months and this was the first live hall practice. Barry had invited me to come and sing. I never did get the chance to sing after they played the first song. They got into it and played one song after another.

I left about an hour after I got there. They were rocking and rolling. I knew that they would make it. And they did. They all worked harder than I was willing to work learning to play the guitar and other instruments. If I would have learned to play the guitar, I still could have joined them as late as six months later. After the six months period, they had it all together and were booked for Friday, Saturday and Sunday, every weekend. These guys were good.

JOINING THE ARMY

In the Tenth grade, Davis Callegan and I were going to join the National Guard. We thought this would help us with grade when we went into the Army. We would have stripes after basic training and be ahead of the other guys. When hearing about this at school, some girls called us draft dodgers or weekend wonders or something else. So we decided not to join. That sure turned out to be a big mistake for me. Until this day, I wished I would have joined the National Guard when I was seventeen.

Davis and I had been planning for a couple of years on joining the Army when we got out of high school. Donald (Duck) Aucoin did not have any plans, so we talked him into joining with us. Davis and I were already nineteen, Duck was seventeen and had to get his momma to sign for him to join which she did.

We signed up to join on the buddy system which meant we could stay together during basic training. Since we were volunteering for three years, we could go to the school of our choice. We all wanted to go to school for operation and maintenance of heavy equipment. There was so much farm land in South Louisiana being sold and developed; we thought that this would be a good profession to get into.

Of course, our timing was off. At the time we were going into basic training, we would not make the start date for the Operation and Maintenance School, so we had to pick schools which would coincide with the time we finished with basic training. Duck picked small airplane mechanic school in Alabama. I picked radar technician school. I would have nine months of schooling after basic training in Fort Monmouth New Jersey. I do not remember which school that Davis picked to attend. The one catch to allowing three- year recruits the schooling of their choice was, if you failed or dropped out, you go straight into the infantry. This was the fighting unit. The ground unit, if a war started, you are the first to go fight. So there was some incentive to not fail your school.

GRADUATION MAY 1962

I had been dating this girl in Plaquemine for several weeks. I cannot remember her name. I met her at a Youth Center Dance in Plaquemine. It was hard for me to meet girls because I was bashful. Davis and I went to many Saturday night dances and I was afraid to ask girls to dance. I knew how to slow dance because my sister taught me when I was fourteen years old. I could not jitterbug very well though. When the twist by Chubby Checker came out I was happy because this was something that I could do. But the twist was too late to help me at the Youth Center dances.

I became friends with girls by meeting them through their guy friends. I would dance with the girls I knew. The Katy Hawkins songs was when the girls would ask a guy to dance. I met a few girls who asked me to dance.

The killer for me was when I got up the nerve to ask a girl to dance and she said NO, for any reason; I withdrew and did not ask another girl to dance for several weeks. I would not even go to the dances. My buddy Davis would tell me at school on Monday that so and so was begging him to bring me to the dance the next Saturday to see me. So I would go and so and so would not even be there or did not care if I was there or not. This is how Davis got me to go to the dance when I did not want to go. I fell for it every time.

Me shortly before graduation

 He always had one of the good looking so and so that wanted to see me.

 The way I met the girl I invited to my graduation was I picked up Russell Pollet in White Castle hitch-hiking to Plaquemine one Saturday night. I took him to the Youth Center dance. Upon arrival I decided to go in and see who was there. After we paid to get in, Russell said come with me. I followed him all about the place. He was looking around. He finally stopped at this cute girl. He talk to her then called me over and introduced me to her. He then left us alone. I asked her how long she knew Russell and she said that she did not know him from Adam until he walked up to her, got her name to introduce her to me. I thought that damn crazy Pollet, I wish I could do that. We danced and talked for the balance of the night. I offered to drive her home. She wanted to walk and ask me if I would walk her home. She said that she lived close by. I agreed to walk her home. But this meant that my daddy's car would be at the Youth Center. Russell had the answer for this. So I let Russell take the car after he got the directions and address to this girl's house to pick me up later. We started walking and walking and walking. She must have lived two miles away. We finally got to her house. We sat on the porch talking until Russell showed up with the car all in one piece, thank God. I got her telephone number and a date for the next week. I saw her several times before my graduation night.

Our class was to be the first class to graduate on the football field at night. We had practiced it several times, even sang the three songs all the way through. All we had to do was pass all our grades. We had thirty two in our graduation class.

The afternoon of graduation, I went to Plaquemine to pick up my date and bring her to our house on the plantation to meet Momma and Daddy. Later that afternoon as I was getting ready, Mrs. Olivia Falcon arrived with her daughter, Wyonna and Punkie Hymel. Wyonna and Punkie graduated the year before. We were the same age and I should have graduated with them but pulled that stupid stunt in the third grade. Punkie was a really pretty girl and I wished that she or Wyonna was my date for this night. They stayed over a while then left. I finished getting dressed after they left.

We all went to the graduation. I was not feeling well. I had a headache and just felt faint. We were all announced and marched out onto the field and the program started. I started feeling better and whatever it was went away. We sang our first song, then some talking, than sang our next song. The music teacher, whose name I cannot recall, put in a lot of work getting us to this point. She did a marvelous job.

We received out diplomas one at a time, sang our last song and marched off the field to the spot where the ceremony was over.

At this time, all the families from the bleachers came onto the field. We all hugged and congratulated each other for a half hour or so. Some of the students had parties planned. We went home and had cake. A few folks came over to our house and after they left, I changed clothes.

The only place opened all night was the bowling alley in Plaquemine. If you did not have an all night party and most parents would not allow that, you went to the bowling alley and stayed out all night.

I brought my date home before one a.m. because that was her curfew. I met up with eight or ten of my classmates at the bowling alley and us guys and gals bowled all night to celebrate our getting out of high school. Yes, I did say bowled and not balled. I was now nineteen years old (made it two weeks before graduation) and I had never balled yet. Came close a few times but no cigar. I have no regrets- well maybe one. I regret that I was so bashful. I wished that I was more outgoing like my buddy Davis. Right or wrong, we all want to be like someone else at sometime in our life.

AFTER GRADUATION - ARMY BOUND

The day after graduation, Davis Callegan, Donald (Duck) Aucoin and I went to Baton Rouge and signed up to join the Army. We had to take all kinds of test. After this, there was a weekend which we hung around White Castle telling folks by. One Monday, we went to New Orleans to the Customs House. There we would have two more days of testing and physicals.

The Army put us up in a hotel near the Customs House. We may have been in the French Quarter, but we did not know where we were. Our one night in the Big Easy, Davis wanted to go to Bourbon Street. Duck and I said NO. Duck was only seventeen and he did not like to spend money and I did not like to spend money either. Not the kind of money that we heard was spent on Bourbon Street. Mr. Deep Pockets Davis always had plenty money when compared to us. All three of us ended up going to a movie. We saw West Side Story. It was about gangs dancing around in the streets and making like they were going to fight with knives and making hand jesters. They were California gangs I guess that some how made it to New York City. They seemed sissy with all that dancing and prancing around. They would not have as good a chance of surviving as a snowball in hell if they would fight the gangs of today. I often regretted not going to Bourbon Street and finding out what it was all about. That is an experience I will never have for I will never be that age again.

We came home after the second day. We spent one day home and the next day, Daddy and Momma drove Duck and I back to the Customs House in New Orleans. Davis decided not to join at that time. Duck and I was sworn in with a bunch of other recruits and got our orders. Seven days after graduating, I was in the Army.

The fourth week in basic training, something was happening to me and I did not know what it was.

THIS IS THE END OF MY FIRST BOOK

www.ingramcontent.com/pod-product-compliance
Lightning Source LLC
LaVergne TN
LVHW021234080526
838199LV00088B/4339